ULTRAROYALISM IN TOULOUSE

THE JOHNS HOPKINS UNIVERSITY STUDIES IN HISTORICAL AND POLITICAL SCIENCE

NINETIETH SERIES (1972)

1. The Savage Ideal: Intolerance and Intellectual Leadership in the South, 1890–1914

BY BRUCE CLAYTON

2. Ultraroyalism in Toulouse: From Its Origins to the Revolution of 1830

BY DAVID HIGGS

DAVID HIGGS

ULTRAROYALISM
IN TOULOUSE

FROM ITS ORIGINS
TO THE REVOLUTION OF 1830

THE JOHNS HOPKINS UNIVERSITY PRESS
BALTIMORE AND LONDON

126383

Manufactured in the United States of America

The Johns Hopkins University Press, Baltimore, Maryland 21218
The Johns Hopkins University Press Ltd., London

Library of Congress Catalog Card Number 72-4021

ISBN 0-8018-1432-4

Library of Congress Cataloging in Publication Data
will be found on the last printed page of this book.

CONTENTS

ACKNOWLEDGMENTS

ABOVE ALL, I wish to acknowledge my gratitude to the late Professor Alfred Cobban for his teaching, understanding, and encouragement during and since my studies at University College, London. I want also to thank my fellow students and friends from Professor Cobban's seminar at the Institute of Historical Research, who will recognize in these pages many themes which were discussed both there and in less academic surroundings.

I owe a very special debt of gratitude to the late Comte de Villèle who very kindly allowed me to consult his private archives and whose family extended such a generous welcome to me. I also wish to thank the Marquis de Beaumont, Vicomte de Castelbajac, and M. Vivie de Régie, who gave me encouragement, hospitality, and valuable information on matters of family history. Professors Godechot and Sentou of the University of Toulouse were generous in suggesting avenues of investigation.

My thanks are due to William J. Callahan, Olwen Hufton, Keith Baker, Harvey Mitchell, Martyn Lyons, Robert Forster, and Richard de Lavigne, who offered helpful criticisms of draft sections of the manuscript. I am very grateful to M. de Saint Blanquat and his staff at the municipal archives of Toulouse, and to all those who constantly gave me help at the departmental archives of the Haute Garonne and at the French National Archives, as well as the other archives and libraries I have used. I am grateful to the Canada Council, the Central Research Fund of the University of London, and the Summer Research Fund of the University of Toronto who made it possible for me to undertake travel to France for research. I wish to thank the Social Science Research Council of Canada for a grant that made possible the publication of this study. I wish also to thank Christine Purden and Linda Vlasak for their help in improving the manuscript.

D. H.

ABBREVIATIONS

A number of abbreviations are used in the text to indicate archives, libraries, and newspapers which are often cited. They are:

AB   Private archives of the Beaumont family

ADHG   Archives départementales de la Haute-Garonne

AG   Archives du Ministère de la guerre, Vincennes

AMT   Archives municipales de la ville de Toulouse

AN   Archives nationales de France

AR   *Ami du Roi. Journal du Midi* (editor Augustin Manavit), 1815–19

AV   Private archives of the Villèle family

BM   British Museum

BMT   Bibliothèque municipale de Toulouse

BN   Bibliothèque nationale de France

BUT   Bibliothèque de l'université de Toulouse

EM   *Echo du Midi* (editor Augustin Manavit), 1821–28

JPLT   *Journal politique et littéraire de Toulouse et de la Haute-Garonne* (editor Jean-François-Joseph Vieusseux), 1815–30

ULTRAROYALISM IN TOULOUSE

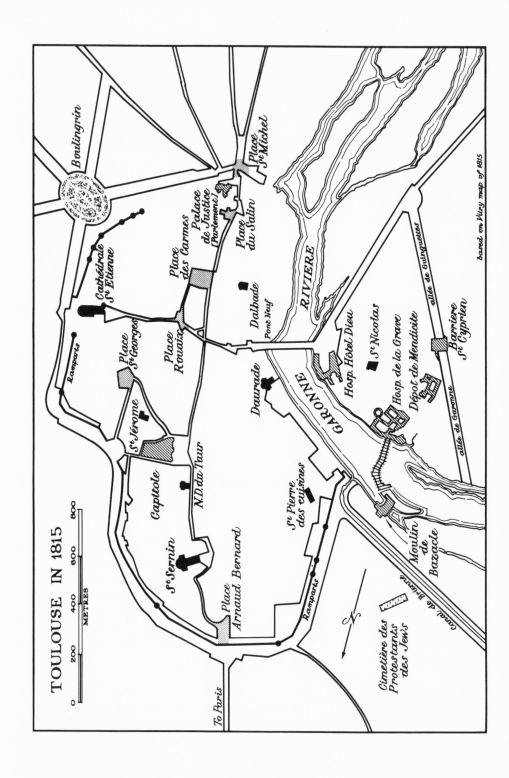

TOULOUSE IN 1815

METRES

0 200 400 600 800

To Paris

St Serpin

Place Arnaud Bernard

Capitole

N.D. du Taur

St Jérome

Place St Georges

Place Rouaix

Cathédrale St Etienne

Ramparts

Boulingrin

Place des Carmes

Palace de Justice (Parlement)

Place du Salin

Place St Michel

Dalbade

Pont Neuf

Daurade

St Pierre des cuisines

Ramparts

Hosp. Hôtel Dieu

St Nicolas

Hosp. de la Grave

Dépôt de Mendicité

Barrière St Cyprien

R. RIVIERE

GARONNE

allée de Guinguettes

allée de Garonne

Moulin de Bazacle

Canal de Brienne

Cimetière des Protestants des Juifs

based on Vitry map of 1815

INTRODUCTION

FRANCE HAS PRODUCED a rich and varied crop of "true" conservatives who find it impossible to accept gradual, empirical reform. This fact has vexed most Anglo-American historians almost as much as the constant appeal to violence in the French revolutionary tradition. However perplexing the "jusqu'au bout" ideal is to many foreigners and even some Frenchmen, its origins and nature are an engrossing study. The social background of the politics of frustration in France is part of the explanation of the attitudes which the far Right derived from explanations of past events. These attitudes are not only to be found codified in the arguments of the theocratic reactionaries of whom the most famous are Maistre and Bonald, but in the social roots of that nostalgia which affects nations as well as individuals. The *émigrés*, the ultra-royalists, the Carlists and supporters of Henri V, the *Action française*, and elements of the O. A. S. display a widely differing set of concerns, but they all exemplify a persistent type in French political life, those whom a Gaullist deputy once described as the *"éternels vaincus."* These men, consistently defending untenable positions in a heroic, if obtuse, manner have fought an unsuccessful rear-guard action to defend a vanishing social order. Whether the explanation of their hostility is to be found in economic trends, social tensions, or institutional failures, their private jeremiads fit into a public framework. Their concerns are as important as those of more successful groups in the explanation of historical change in France since the Revolution. Lost causes are an integral part of those

1

which have been won by their defeat, and deserve equally close examination.

France, like other nations and societies, has produced a variety of theories of decline, corresponding to her changing political fortunes in Europe and the world.[1] Eighteenth-century pessimism was insignificant by comparison with that induced by the course of the Revolution. It was not only Lammenais, de Musset, the returned *émigrés*, and the rarified world of the intelligentsia who suffered from the *mal du siècle* following Waterloo. The Revolution represented another, at least temporary, victory of the state apparatus over local community and privilege, and it stimulated the longing, apparent in all parts of the country after the fall of Napoleon, for a return to older forms of society and government that were essentially provincial and rural. The dockers of Marseille, the fishermen of Brittany, the peasants of the Auvergne, saw plainly enough that the Revolution had not solved the problems of poverty and economic distress. Like the nobles, the ex-parlementarians, and the descendants of other local oligarchies, they were hostile to the ascendancy of Paris. On all levels of French society, there were those who selectively remembered the best of the Old Regime, dwelt on the most obvious failures of the Revolution's religious and welfare policies, and blamed facile utilitarians who did not understand tradition for the destruction of the pre-1789 institutions.

The *locus classicus* of this nostalgia in nineteenth-century France was the Paris salon of that undignified deputy, M. Piet. He possessed, happily, a room large enough to accommodate his ultraroyalist colleagues at the *Chambre Introuvable*, who gathered there to plan parliamentary strategy. The lawyers, doctors, country gentlemen, and aristocrats, disapproving of the policy of Louis XVIII which they thought mistakenly conciliatory, formulated the basic themes that constantly reappeared in their critique of technological modernization and egalitarianism.

The most able among this company was Joseph de Villèle, a very short man with a pock-marked face and a strong southern accent, deputy and mayor of Toulouse. He was level-headed, of austere morality, pragmatic in his ideas, and intent more on balancing the budget and reducing taxation than on composing rhapsodies

[1] K. W. Swart, *The Sense of Decadence in Nineteenth-Century France* (The Hague, 1964); R. Rémond, *La droite en France*, 3rd ed. (Paris, 1968).

2

about royalist fidelity. The monotone quality of his personality together with his remarkable organizational abilities in financial matters contributed to his success among the ultras. The most talented man there, at least in the eyes of literary historians, was the Breton noble Chateaubriand, vain, unreliable—and a brilliant writer. These two men represented the extremes of ultraroyalism: one was the pragmatic defense of the position of the landowner and noble in post-revolutionary French society; the other, an emotional invocation of the past and a self-glorification on the level of heroic fantasy. The mass of the deputies were uncertain which of these two ways they should follow. They praised rural values, ancient precedents of noble liberty, familial discipline, and an hierarchic society which they claimed to be in the best interests of the majority. They hated the Revolution that had broken the orderly community they believed to have existed in France. Even those who had not suffered the loss of property or relatives were mesmerized by the image of the guillotine. As with Chateaubriand, Labourdonnaye, or Montlosier, their own biographies became more mythic with each retelling. To reinforce the strength of their version of the Revolution, they dramatized the extent of their revulsion against the recent past; each and any accommodation was seen as a betrayal. Many ultras remembered the suspicions expressed in the entourage of the Comte d'Artois at Versailles concerning the "liberal" opinions of his older brother the Comte de Provence in 1789. Now that he was no more a poetaster but a king marked by long years of exile, they still felt they knew much better than he what really ought to be done. Until Louis XVIII came to his senses, they would shout the famous exclamation of Béthisy: "Vive le Roi, quand même!"[2]

During the Bourbon Restoration of 1814–15, with its response to the preceding quarter-century of revolutionary upheaval in France, local variations appeared within the royalist crescent in the South that reached from one of its tips in Brittany, down to Bordeaux, had its heartland in the triangle of Toulouse–Mende–Montpellier, and extended across the *garrigues* to the Rhône, from Aix-en-Provence and Marseille to Lyon and up to its second tip in Burgundy. In this area, the most persistent supporters of ultraroyalism,

[2] Nora E. Hudson, *Ultraroyalism and the French Restoration* (Cambridge, 1936); J.-J. Oeschlin, *Le mouvement ultra-royaliste sous la Restauration; son idéologie et son action politique (1814–1830)* (Paris, 1960).

3

deeply suspicious of Paris and the revolutionary North, were to be found in the early decades of the century. The Duc d'Angoulême remarked in 1815 that the Bourbons preferred departments to provinces, but this was untrue of the enthusiastic supporters of Restoration which was perceived as a return to past regionalism rather than as a victory for the centralizing ambitions of the Old Regime monarchy. Ultraroyalism found its strength in departments with the least technological and agricultural development: the more illiteracy and poverty, the more likely was popular royalism to flourish. Enthusiasm for the Bourbons was also found where the local economy had suffered most from the Revolution and the Continental Blockade. Once Louis XVIII was again on the throne, poor roads, linguistic variations, local customs, and a larger measure of regional representation reinforced this trend toward decentralization, and the nobles and notables began to emphasize more strongly the distinctive traits and traditional personalities of their own areas.

The Napoleonic maritime blockade stifled the Atlantic commerce of western and southern France just as the Revolution had disrupted trade from the South-West into the Levant and caused economic hardship. Northern authority in the form of troops, revolutionary officials, tax collectors, prefects in uniforms, and their bureaucrats, all seemed to have diminished and humbled the proud municipal traditions of the Midi. They were resented. Gangs of royalist thugs appeared during Thermidor to terrorize Jacobins, grain dealers, buyers of confiscated property, and all those who seemed to be supporters of the revolutionary changes in society. These bands had names like the Nîmes Onion-Eaters (*cébets*), the Arles Rag-Pickers (*chiffonistens*), the Ostlers of the Cévennes (*palefreniers*), and the Companions of the Sun (or of Jéhu)— names which showed the frustration and hostility of a portion of the common people to the Revolution. These outbursts of violence were poorly coordinated, despite the conspiratorial theories advanced by the revolutionary officials, and they were betrayed by geography. Tocqueville can be rephrased in saying that tyranny is best exercised over flat land; to keep order, Paris put to good use the army and the excellent roads constructed in Languedoc under the Old Regime. The poor military communications typical of the Vendée, Brittany, the Lozère, the Ardèche and the Pyrenees made easier the resistance of the population, but this resistance remained

4

sullen and localized, never building up into a unified opposition to the central government with its network of officials and interested partisans, its army and police. The Jacobins defeated the Federalists, rebellious peasants, and royalists because they all were too local in their resistance activities. The royalist dislike of centralization, which they dimly sensed as the cause of their failure, explained the desire to duck the issue by relating to an ideal past which had none of the frustrations of the present.

Regional politics make sense only in relation to the urban centers which coordinate and reinforce them.[3] This is particularly true of Haut-Languedoc between 1750 and 1850, an area dominated by Toulouse that was at the time called the capital of the Midi. The city drew its prestige from the institutions of a traditional society and its prosperity from a rural-based economy.

The rulers of the city showed this in their outlook. Disorder, crime, religious controversy, and intellectual debate were blamed either on outsiders or on the wickedness of the lazy and immoral. The rulers of Toulouse in the Old Regime stressed obedience and morality in their approach to public order, and only dimly, if ever, realized that the strains and changes of population growth, the breakdown of family discipline in a large city, and rivalries between professional and religious groups were not solved any better by pious exhortation than by repression. If some younger judges and liberal-minded advocates displayed a fashionable interest in philanthropy and criticized the political views of their elders on Jansenist and governmental matters, this had little effect on the ruling circles of the city. Even by the standards of the Old Regime, Toulouse was notorious for the savagery of its punishments of criminals. Many unfortunates had preceded and many followed Calas to the Place Saint Georges during the eighteenth century where they were broken alive on a wheel. The parlementarians, the local aristocracy, and the municipal officials set their faces against change and turbulence in a city which attracted peasants, artisans, vagabonds, criminals, university students, merchants, seminarists, and hopeful candidates for official jobs. The elites of Toulouse maintained an essentially rural outlook on society.

The Revolution asserted the victory of town over country and

[3] R. N. Morris, *Urban Sociology* (London, 1968); Gideon Sjoberg, *The Preindustrial City, Past and Present* (New York, 1960).

5

humbled the southern regional centers before the northern capital. The subsequent resentment of Paris surfaced in 1814 and 1815 when Toulouse, one of the "faithful" cities where people and nobility were of a common opinion, showed great enthusiasm for the Bourbon Restoration. The reasons for that fidelity and its expression reveal much about the reactionary mind in France. Charles de Rémusat, *littérateur* and a minister of Louis Philippe, wrote in his memoirs:

> Apart from some spiteful Jacobins and some loitering Bonapartists, the one and the other fairly rare, the Revolution produced nothing at Toulouse. . . . the higher classes were royalists by pretension and ignorance, the lower classes in imitation of the upper classes and by Spanish devotion. But even royalism insofar as it had serious and good qualities could not count on effective loyalty, all the more reason why the law, liberty, the motherland herself, did not have partisans.[4]

As a young man, de Rémusat had experienced the fevered emotions of Toulouse during the White Terror of July and August 1815 and, like his father who was prefect there during those frightening days, he was unsympathetic to extremism. In fact, he had a very low opinion of the general character of the people of Toulouse. In the first half of the nineteenth century, the city was an offense to the liberal mind.

Toulouse was conservative in its economy also. The surrounding countryside was generally inactive; in the foothills of the Pyrenees there were only small rural industries in the environs of Saint Gaudens, Volvestre, and around Castres and Albi on the plain. In the Gers and along the length of the Garonne, from Cuzères to Toulouse and beyond to Grenade, only small artisans existed, dependent on a limited local market.[5]

This industrial backwardness was matched in agriculture. Until the last third of the nineteenth century the system of *métayage* (share-cropping) was practised on the alluvial soil of the Lauraguais and the rolling hills of the Toulousain. This reliance on share-cropping put a distinctive stamp on local agriculture and the society supported by it. It also marked the relationship of Toulouse to its

[4] Charles de Rémusat, *Mémoires de ma vie* (Paris, 1958), I, 223–24.
[5] R. Brunet, *Les campagnes toulousaines, étude géographique* (Toulouse, 1965), pp. 298–99.

6

surrounding countryside and less important towns, for they served as markets for local produce. Certainly merchants, lawyers, and professional men showed little inclination to question the nature of the sluggish agricultural economy. Various reasons have been advanced for the characteristic lack of innovation or drive among those who controlled the local economy, ranging from inherent inaptitude, scarcity of raw materials, and shortage of available capital due to its immobilization in landed investment and real estate, to a desire to ape the manners of the landed gentry.[6] The inefficiency of local agriculture, producing so little surplus, was in large part the consequence of the *métayage* system, the economic backbone of the area. The share-croppers were generally ignorant men, trying to make a living for their families on a plot of land given to them on a limited lease, under conditions which became harsher during the first half of the nineteenth century. A *métayer* of fifty years in 1830, surveying the political changes in France which had taken place during his lifetime, might be excused for seeing some good points in the years of his youth before the Revolution. The fact was that the political changes affected him very little, whereas the continuing population pressures in the countryside encroached increasingly on the peasants. If Old Regime landlords had shown themselves ever more exacting in the leases concluded with the tenants who worked the wheat lands in conjunction with growing maize, rye, vegetables, fruit, and fodder, the Revolution had brought the exactions of the *armées révolutionnaires* which forced peasants to sell produce for almost worthless paper *assignats* and to provide horses, mules, sheep, poultry, and game wherever these were raised in the department. Few *métayers* were in a position to buy confiscated property which was put on sale. The clergy owned little land in the area, so that the disruption of the Church was generally unpopular in a pious region. During the Empire, the new landowners together with the nobles who had retained their estates increased pressure on the share-croppers. Customary rights came under vigorous attack, gleaning privileges

[6] A. Armengaud, *Les populations de l'est aquitain au début de l'époque contemporaine* (Paris, 1961); A. Armengaud, "A propos des origines de sous-développement industriel dans le sud-ouest," *Annales du Midi*, LXXII (1960), 75–81; François Crouzet, "Les origines du sous-développement économique du sud-ouest," *Annales du Midi*, LXXI (1959), 71–79; Daniel Faucher, "Réflexions sur le destin de Toulouse," *Revue de géographie des Pyrénées et du sud-ouest*, XXX (1959), 101–15; R. Brunet, *Les campagnes toulousaines.*

were changed in 1807, and the right of common pasture was curtailed, even to the roadside grass verges. The quaint "feudal" nomenclature of the leases had disappeared after 1789, but the same exactions, becoming increasingly severe, existed in the leases which were concluded between rich and poor Frenchmen who were equal in law. In short, the economic situation of the *métayer* steadily worsened.

There were not only share-cropped farms in the Toulousain. A variant form of land rental existed which, like the *métayage* system, left free the whip-hand of the unprogressive landowners of the region. This was called *faire valoir à maître-valet*: unlike the *métayer* who received a percentage of the crop (between a half and a quarter), the *maître-valet*, on the other hand, was given the necessary tools, an agreed amount of the produce after the harvest, and a cash payment. At a time of increasing rural population, the landowners favored the *maître-valet* system, for they could constantly force downwards the fixed cash payments made under this system. Because there was a surplus of peasants looking for a living or terrified of losing at the expiration of the lease the *métairie* which they worked, they made no effective resistance to this exploitation. More than one committed suicide in despair after he had been dismissed by the landowner. Improvement in the profit margin of an estate was habitually made at the expense of the tenant, and only a small and notable minority of farmers in the region, like Philippe Picot de Lapeyrouse, Joseph de Villèle, or Louis-Philippe Couret de Villeneuve, made an effort to improve yields or cultivation methods. The *métayers* and *maître-valets*, demoralized by short leases and frightened by innovations which might not work as well as tested methods, contributed little or nothing in the way of improvement to the farms they worked. In consequence, during the first half of the nineteenth century, the agricultural yield of the Toulousain fell steadily in comparison with the national average.[7]

[7] R. Forster, *The Nobility of Toulouse in the Eighteenth Century* (Baltimore, 1960), pp. 55–56; Philippe Picot de Lapeyrouse, *The Agriculture of a District in the South of France* (London, 1819); L.-P. Couret de Villeneuve, *Essai d'un manuel d'agriculture . . . domaine d'Hauterive, commune de Castres. . . .* (Toulouse, 1819); G. Frêche, *Le prix des grains, des vins et des légumes à Toulouse, 1486–1868* (Paris, 1967); Michel Morineau, "Y a-t-il eu une révolution agricole en France au XVIIIe siècle?" *Revue historique* 486, (avril–juin 1968): 299–326.

This wretched peasantry was bound to the landlords in tight servitude. In 1808, the prefect of the department noted that the agricultural system of the area placed the population under the direct influence of the landlords, most of whom were nobles.[8] This subjection of the peasantry continued and was romanticized by royalists as an ideal relationship between the lord and the peasant. The children of the nobility were put out to suck at the breast of a sturdy peasant wet-nurse; the first words that many of them learned were in *occitain*. A writer on the agricultural system of the Lauragais, Pariset, wrote of the peasants' deference for their "natural" superiors, of whom they had personal knowledge, with whom they had frequent contact in the countryside, and who often shared their memories of common childhood games. He cited the proverb, "A l'escuato cal uno centeno"—the skein must be tied with a string (to keep the threads together)—as an example of the instinctive search for order among the common people.[9] By the time Pariset was writing in 1867, the statement was anachronistic, for during the Second Empire the landowners of the Toulousain were reaping the harvest of their exploitation. The countryside was depopulating in consequence of the young people's escape from the rigors of share-cropping. Large estates, no longer able to rely on plentiful cheap labor, unable or unwilling to muster capital, splintered rather than modernized.

Ultraroyalism in Toulouse was nourished from several sources of nostalgia for the past, rural and urban. The share-cropper, the parlementarian, the nobleman, the ecclesiastic, the artisan, and the poor—all could remember what seemed to have been better days while forgetting the conflicts and tensions of the society that had existed before 1789.

Little sense of new ways of dealing with the disruptions caused by the Revolution appeared in the city. Few ultras saw that the *Chambre Introuvable*, elected in 1815, was espousing ideas differing little from those of the aristocratic revolt in the years before the Revolution. One royalist engineer in Toulouse appreciated this similarity and was afraid that history would disastrously repeat

[8] Joseph Lacouture, *Le mouvement royaliste dans le sud-ouest, 1797–1800* (Hosségor, 1932), p. 154.
[9] F. Pariset, *Economie rurale, mœurs et usages du Lauragais, (Aude et Haute-Garonne)* . . . (Paris, 1867), p. 33.

itself.[10] Most of his colleagues on the municipal council disagreed, however, and were convinced that it was their duty to resist further change, since the present misfortunes of France resulted from bad innovations—or so they thought. The ultras dismissed as so much intellectual legerdemain those social and political theories which appeared in the Revolution. In this study I wish to examine in more detail the origins of this hostility in the local past and the form which ultraroyalism took in Toulouse.

[10] Aubuisson de Voisins to Laîné, September 5, 1815, cited in: E. de Perceval, *Un adversaire de Napoléon; le vicomte Laîné* (Paris, 1926), II: 68.

I

LOUS SEIGNOUS

THE ULTRAROYALISTS of 1815 were those who, like Joseph de Villèle, hoped to see a return to what had existed in France before the Revolution of 1789, or rather to their idealised memory of it. The complexity of their feelings about the past becomes apparent when compared with the reality. Much of their ambivalence towards the repressive post-revolutionary state—its army, judicial system, bureaucracy—paralleled their moral attitudes toward religion, education, and the family. Ultraroyalism was basically an interpretation of the past applied to the present, but an overview of the social situation of pre-revolutionary Toulouse is necessary for a full understanding of the forms taken by that reaction. Toulouse provided an urban focus for the wealthy nobility with country interests to an extent unusual for cities of its size in the Old Regime. In their rosy recollection of the past the local ultras found ample ammunition for their attack on egalitarianism, urbanisation, technology, intellectualism, and almost every other component of what is often called by sociologists "modernization." The difficulty of their position came from the contrast between what they wished the past to be and what it was, and the social consequences of that opposition.

No single feature of pre-revolutionary Toulouse compared in importance with the existence of the Parlement, founded within its walls in 1443 as the second sovereign court of France. It was an appeal court for fourteen seneschalsies, seigneurial and other lesser courts. It drew litigants to the city from the three million inhabi-

11

tants of Languedoc, Rouergue, and parts of Gascony and Quercy which were its jurisdictional area. It included the following courts: the plenary *Grand'chambre*, a criminal court called the *Tournelle*, the first and the second *chambre des enquêtes* and one *chambre des requêtes*. There was also a court which sat during the judicial holidays, called the *chambre des vacations*. The chancellery had thirty-three places which conferred ennoblement through the office of *secrétaire du roi*.[1]

Even more impressive than the rambling intricacies of the organisational structure of the Parlement was the local power of the parlementary families. First President Jean-Louis-Augustin-Emmanuel de Cambon, swathed in his vermillion robes of office, surrounded by the councilors who judged cases in the various *chambres*, seemed like a prince in the company of so many vassals. The parlementarians were easily the wealthiest group in the city and they led dignified and comfortable lives between their estates and townhouses. United by professional experience, by a common educational background, and in large measure a common political viewpoint, they were further united by frequent intermarriage until they became almost a caste. Councilor Jean-François-Denis d'Albis de Belbèze, for example, had a councilor for maternal grandfather. His father was a councilor (son of a *secrétaire du roi*), and he himself married into a parlementary family in which a brother-in-law became *avocat-général*. The robe nobility was a more tightly unified and interwoven group than their peers in the second estate at large.

The Parlement of Toulouse was one of the most disobedient of the sovereign courts that existed in France in 1789. As a result of its resistance to the fiscal edicts of 1763, the *lieutenant-général* of Languedoc duc de Fitz-James was forced to go back to Paris. Subsequently the Parlement humiliated its First President for his cooperation with the Duke and caused his resignation in 1768. In the remonstrances sent to the King, the Parlement struck out at ministerial "despotism" and invoked a kind of baroque federalism in which it depicted itself as guardian of provincial rights which were enshrined in antique precedents. Simultaneously and perversely, the Parlement was hostile to the provincial Estates, which met

[1] Axel Duboul, *La fin du parlement de Toulouse* (Toulouse, 1890), pp. 41–42.

annually at Montpellier, on the Mediterranean coast. These Estates were, in the view of one young councilor, "a body composed of bishops of no interest, of barons of no credit, and of municipal officials with no liberty."[2] On the other hand, Bishop Beausset of Alais described the Estates in 1786: "Defenders of the peoples confided to our care, we seek to conciliate their interests with the needs of the state of which we are members, and with the requests of the prince of whom we are subjects."[3] The parlementary opposition to this body which might have been an ally in the continuing struggle against royal authority derived from more than mere jealousy. It came from the rivalry, so acute in the south generally, between urban centers. Montpellier was the seat of the Estates, the Intendant, a university, an Academy of Sciences, a *cour des aides* which heard appeals on matters of indirect taxation, a *présidial-sénéchaussée* (a lower court hearing both criminal and civil cases), and had a more flourishing commerce than was to be found in Toulouse.

Archbishop Dillon spoke of Languedoc as "forming a second motherland in the breast of the common motherland."[4] The parlementarians applauded the sentiment of the president of the Estates but they had no intention of allowing any other institution to gain a paramount position in provincial affairs. The Parlement played a more important role than the Estates in contesting the financial policy of the monarchy, fighting administrative reorganization of local government, and defending the interests of landowners and merchants. The parlementarians of Toulouse were as suspicious of Montpellier's pretensions as they were of those of Versailles. They thought of themselves as the champions of local interests, and accepted the "exile" to their country estates caused by their struggle with the ministers of Louis XVI. Their return, significantly, provided their fellow citizens an opportunity to display affection for their foremost champions; when the "exiles" entered the city walls, the townspeople, municipal officials, and members of the thousand-strong university roared their approval of the "Fathers of the People."

[2] Claude de Vic, *Histoire générale de Languedoc ... continuée jusqu'en 1790 par E. Roschach* (Toulouse, 1872–1904), vol. XIV, cols. 2231–32.
[3] Renaud de Vilback, *Voyages dans les départements formés de l'ancienne province de Languedoc* (Paris, 1825), p. 218.
[4] *Ibid.*, p. 212.

The second major presence in Toulouse was the Church, boasting fifty-two religious houses. The inhabitants of its ten parishes were proud of the famous relics to be found in the romanesque basilica of Saint Sernin, of the Black Madonna of La Daurade, and of the numerous chapters and the wealth of the cathedral of Saint Etienne. A good third of the urban property in Toulouse belonged to the churches, convents, and monasteries of the city. At the end of the seventeenth century, the Intendant said that half the city was filled with convents. The Church was not a great landowner in the countryside: it owned less than seven per cent of the Toulousain.

The Church was more than a religious and economic fact, it was a focus of loyalties and an object of social ambitions. Lay confraternities of penitents, known as blue, white, black, or grey penitents according to the color of their ceremonial costumes, provided festive occasions and an opportunity to engage in processions and good works. There were also confraternities of artisans, joiners, wig-makers, porters, and tailors that provided mutual aid to members. Toulouse was described by contemporaries as positively Spanish in its taste for elaborate ceremonies in which these associations played conspicuous parts. On more than one occasion a confraternity was reprimanded for prolonging a feast-day banquet until a scandalously late hour. Besides these lay associations, there were the seminaries which made it possible for the sons of artisans and lesser officials to rise in the world by becoming a curé; the sons of parlementarians, like Philippe Dubourg, looked forward to a possible bishopric.

The municipal government, the *capitoulat* of Toulouse, was the third most prominent institution in the city. The reforms of 1778 distinguished three classes among the eight *capitouls*: nobles, those who had already served as *capitouls*, and notable citizens. Each *capitoul*, of whatever class, had to be born in Toulouse and domiciled there for at least ten years, as well as to have some practical experience of local government as a member in a subsidiary municipal council. The *capitouls* controlled the city budget (although the permission of the Intendant was needed for major expenditures), rendered justice in civil and criminal cases (although the *présidial-sénéchaussée* disputed the limits of their jurisdiction), and directed eleven police commissioners, four hundred *dizeniers* or police auxiliaries, and the men of the Watch. They were able to call on thirty companies of the *garde bourgeoise*.

14

The *capitoul* was a man of importance. The office was very attractive to many of the lesser notables of the city, both because of the esteem which was attached to it and, more especially, because it was ennobling. Many local families owed the origin of their nobility to the *capitoulat*, subsequently polished by other respectable offices and the purchase of seigneuries. The merchant Joseph-François Gounon-Loubens, for example, the only businessman to become *capitoul* between 1778 and 1789, was involved in charity work and had purchased a seigneurie. Many advocates and notaries, even doctors, came to rise in local society through municipal office.

The regional capital had other important offices, especially those of the lower courts of justice. The *présidial-sénéchaussée*, the office of the *Eaux et Forêts*, the *trésorerie particulière*, and the offices of the various *receveurs* provided employment for over two hundred and fifty men. Minor posts of *huissier*, *greffier*, and *octroi* collectors at the gates of the city, together with copy-clerks and office boys, multiplied the number of menial jobs.[5]

The royal authorities were not particularly prominent in the city. The governor of Languedoc had his official headquarters and a small staff there, but was rarely resident. Toulouse enjoyed the privilege of not lodging soldiers within the walls of the city. In 1746, when troops had been billeted, a protest was sent to the king pointing out that the soldiers, far from keeping the peace, in fact caused fires and brawls, and frightened off the university students which caused a decline in wheat sales normally consumed by the scholars. The *capitouls*, together with nobles and others who possessed noble fiefs, were perfectly capable of maintaining order:

Toulouse, large as she is, is filled only with monasteries or judicial officials exempt from billeting. The remainder of her citizens are merchants or artisans. Does Your Majesty find it just to subject city merchants needlessly to lodge soldiers? Is it not to be feared their commerce will be disrupted? Few artisans can provide billets: the majority have only sufficient beds for themselves. The remainder of the people is in such misery that they are reduced to sleeping on straw.[6]

[5] E. Lamouzèle, *Essai sur l'administration de la ville de Toulouse* (Paris, 1910); J. Coppolani, *Toulouse, étude de géographie urbaine* (Toulouse, 1954), pp. 80–84.
[6] *Capitouls* and Toulouse syndic to Louis XV, in de Vic, *Histoire générale*, vol. XIV, cols. 2163–64.

The complaint had been heard, so that the *capitouls* and the parlement remained the most visible authorities in the city.

The local nobility was very punctilious in exacting respect for its titles; the famous "cascade of disdain" was, as one noble put it, the city's moral flaw.[7] Disputes over precedence took place among clergy, officers, *capitouls*, and parlementarians. It was a fine art of the salons to evaluate the social standing of the nobility, although standards were hard to set after centuries of intermarriage between robe and sword families. Even thoroughbreds, presumably like the pamphleteer who denounced the mercenary, vulgar origins of the robe nobility, ruefully admitted that "mulatto (*mulâtres*) nobles prevail by their number."[8] The forty-two member *conseil politique* which discussed municipal matters was dominated by the nobles who owned approximately forty-four percent of the land area of the Toulousain, including the best land. Although the nobility was the richest group in local society, seigneurial rights made only eight percent of the average revenue of a noble estate.[9] Since the Province of Languedoc was an area of *taille réelle* (where commoners could own privileged "noble" land, and nobles held "common" land, and tax was levied on land rather than the privileged status of the owner), there was less psychological friction over the issue of noble fiscal privilege.[10] The nobility placed its offspring in buttressing positions: President Dubourg, for example, had one son who was a vicar-general, another one in the navy, and a third one in the Parlement. Few, if any, other areas of France showed such a clear socio-economic primacy of the nobility in urban and rural society.

The parlementarians were not menaced in their ascendancy by the city merchants, whom they had superseded by the end of the

[7] J.-B. d'Aldéguier, *Histoire de Toulouse* (Toulouse, 1834), IV, 291.

[8] *Dénonciation d'un Languedocien à sa province* (Toulouse, 1789), p. 4; Alphonse Brémond, *Nobiliaire toulousaine*, 2 vols. (Toulouse, 1863); Louis de Laroque, *Catalogue des gentilshommes en 1789* (Paris, 1866), vol. I, *Généralité de Toulouse;* Jules Villain, *La France moderne . . . Haute-Garonne et Ariège* (Montpellier, 1911–13).

[9] R. Forster, *The Nobility of Toulouse in the Eighteenth Century: a Social and Economic Study* (Baltimore, 1960), pp. 38–39.

[10] Georges Frêche, "Compoix, propriété foncière, fiscalité et démographie historique en pays de taille réelle (XVIe–XVIIIe siècles)," *Revue d'histoire moderne et comtemporaine*, XVIII (juillet–septembre 1971), 321–53.

seventeenth century in control of civic institutions.[11] The woad
industry that had produced a number of local fortunes collapsed
when cheaper imported dye became available. Lamoignon de
Bâville, intendant of the province at the end of the seventeenth
century, thought that the people of Toulouse were unsuccessful in
commerce because they were hostile to strangers. Perhaps a kind of
regional xenophobia was one of the reasons for the failure of new
commercial ideas to establish themselves. Many pre-industrial
French cities with similar institutions had more flourishing commercial and artisanal alternatives. Whatever the causes—undoubt-
edly complex, as Arthur Young pointed out—industrial and commercial activity was scarce in the city in June, 1787.

What manufactures did exist—silk upholstery (employing 260
workers in 1788[12]), brandy distilling, wallpaper printing, taper-
making, and lead work—they looked to the aristocracy and clergy
for their best customers. In the eighteenth century, local merchants
were dealing primarily in these products. Although there was a
constant trade in other articles, especially cloth, to Spain and the
Levant, it was of small volume. The four great annual fairs were
Jour des Rois (January 6), *St. Jean* (June 24), *St. Barthélemy*
(August 24), and *St. André* (November 30). Few of those who did
attend stayed in Toulouse to prosper. Colbert established a gunpowder factory there in 1667 and, some ten years later, a tobacco
plant to process the crop harvested on the plain of the Garonne.
On the Ile de Tounis, a small island in the Garonne River, silk
workers from Tours were set up in business to manufacture a cloth
of which the warp was silk and the woof was wool. Cheap cloth
was produced, and some Toulouse *grisettes*, *ferrandines*, and
mignonettes were sold as far afield as Italy and South America.
These materials were already declining in popularity before the
Revolution, outmoded by technical progress. On the eve of the
Revolution,[13] some thirty manufactures in the city employed five to
six thousand workers. The state monopolies were the largest em-

[11] Micheline Thoumas-Schapira, "La bourgeoisie toulousaine à la fin du
XVIIe siècle," *Annales du Midi*, LXVIII (1955), 313–29.
[12] P. Wolff, *Histoire de Toulouse*, 2nd ed. (Toulouse, 1961), p. 249.
[13] J.-F. Baour, *Almanach historique* (Toulouse, 1791), *AMT*.

ployers, a fact which was still true in 1866 under the Second Empire.[14]

Very few businessmen had fortunes which equalled those of the average noble, and most of them were very much less wealthy.[15] What money they had amassed through economic activity was often used by them to rise in the social system by the classic method of purchasing a seigneurie or an ennobling office or by contracting an advantageous marriage.[16] Commoners, like nobles, were consumed with a passion for land and invested their capital in it. There was also a substantial local clientele seeking *rentes* on the Estates of Languedoc or shares in the Bazacle mill, both dependable and secure forms of investment. In consequence, there was no substantial capital concentration in Toulouse, since these funds were quickly channelled into land and safe investments. The only banking house in the city, owned by the Protestant family Courtois, was small and primarily involved with personal loans.

The commoners and nobles who mixed in the twelve masonic lodges of the city and in civic activities shared a similar socio-economic outlook. There was no economic rivalry between the two groups, although differences were plain in their attitudes toward social status. François de Boutaric, one-time professor of French law at the University of Toulouse, published a book on feudal rights and noble privileges, the *Traité des droits seigneuriaux et des matières féodales*, which went through several editions during the eighteenth century. Members of the Third Estate resented these noble privileges, and showed their vexation in petty disputes over honorifics and matters of precedence, but it was a resentment which sprang from a desire to share these privileges and not from a demand for an alternative social order. Fashionable young lawyers like Mailhe and Barère were typical spokesmen of those in the city who wanted to see the nobility pay a more just portion of taxation and who resented the occasional arrogant slight by the well-born.

[14] The four state monopolies in 1866 (tabac, arsenal, cannon foundry, and gunpowder factory) employed more workers than the 2,286 "industriels" of the city combined, including artisans and millers. E. Roschach, *Géographie de la Haute-Garonne* (Paris, 1866), pp. 135–36.

[15] J. Godechot and S. Moncassin, "Structures et relations sociales à Toulouse (1749, 1785)," *Annales historiques de la Révolution française* (1965), pp. 129–69.

[16] C. Marinière, "Les marchands d'étoffes de Toulouse à la fin du xviii siècle," *Annales du Midi*, LXX (1958), 251–308.

However, most of the prosperous professional men and merchants had no desire for any radical change in the institutions of Toulouse.[17] The deputies sent to Versailles were an undistinguished group, with the dubious exception of Roussillou, an assiduous committee man. This befitted a city where the Third Estate endorsed the preservation of urban privileges, the Parlement, and the rejection of the proposed departmental system.[18]

The "people" of Toulouse—artisans, servants, agricultural laborers—were vivacious and wiry, darker in complexion and hair color than their Parisian counterparts, and also generally shorter. They spoke an occitain *patois*, and were noted for ostentatious, ritualistic piety and a passion for singing. They disliked foreigners—those from outside the city—and had not completely forgotten their historic animus against the local Protestants and Jews. Other prejudices were reflected between the different suburbs, each of which had a special character. Arnaud Bernard, Saint Michel, and Saint Cyprien, all lying on the periphery of the historic core of Toulouse, were considered lower-class areas, more likely to have recently arrived migrants from the countryside. The loyalty of each district (*capitoulat*) was bound up with the parish festivals called *fénétras* and reinforced by the boisterous rivalries of apprentices or street gangs.

The common people found their livelihood closely connected to the system of land ownership and the social patterns which resulted from the ideas on status.[19] In eighteenth-century Toulouse, life was hard, assuaged by cheap wine and prostitutes, both readily available. The recent immigrants from the countryside found it difficult to get work in the static guild-dominated artisan sector. One of the peculiarities of the city was the large number of people who still left the city daily to work in the fields of the *gardiage*, the area im-

[17] Armand Brette, *Recueil de documents relatifs à la convocation des Etats Généraux de 1789* (Paris, 1894–1915), I, 167, n. 2.

[18] Comité de la Haute-Garonne, *Cahiers paroissiaux des sénéchaussées de Toulouse et de Cominges en 1789*, published by F. Pasquier and F. Galabert (Toulouse, 1928), pp. 84–86; Pierre-Henri Thore, "Essai de classification des catégories sociales à l'intérieur du tiers état de Toulouse," *Actes, Congrès des sociétés savantes de Paris et des départments, 78th session, Toulouse* (Paris, 1954), pp. 149–65.

[19] Godechot and Moncassin, "Structures et relations sociales," p. 152. In 1787, 7 percent of the population were servants, a decline from the 11 percent of the late 17th century.

mediately outside the walls.[20] Many residents inside the city walls kept pigs and poultry in the gardens that remained from an earlier, more spacious city. There was a wide range of artisan activities since it was characteristic of local villages to have few craftsmen. When villagers went to market in Toulouse, they took not only produce to sell, but also the old tools and furnishing which needed repair or which they exchanged. Most of the local corporations had been founded in the sixteenth century and the rivalries between them were long established. A number of them were in financial difficulties before the Revolution. Group interests were only dimly perceived among the city workers.

There was scant change in this economic and social situation during the eighteenth century, save in the vital respect of the constant population influx, a result of the population increase in the countryside. The migration to Toulouse was drawn from overcrowded rural areas, especially from the Lauragais with its great estates owned by parlementarians and its peasantry living in wretched conditions, and from the poor mountain villages in the Pyrenees and as far off as the Massif Central. It provided a supply of agricultural laborers who lived inside the city but worked in the market-gardens which surrounded it, of maidservants and menials, porters, prostitutes, and beggars. The individual often experienced a range of situations depending on circumstance. These people were unable to demand better wages or living conditions since the refusal of one was easily repaired by the use of another candidate for each position. Less than twenty-three percent of the Toulousain belonged to the peasantry at mid-century, and this property was in land parcels which did not support substantial living for the average family.

The consequence of this situation was pervasive poverty. The inquiry of 1763 showed that, of fifty-seven rural parishes in the Toulouse diocese, twenty-three were without any charitable institutions, while fourteen of the remainder had the use of completely inadequate revenues of less than one hundred *livres*.[21] The local curés saw the establishment of industry as the only answer to this

[20] The *gardiage* was land surrounding the city suburbs of St. Michel, St. Etienne, Arnaud Bernard, and St. Cyprien; it included several villages, hamlets, and isolated farm houses, but was within the municipal jurisdiction.

[21] J. Adher, "L'assistance publique au XVIIIe siècle; l'enquête de 1775 dans le diocèse civil de Toulouse," *La Révolution française*, 70 (1917), 132–66.

rural poverty, but this was as absent in the country as it was in the towns.

In Toulouse, forty religious institutions provided assistance to the indigent.[22] They tried to deal with problems of beggary, prostitution, and unemployment. Their efforts were supplemented by private charity, much of it provided by the parlementarians and by the penitential confraternities, so typical of the eighteenth-century south.[23] The common people could not easily conceive of an alternative to traditional patrons for the provision of relief in the form of alms or food. It was popularly believed, probably correctly, that the nobility was more charitable than merchants or professional men. The poor hoped for the maintenance of what has been described in eighteenth-century England as the "moral economy," since their position was disadvantaged in both town and country. The clerical and parlementary self-congratulation on the mission of mercy carried out by the rich towards the poor was exaggerated; and the indigent, queuing for food and hectored by denunciations of laziness, were, understandably, not always overwhelmed with gratitude. However, when survival is at issue, there is a clear knowledge of dependence. The Declaration of the Rights of Man was not a substitute for distribution of free food or alms. Innovations which disrupted the old system of charity were resented. This was true, for example, in the two major hospitals in the city, the Hôtel Dieu and the Hôpital Saint Joseph de la Grave. Both were located in the working-class suburb of Saint Cyprien across the Garonne, possibly to keep pestilence away from the rich.[24] The Grave accepted the "deserving" poor, orphans, the senile, lunatics, and sick beggars and thus doubled some functions of the Hôtel Dieu. Both hospitals enjoyed a special local prestige as a place where the poor of Toulouse could find medical care and assistance. During the eighteenth century, the patients' food was gradually improving, and an effort was being made to mitigate the worst overcrowding in beds and bad sanitation.

At the lowest levels, the line between the worker and the beggar

---

[22] J. Contrasty, "Les foyers toulousains d'enseignement et de bienfaisance détruits par la Révolution," *Revue historique de Toulouse*, 21 (1934), 165–85.

[23] Maurice Agulhon, "La sociabilité méridionale au XVIIIe siècle," *L'information historique* (November–December, 1968), pp. 224–26.

[24] François Buchalet, *L'assistance publique à Toulouse au dix-huitième siècle* (Toulouse, 1904).

was often hard to establish among the population of Toulouse. In wheat-growing areas, a number of seasonal migrant workers moved about, looking for harvest and other seasonal jobs, but not assured of any permanent employment. At a time of high bread prices, as in 1788 and 1789, this group relied on begging. Their wages in any event were wretched: the Parlement fixed maximum wages in 1715, 1721, and 1762, with enforcement by flogging and imprisonment. In 1773 it was reported that "an unfortunate who has a family earns only fifteen sols daily and consequently he cannot get bread to nourish them."[25] The local diet was not particularly good. In 1783, the subdelegate of the intendant in the *généralité* of Toulouse said that little wheat was eaten by the common people of his jurisdiction, although rye and various kinds of mixtures of maize and other coarse cereals were used.[26] Drink offered a release from daily problems: wine was cheap in a time of over-production. The subdelegate thought people drank in order to forget the misery which burdened them on all sides.[27]

The reliance of the poor on the traditional sources of charity was as marked in Toulouse as in many other French towns. The city curés petitioned in 1788 for an improvement in the parish welfare system. They pointed out how acute was the need at the time when the parlementarians were exiled for their resistance to the judicial reforms enacted in May, 1788:

We come to implore your goodwill and the paternal sentiments of your heart in favor of a multitude of our parishioners who are plunged by the present misfortunes into the abyss of the deepest indigence. We cannot, without becoming overcome and shedding tears, present the fearful picture which is offered to us daily by whole families, burdened with children whose support and nourishment they cannot provide because of the present revolution, or the distress of some of those who find work in defending legal cases, and especially of the large numbers of co-workers they employ; of artisans without work, laborers of all sorts without bread or aid. If, before these changes came about, we used to be hardly able to assist those unfortunate of whom this large city offers so touching a

[25] Henri Bourderon, "La lutte contre la vie chère dans la généralité de Languedoc au XVIIIe siècle," *Annales du Midi,* LXVI (1954), 159.
[26] Louis Théron de Montaugé, "Sur la condition des paysans dans le pays toulousain au XVIIIe siècle," *Mémoires de l'Académie des sciences, inscriptions et belles lettres de Toulouse,* 6 ser., t. iv (Toulouse, 1866), pp. 710–47.
[27] Buchalet, *L'assistance publique à Toulouse,* p. 27.

spectacle, and to whom we are by our calling pastors and fathers, we now find ourselves absolutely unable to meet their pressing needs because of the exile of those whose charity offered us assured resources.[28]

The clergy saw the importance of the parlementarians as a source of work and charity for the city poor. Food riots, quite frequent in times of shortage, showed that a hungry populace would not suffer quietly for ever. The charity system was a means of social control as much as it was a fulfillment of traditional catholic charitable injunctions. The point was nicely expressed by the apostrophe in the city curés' petition cited above; their double meaning was clear enough to the city notable:

Of all the virtues, none is better suited to persons of consequence than charity [*bienfaisance*]; by it they approach in some sort of the Divinity; only by it do they raise themselves above the remainder of men.[29]

The idealized memories of the independent traditions of the Parlement, the splendors of the churches, the piety of the religious houses, the social welfare system, the *capitoulat*, the network of ceremonial, and the guild loyalties were to be constantly invoked by the ultras after 1815. Memories are notoriously short in popular politics. Once a myth has gained currency, at the same time, it becomes persistent. In a later chapter the main characteristics of this nostalgia for the Old Regime are discussed at greater length. Then it will become evident how the social characteristics of Toulouse prior to 1789 remained typical of its inhabitants long after the revolutionary decade.

[28] *Très humbles et très-respectueuses supplications de messieurs les curés de Toulouse à M. le comte de Périgord, commandant en chef pour le Roi ... en Languedoc* (Toulouse, 1788), pp. 3–4.
[29] *Ibid.*, p. 2.

II

THE REVOLUTION: *SANS RELIGIOU*

Iᴎ ᴛʜᴇ ғɪʀsᴛ ᴅᴀʏs of 1789 it was reported that the Estates of Languedoc, due to open their session on January 15, were planning to represent the Province at the Estates which Louis XVI had called to meet in Versailles in the following May. The spokesmen of Toulouse, its nobles, the cathedral chapter and clergy, and its merchants and notables, all objected strongly.[1] Their criticisms were carried into the sessions of the Estates at Montpellier; Jean-François Gounon-Loubens, *capitoul*, bitterly attacked the representatives of the Third Estate for not better protecting those traditional interests which the barons of the Estates were trying to usurp.[2] Regional rivalries in the Province as well as differences between the social groups in Toulouse were to become more apparent in the course of the "Year of Liberty." The clergy advocated in their *cahier* educational reforms and an increase in the number of schools giving elementary education to the children of the poor, the nobility called for fewer ennoblements, but both orders held fast to their fiscal and social privileges. The Third Estate took a more hardy view of reforms required in the kingdom, but while it requested equal access to jobs in the legal system and reforms in taxation, it also called for the maintenance of the Parlement, the guaranteed permanency of its members as a protection against

[1] *Arrêté et supplications du parlement de Toulouse, concernant les Etats du Languedoc*, du 21 janvier 1789 (2 fascs).

[2] Joseph-François Gounon-Loubens, *Discours prononcé par Mr. Gounon-Loubens*, capitoul de Toulouse, aux Etats de Languedoc (Toulouse, 1789).

threats of dismissal, and no change in its jurisdictional area. The parlementarians did not have a unified outlook on politics, naturally enough, but the majority was soon more anxious than elated over the news from Versailles, over the development of Revolution, and over the local food shortage.[3]

The local elite, of which the parlementarians were the most important figures, tried to assert their authority. The Parlement devised a ration-card system enabling indigents to buy cheap bread during the food crisis. The rich and the respectable vied with each other in good wcrks. The elderly advocate Fauré wrote in May: "Other charitable persons give lots of money to the curés who then distribute it in kind to ashamed families and in bread to the poor. There is no well-off person without dependents."[4] Despite this charitable response to popular hardships and the expectation that the changes taking place in France as a result of the work of the Constituent Assembly would not alter the basic certainties of local life there were obvious grounds for increasing unease. The Great Fear of early August that swept through much of France affected also Toulouse. No lesser person than the First President de Cambon led a thousand men, reinforced with detachments from the *maréchaussée* and the town guard, against the brigands rumored to be advancing in strength from the direction of Montauban, burning and looting as they came. The collective panic had barely subsided before another and more substantial shock was experienced with the news of the hectic deliberations of the night of August 4, 1789, when the legal basis of the feudal system in France was largely abolished. Although the owners of seigneurial rights in the area of Toulouse found their losses almost balanced off by the abolition of the tithe on their land revenues, and need not have felt any hostility on fiscal grounds, the abolition of many of the most antique forms of French life was alarming. The parlementarians in particular were hostile, not merely for the selfish reason that their own position was dependent on the legal system which would favor their interests and careers but because the whole parlementary critique of the monarchy rested on a theory of society and history which was now being declared redundant. They were not alone in

[3] Claude de Vic, *Histoire générale du Languedoc . . . continuée jusqu'en 1790 par E. Roschach* (Toulouse, 1872–1904), vol. XIV, col. 2873.

[4] Louis-Joseph Fauré, *Notes et réflexions d'un bourgeois de Toulouse au début de la Révolution . . .*, ed. F. Pasquier (Toulouse, 1917), p. 25.

apprehension at what the immediate future would bring to a city which was widely known to depend upon its institutions for much of its revenue. There was no spontaneous overthrow of the municipality in Toulouse after July 14, such as took place in a number of French cities. The Patriots in the capital quite rightly saw evidence of a recalcitrant spirit in Toulouse in the continued existence of the *capitoulat* and the *parlement*.

The decree of the National Assembly of November 5, 1789, sharply reminded the courts and municipalities of the Kingdom that they must obey the representatives of the nation promptly. Less than a month later, the thirteen Parlements of France were sent on vacation and thus their opportunity to obstruct new legislation was reduced. The law of December 14, 1789, reorganized municipal government and doomed the *capitoulat*. As the nobles of Toulouse exchanged their New Year gifts and visits at the beginning of 1790, many agreed that the Old Year had seen a number of remarkable changes for the worse.

The parlementarians were determined to make an example of local supporters of the Patriots and to show their disdain for the new legislation. The *procureur général* Rességuier, particularly forthright in his criticism of revolutionary ideas, pressed for the prosecution of a book seller of Toulouse, Brouilhet, who was accused of publishing sedition in his *Journal Universel et Affiches de Toulouse et du Languedoc*. Brouilhet showed that his newspaper was, in fact, entirely a pastiche of extracts from journals published in Paris. Nevertheless, disregarding article seven of the *Declaration of the Rights of Man and of the Citizen*, which provided for freedom of the press, the vacation court at the end of January sentenced Brouilhet to pay a fine of one thousand livres to benefit the two main hospitals in Toulouse, and ordered the suppression of the *Journal*.[5] The time for such gestures was fast running out, as they increased hostility toward the Parlement among those in the city who had thrown their lot in with the Revolution. In Paris also newspapers like the *Courrier français* were writing that old-style magistrates were enemies of the Revolution.

The parlementarians participated only little in changes going on in the city and this seemed to give substance to the above suspi-

[5] E. Lamouzèle, "Le premier procès de presse à Toulouse sous la Révolution," *Revue des Hautes-Pyrénées*, XVII (1922), 41–53.

cions. President de Cambon was soon replaced as Commander of the National Guard. Although some of his colleagues joined this organisation, they played nothing like the part to which their former importance might have entitled them. In fact, it was their underlings who pushed themselves forward. Less than two years had passed since the advocates of the Parlement agreed not to serve in the new courts established by Loménie de Brienne in his effort to break the resistance of the old judiciary to his reforms. Now the memory of that outmoded loyalty was fast fading.[6] Malpel, Romiguières, Mailhe, and Rouzet, all advocates and future deputies, began to take a disquieting ascendancy in political meetings in the city. These men not only embraced Patriot principles but they had a sense of opportunism which the parlementarians lacked. Without the wealth and the constricting self-esteem of the judges they quickly followed the newly opened paths. Moreover, in the general atmosphere of change in France, it was natural that the rhetoric of egalitarianism found some audience in Toulouse, even if the majority believed that local prosperity rested on old institutions. Only commoners were elected to the new municipality which refused to officially inform the Parlement of the election. This new spirit of independence did not pass without notice.

Misgivings were expressed vehemently in the influential salons of the parlementarians and noble ladies, like that of the wife of a baron of the Estates of Languedoc, Mme. Montesquieu-d'Hautpoul. Early in 1790, the municipality asked the National Assembly to leave the Parlement intact. Was it not true of Toulouse that "all her fortune and hopes rested on this antique base"?[7] The pace of change forced by Paris was so rapid that its local opponents were at a loss to halt it. Archbishop Fontanges denounced the false principles of the Revolution in September, 1789, and again in January, 1790, and he had the satisfaction of a majority of his clergy rejecting the Civil Constitution, but the sale of church property and the closure of religious houses went forward. In February the guilds were abolished, to the regret of their former masters. A group of 370 angry catholics met on April 18, 1790, to demand of the King and the National Assembly that religious houses be preserved and

[6] *Lettre des avocats au parlement de Toulouse à Monseigneur le Garde des Sceaux sur les nouveaux édits transcrits ... dans les régistres du Parlement le 8 mai 1788* (Toulouse, 1788).
[7] Vic, *Histoire générale*, vol. XIV, cols. 2874–75.

THE REVOLUTION: *Sans Religiou*

Roman Catholicism recognized as the established religion. Their meeting was intimidated by the noisy intrusion of outsiders, but two days later they met again and almost two hundred of those present signed a petition requesting a plenary meeting of the commune of Toulouse. More of the leading parlementarians and the prominent clergy were present at this second meeting and signed. There was at least one artisan who described himself as such: Loustiac, *dit* Alcoix, shoemaker. When, predictably, the municipality refused to convene the commune, the statement was made that this decision might produce a dangerous backlash. A month later, a printed petition was sent to Paris in support of the Catholics of Nîmes (who had protested against the religious policy of the National Assembly in a widely circulated *Adresse*), and eleven hundred Catholics were claimed to have signed it. Of the signatories, 339 gave their occupation and thus showed the hostility of the religious policy of the Revolution among those groups recently affected by the abolition of the guilds. Over half of them came from commerce, food trades, tailors and wigmakers, and others involved in clothing and personal appearance. Almost fifty members of the legal professions also signed. There were some seventy nobles among the petitioners.[8] The municipality brushed aside the significance of this number of signatures and claimed that the petition was the result of house-to-house canvassing. Moreover, this activity was seen as showing a very sinister intent: "The ultimate goal of these secret intrigues is to form in the bosom of Toulouse a party hostile to the regeneration of France. . . ." The recently formed Directory of the new department of the Haute-Garonne feared that a fusion of religious and economic discontent might produce violence in a city which had always been "too disposed to fanaticism."[9] Pamphlets critical of the Revolution constantly harped on the theme of economic disruptions which followed abrupt institutional changes. *Les Quatre Evangélistes*, a local paper which tried to imitate the style of the conservative *Actes des Apôtres*, pointed out the

[8] *Procès-verbal et adresse des citoyens actifs et catholiques de la ville de Toulouse pour demander la conservation des Etablissements religieux, séculiers, et reguliers, et que la religion catholique, apostolique et romaine soit declarée la religion de l'état avec differentes pièces rélatives à cet objet* (Toulouse, 1790).

[9] Directoire du departement de la Haute-Garonne, Rapport . . . 24 avril 1790, AN, F^{19}427.

distress of the former employees of the parlementarians, as well as the economic difficulties caused by the disruption of the church.

The Catholics of Toulouse provided, as everywhere in France, a focus for those who felt some grievance against the Revolution. This remained true throughout the Revolution as royalism and hostility to the constitutional church tended to become interchangeable. On the other hand, the parlementarians played a minor part in the opposition to the Revolution after the sovereign courts had been suppressed by Letters Patent in September, 1790. The skeleton court that had kept the administration of justice going since the suspension of the previous year made one last gesture of defiance in the manner of the remonstrances. They were encouraged in their intemperate action by high feeling in the city where seven hundred families directly or indirectly suffered loss of prestige and income through the abolition.[10] This Vacation Court did not mince words. Only two of the councilors disassociated themselves from the action of their colleagues who declared, "Considering that the French Monarchy is at the moment of its dissolution' and that soon there will not remain any vestige of its most ancient institutions," the inhabitants of Languedoc, Quercy, Comminges, and Foix wished to preserve their cherished Parlement. It was an abuse to strip the clergy of their property, and the nobility of those "distinctions inherent to the essence of every monarchist state." Moreover, the reorganization of justice would produce an increase in the burden of taxation. The judges reaffirmed their duty of upholding the rights of the Crown, together with the liberties and franchises of the French people, and claimed they would remain faithful to these principles to their last breath.[11] Few of the judges could have suspected that this declaration would, in fact, cost them their lives. This was to occur within three years. The National Assembly, perplexed by news of the religious resistance in Toulouse, took a very dim view of what Mailhe, a radical advocate before the Revolution and now *procureur-général-syndic* of the Haute-Garonne, denounced as a collection of "the most unconstitutional and seditious maxims ... the height of the outrages of the former parlementary

[10] Axel Duboul, *La fin du parlement de Toulouse* (Toulouse, 1890), pp. 41–42.
[11] *Arrêtés du Parlement de Toulouse séant en vacations, 25 et 27 septembre 1790* (Toulouse, 1790).

aristocracy."[12] Prince de Broglie called for the arrest of those judges who had signed the declaration. They were thrown into confusion by this sharp reaction. Some crossed into Spain, where they gathered at Vitoria, and others were arrested but shortly thereafter released. Until the amnesty of September 15, 1791, a number of the more determined and energetic judges remained outside France. When they did return, it was to a city much different from that which accorded them a civic welcome in 1788. The municipality was frightened by the storm of Parisian rage against the parlementarians and followed Mailhe in censuring them.

There were of course in Toulouse those who favored the Revolution, who were fired by its principles, and who saw new career opportunities in the reorganization of French government. They found their forum at the meetings of the *Amis de la Constitution*, the only political club in the city, founded by a group of artisans in May, 1790, that became the *société populaire* of 1793. The *feudiste* Gélas, for example, joined the *Amis* in 1790, was a deputy to the Federation and played a major part in the *armée révolutionnaire*.[13] In revolutionary activity he found a substitute for his vanished sources of employment as a specialist on feudal law. The judicial system was changing rapidly, especially with the laws of September–October, 1791, which carried through a complete revision of what remained of the Old Regime organization. Artisans, merchants (especially from among the small Protestant community, following the lead of Pastor Julien), and some professional men joined notaries and advocates in the club, but there were few laborers or former servants among them. The *Amis* were particularly vehement on the point of the Civil Constitution of the clergy, perhaps because many members invested in buying the confiscated property which was put on sale. They denounced those Jacobins in Paris who had resigned in protest against a petition calling for the deposition of Louis XVI and who were known as *Feuillants*. In January, 1791, eight months before the mother society in Paris took the same step, the public was admitted to their meetings in order

[12] *Réquisitoire fait par M. Mailhe, procureur-général-syndic du departement de la Haute-Garonne, le 2 octobre 1790, devant MM. les administrateurs composant le Directoire de ce Département* (Toulouse, 1790).

[13] P. Gérard, "L'armée révolutionnaire de la Haute-Garonne," *Annales historiques de la Révolution française* (1959), p. 8.

to give wider circulation to their arguments against the nonjuring clergy and against local conservatives. The members demonstrated with their supporters, four hundred strong, in October, 1791, against the reopening of those churches which had been closed, and a month later denounced the Capucines who refused to take the oath to the Constitution and who said Mass in the chapel of the La Grave hospital. The chapel was a meeting place for critics of the religious policy of the Revolution, and increasing numbers of people attended these religious services. It was a tacit criticism of the Revolution to go to these Masses, and the municipality tried to exclude outsiders from the congregation on health grounds. Nevertheless, many local catholics petitioned for an access to these services.[14]

The religious question sustained tension on a variety of issues. The revision of parish boundaries and the reduced number of churches open for worship was part of the increasing rigor shown toward defenders of the old order. Precisely because these were so numerous, the partisans of the Revolution were harsh in trying to enforce obedience. The decrees of August, 1791, exiling non-jurors three leagues from the city, caused fears of "dangerous moves on the part of the people." When Hyacinthe Sermet, an ex-monk, was enthroned with the new title of Metropolitan Bishop and gave his allegiance to the Civil Constitution of the Clergy, many laymen in Toulouse supported the majority of the diocesan clergy who refused to accept his authority. Foremost among these priests was an angular young abbé, Marie-Jean-Philippe Dubourg, one of twenty children of a councilor at the Parlement. He had been a cathedral canon at Saint Etienne in a chapter whose membership was a roll-call of parlementary names, and he became a protégé of Archbishop Brienne, and of his successor, Archbishop Fontanges, to whom he was related through his mother. By 1789 he already bitterly regretted such juvenile enthusiasms as his brief membership in the masonic lodge *L'Encyclopédique*, in which one of his lodge brothers had been Bertrand de Barère, later to be a member of the Committee of Public Safety. Dubourg played an important role in the counterrevolution by coordinating the clerical resistance in Toulouse. His brothers were émigrés in the company set up by Comte

[14] *AN*, F^{19}427.

de Panetier in Spain, and received letters from him full of exhortations to practice their religion faithfully.[15]

The sale of church, noble, and émigré property, the changed demand for goods and services resulting from the disruption of the judicial system, and the effects of food shortage and dearth of currency all affected the city economy. It would be wrong to suggest that none profited from the new situation. Changes in the guild system, for example, were to the advantage of apprentice barber-wigmakers who described their former masters as men living on Old Regime abuses. Louis XVI had granted, by an edict of September, 1784, ninety-two privileged positions of barber-wigmaker in the city at a cost of 1,200 livres each. The owners of these licenses kept their apprentices in a state almost of slavery it was claimed. Many of the journeymen (*compagnons*) were grown men, married and members of the National Guard, who rejoiced in their liberation "as though more than ten centuries removed from an oppressive regime."[16] The masters for their part were appalled at the implications of economic liberalism; their ability to control the guilds had been weakened by internal dissensions before the Revolution and was now completely undermined by revolutionary legislation. If the masters were unhappy at the progress of the Revolution, those journeymen who were now able to set up their own shops could enjoy the initial elation—as long as they had customers. The sale of church property, especially that which belonged to the regulars and to the cathedral chapter who held in both town and country more than the secular owners did, was gratifying to those who had the money to buy, although priests and pious laymen were outraged. Some noble property was sold and caused a double dispossession to members of the family who were in religious orders. A number of nobles were completely ruined by confiscations: Thésan, Tournier-Vaillac, Dugarreau-Lassaguier, and Varès-Fauga among others. The professional men of Toulouse profited most handsomely from the sales; a study has shown that eighty percent and more of the lots offered for sale in the district were sold to town-dwellers. Merchants, doctors, prosperous artisans, and

[15] A. Dubourg, *Monseigneur de Bourg, évêque de Limôges, 1751–1822* (Paris, 1907), p. 138.

[16] *Les garçons perruquiers de la ville de Toulouse ... à MM. le maire et officiers municipiaux, 8 avril 1790* (Toulouse, 1790).

others were able to satisfy their desire to increase their land-holdings.[17]

This was not true of the wretched *métayers* of the countryside around Toulouse. These unfortunates had no reason to find the new landowners any different from the old. In fact many of the new owners showed themselves more exacting than the agents of the clergy or the noblemen had been in the years before the Revolution—if that was possible. Neither did the nobles who stayed in France profit from the sales opportunities, although twenty-one nobles did buy larger-than-average lots of the total 1,560 adjudications in the Toulouse district. The many nobles who stayed in the district throughout the Revolution were more involved in keeping out of hot water with the revolutionary authorities and in protecting their property from requisitions and confiscations. Joseph de Villèle's father, a model farmer, owned a house in the most aristocratic district of Toulouse, on the rue Vélane, as well as a large estate at Mourvilles-Basses, some sixteen miles from the city. He was a model of the way in which the noble kept his property intact. He explained in 1799 how he had preserved his estate and property against the attacks of "some so-called *patriots*, discriminatory and exaggerated in their attitudes, who for ten years I have resisted, laws and constitutions in my hand, to prevent them from ultra-revolutionising this area in order to put themselves in the place of the landowners."[18] Litigation could be dragged out before the new courts as well as the old, republican divorce proceedings (invalid in the eyes of a Catholic) could transfer menaced property to a wife, intermediaries could be used to repurchase estates which were placed on sale, bribes could be tendered and influence solicited, all possible devices used to protect the noble estate. After the Revolution, it was clear that, with few exceptions, the local nobility had been able to preserve the bulk of its property and wealth.

Between 1789 and the end of 1791, the parlementarians who had so zestfully defied the royal government in 1787–88 realized they were previously following a mistaken course. From their point of view, the best thing about the Old Regime was one of its major

[17] Henri Martin, ed., *Département de la Haute-Garonne. Documents rélatifs à la vente des biens nationaux, district de Toulouse* (Toulouse, 1916).

[18] Henri de Villèle to Minister of the Interior, 28 thermidor VII, *AN*, F⁷7602.

abuses, the pervasive legalism and antiquated judicial system which employed them. The innovations already made in the structure of French government had been made at the expense of their privileges and further change might, it seemed increasingly likely, be at the expense of their lives. Younger parlementarians now joined the National Guard company, commanded by President d'Aspe of a family from Auch, a man who served in the cavalry as a young man and who prided himself on his military dash. This company was soon known as the "Black Company" because of the extent of its association with the parlementarians and the various clerks, scriveners, and young law students who made up the *basoche*. Clashes between the Black Company and members of the *Amis de la Constitution* and their supporters became fairly frequent. On March 17, 1791, these exchanges of blows and curses reached a climax in a real fight: a man was killed by the Saint Barthélemy gate, and two of his companions were seriously wounded, one of them fatally. All three of these men were from the Saint-Nicholas legion, recruited from the working class district of Saint-Cyprien across the Garonne. The fight thus doubled the traditional rivalry between the workers of Saint-Cyprien and the servants and inhabitants of Saint Etienne. The master barber-wigmakers, porters, cooks, valets, and butlers were allies of their employers against the Canal du Midi stevedores (*crocheteurs*), the river men, and the artisans and common laborers of Arnaud Bernard, Saint-Michel, or Saint-Cyprien, all essentially lower-class districts. As a result of the fight, the d'Aspe legion was dissolved and the Departmental administration was well aware that the parlementarians commanded enough working-class sympathy to make it a distinct possibility that they could turn public discontent with the various innovations and shortages into dangerous channels.[19] Many men and women in the streets of Toulouse lacked work and any clear appreciation of the relevance to them of revolutionary slogans coined in the cold, half-understood language of the North. What is striking, however, is the ease with which the Black Company was brought under control. Neither President d'Aspe (who was guillotined in 1794), nor his associates made any further significant effort to coordinate armed resistance to the Revolution. The inability of parlementary counter-

[19] *ADHG*, L 268; *AN* Dxxix bis 11, 119; ——bis 21, 224; *Nouvelles tentatives des aristocrates de Toulouse* (Bordeaux, 1791).

revolutionaries to carry out illegal measures of resistance with any decisiveness, their most salient characteristic, had already become obvious.

Of the total 1,157 émigrés from the Haute-Garonne, more than a quarter were noble.[20] Most of them went to Spain across the Pyrenees or stayed close to the border where they could receive news from relatives via the Val d'Aran. When prominent individuals like Louis-Gaston d'Escouloubre, the richest man of the Toulouse area and a former deputy to the Constituent Assembly, left the country, attention was drawn forcefully to the vacuum in employment opportunities. In November, 1791, the advocate Fauré wrote anxiously in his diary about the prospects for a future where all the nobility, many bourgeois and even artisans had fled Toulouse, leaving only misery behind.[21] Even if he exaggerated, there were clear gaps in the familiar certainties of Toulouse.

Not everybody was as worried as the sexagenarian advocate. By 1792, the *Amis de la Constitution* enjoyed the local power and prominence which formerly belonged to the members of the Parlement. Just under three hundred strong, they occupied the place in the Toulouse sun which the robe nobles had enjoyed. They addressed to the public proclamations couched in the new revolutionary jargon that seemed almost a parody of the pretentious legal vocabulary of the "lair of chicanery" (as the *ci-devant* Parlement was now often described). Energetically joining the national effort against counterrevolution, they defended the measures that exiled the recalcitrant clergy from the city: "To require legal proofs to establish that the nonjuror priests are involved in conspiracy would be like asking them whether it is daytime at noon."[22] At a time when the city was affected by fears of invasion, food shortages, and anxiety felt by some about the wrath of God and by others about the fears of dearth among the people, the revolutionary administration and its supporters showed they could command and organize their forces much more effectively than their opponents did.

Among the latter, the clergy were the most persistent. In 1792 a clerical Committee of Conscience was said to have been formed to coordinate action. Abbé Dubourg and the Superior of the Irish

---

[20] D. Greer, *The incidence of the emigration* (Cambridge, Mass., 1951), pp. 110–14.

[21] Fauré, *Notes et réflections*, p. 60.

[22] *AN*, F^{19}427; correspondence of April 1792.

Seminary were its leading members. Dubourg was now a Vicar-General, appointed by Archbishop Fontanges before his withdrawal to London, and he remained in hiding in Toulouse during most of the Revolution, mainly in a house on the Rue St. Rémezy, from which he directed charity and propaganda, sent instructions to suffragan bishops, and distributed religious and royalist tracts. He was behind the clashes between the supporters of the nonjuring clergy and the authorities in 1792. As many as four hundred nonjuring priests may have been under his orders.[23]

Of the Ortric brothers, vicars of the Cathedral and sons of the co-seigneur of Bazière, the younger one was an especially active companion of Dubourg in this clandestine activity, moving around the city disguised, according to legend, as a tooth-powder salesman.[24]

The news of the execution of Louis XVI produced no royalist disturbances at Toulouse, although the local authorities themselves were becoming increasingly hostile to the policies pressed by the Jacobins in Paris. The religious resentments were now reinforced by dislike of conscription, requisitions, the *levée en masse*, the presence of a brawling garrison, and the other consequences of the war France was now fighting for her survival. In the eyes of the city authorities, here as in so many other parts of France, it was important to minimize the already numerous causes of dissension among citizens of the Republic rather than to increase them by what appeared ill-considered extremism forced by the Paris Jacobins. In Toulouse, the lack of enthusiasm for many of the main features of the Revolution was easily seen; in mid-March, 1793, a printed handbill attacking conscription was circulated, and in early April there were "attroupements" of the servants of émigrés. To the administrators of Toulouse, determined to maintain the achievements of 1789, it seemed politic not to goad the counterrevolution into action.

On April 24, 1793, the *représentant du peuple* Baudot arrived in Toulouse, one of the energetic Jacobins sent from the capital to rally and direct the war effort throughout France. He wasted no time on conciliatory overtures to the dissatisfied; the next day sev-

[23] G. Cayre, *Histoire des évêques et archévêques de Toulouse* (Toulouse, 1873), p. 468.
[24] A. Salvan, *Histoire générale de l'église de Toulouse* (Toulouse, 1856–61), IV, 539–40.

eral hundreds from among the nobility, artisans, and professions were arrested in Toulouse. Of the almost four hundred people imprisoned for royalism, the nobility numbered 148 and the legal professions 105; there were 56 artisans accused of counterrevolutionary sympathies. Although the charge was vague and based on opinion rather than facts, it is clear that the parlementarians and the older, well-established artisans from the food, clothing, and construction trades were most suspect of hostility to the Revolution. The latter group included Jean Arnal, a handkerchief-maker before the Revolution, who was subsequently employed at the tobacco factory as well as in packing bales of fodder: he had distributed copies of the *Adresse des Catholiques de Nîmes* in 1790. Another one was Jean-Baptiste Cazeneuve, a former agent of a seigneur and now a dealer in wood and sheep. There were also a former *feudiste*, Déaddé, who was an *agent de change*; a cooper suspected of being involved in a massacre of Patriots in his native Montauban; a *"liqueriste et cafétiste"*; a shoemaker; and others. The royalist prisoners were held in the Visitation prison, separated from the clergy, women, federalists, and common criminals who were housed in other jails. Political and personal animosities and spite were rife in the prisons, if the vituperative memoirs of Pescayre are to be trusted.[25]

It does not enter into this study to examine closely the strength of federalism in the city or its destruction by the vigorous action of the *représentants en mission* from other parts of France who had the support of the local *société populaire*.[26] What was evident to the people of Toulouse was the thorough humiliation of the past. Coats-of-arms displayed on buildings were destroyed. One of the *représentants* lived on the Place Rouaix, now renamed Marat, in the splendid hotel of a parlementarian, and enjoyed the extensive wine cellar. The hôtel Rességuier, formerly property of the notably counterrevolutionary *procureur-général* Rességuier, was now used as a troop billet. New street names, the revolutionary vocabulary, the cocky refusal of the old deferential forms of address, in short, the visible upset of the old social certainties gave a sense of exhila-

[25] R. de Bouglon, *Les reclus de Toulouse sous la Terreur. Régistres officiels* (Toulouse, 1893–1912); J. Pescayre, *Tableau des prisons de Toulouse sous le règne de Robespierre et sous celui de ses satellites* (Toulouse, an III).

[26] Madelaine Albert, *Le fédéralisme dans la Haute-Garonne* (Paris, 1931), *passim*. Dr. Martyn Lyons, research fellow at King's College, Cambridge University, is to publish shortly a study of *comités de surveillance révolutionnaire* in Toulouse, 1793–95.

ration to some, but fear and bewilderment to more. The experience with Terror was one of the roots of the ultraroyalist obsession with conspiracy. The success of the Jacobins seemed too total to be merely the result of energy and determination which triumphed over the widespread but cowed hostility of town and country. Indeed, the Jacobins themselves were aware of this explanation: "Without the rage of a handful of patriots that she [Toulouse] contains, not only would she have been unable to send missionaries to the towns of the Midi but she would have been torn like Lyon by aristocratic fury."[27]

The most systematic vehicle of the Terror was the revolutionary system of justice; on November 15, 1793, the criminal court of the department became its revolutionary tribunal, presided over by a former notary, Hugueny, and with a former advocate of the Parlement as public prosecutor. Of the eighty-five cases tried before it, thirty-one resulted in a death sentence, although only ten of the condemned actually lived in Toulouse. The tribunal did not, however, try the most notable Toulouse prisoners, for the leading Federalists and the judges of the Parlement were sent to Paris for the trial which resulted in their execution.[28]

D'Aldéguier, himself imprisoned during the Terror, thought that repression in Toulouse was less bloody than that in Lyon or Bordeaux. He put this down to the "lack of social standing, *médiocrité des existences sociales* which did not inspire any great envy, or to the general attitudes of the population."[29] There may also have been a backlash of opinion against a number of the executions. Regrets were expressed at the death on the scaffold of comte Jean Dubarry, notorious for his connection with the famous mistress of Louis XV and, more recently, as a leader of local catholics. His sumptuous house on the Place St. Raymond had been the setting of many elaborate parties and the cause of much free spending, and his own jovial generosity had made him a popular local personality. There was dislike for the maladroit decapitation, on February 24, 1794, of a handsome twenty-three-year-old descendant from the *capitoul* David (who had played a sinister part in the Calas Affair), who was a nephew of the ex-First President of the Parlement. His struggles on the scaffold and a botched first cut caused a lot of

---

[27] Albert, *Le fédéralisme*, p. 196.
[28] Axel Duboul, *Le tribunal révolutionnaire de Toulouse* (Toulouse, 1894).
[29] J. B. A. d'Aldéguier, *Histoire de Toulouse* (Toulouse, 1834–35), IV, 515.

blood to be splattered on the executioners. Not all present were afficionados of such events; the *société populaire* was so impressed by the unfavorable crowd reaction that they debated how the sight of blood could be hidden from spectators at public executions. In March, 1794, a prominent noblewoman was executed for sending some money to her son, an émigré in Spain. This case excited public sympathy, and the story of her death was long remembered. In the 1830's, the English tourist Mary Boddington was told by a *concierge* that she had seen "as good and virtuous a lady as any in Toulouse pass by with her hands tied behind her back going to execution, and all because she had sent a little money to her son, who was an émigré."[30] Some of the executions which took place in Paris affected Toulouse: the story circulated of how young Armand Dubourg, nephew of the royalist priest and son of the councilor, had followed on foot to the capital the carts carrying his father and other members of the Parlement to trial and execution. He allegedly received a last blessing and a crucifix from his father on the Place de la Révolution, site of the guillotine.[31] Such incidents, constantly retold, were part of royalist hagiography.

The fall of Robespierre renewed hope among royalists, clergy, and former Federalists everywhere in France. In December, 1794, the *société populaire* was purged, a month after the closure of the parent society in Paris. Elegantly dressed dandies appeared on the streets of Toulouse as elsewhere in France, in sharp and deliberate contrast with the drab clothing and scruffy appearance favored under the Jacobin ascendancy; they met in a café on the Place Rouaix. The same square was to be a social center for the ultras two decades later; it adjoined the area of the parlementarian *hôtels*.[32] Laurence, one of the representatives on mission (*représentants en mission*) who were sent by the Thermidorean government in Paris to eliminate in France the local power of the Jacobins, made clear his sympathy for those who had suffered under the Terror.

[30] Mary Boddington, *Sketches in the Pyrenees with some remarks on Languedoc. Provence and the Cornice* (London, 1837), II, 249.

[31] Referred to in the speech on paternal love, read at the Temple of Reason on January 30, 1795. Dubourg, *Mgr. du Bourg*, p. 193.

[32] J. Adher, "La conspiration royaliste dans la Haute-Garonne en l'an IV et en l'an V," *La Révolution française*, 41 (1901), 218–22; J. Beyssi, "Le parti jacobin à Toulouse sous le Directoire," *Annales historiques de la Révolution française* (1950), pp. 28–54, 109–33.

The times seemed propitious to local royalists, and in March, 1795, Antoine Pourquéry Dubourg, a flamboyant minor nobleman from the Lozère, formed a committee to organize those who hoped to restore the Monarchy. Before the Revolution, he had been a guardsman who had acquired a scandalous reputation for seducing the daughter of a financier, who was in a convent. Soon after 1789, he declared his hostility to the Revolution and was involved with the Camp de Jalès, an armed counterrevolutionary assembly which met in August, 1790. After the collapse of that attempt to coordinate armed opposition to the Revolution, Pourquéry Dubourg went into hiding, but emerged in the congenial atmosphere of the Thermidorian reaction and came to Toulouse to the home of his cousin. She was the wife of Alexandre de Sambucy, baron de Meirs, a native of Millau, and son of an officer in the Isle-de-France regiment; he had studied law at the University of Toulouse and had purchased an office of a councilor at the Parlement. Pourquéry Dubourg thus found himself in contact with the robe families of Toulouse through his host, but even more so through Mme de Sambucy who was daughter, sister, mother and cousin-german of five councilors. She was also related to the dean of the company as well as to a President and to the procureur-général Rességuier. Sambucy was imprisoned during the Terror and was only saved from the fate of the councilors executed in Paris by the fact that he was not any longer a member of the Parlement in 1789. The Revolution had disturbed his finances and forced him to live on the dowry brought to his marriage by his wife and to engage in an expensive lawsuit. His wife had a small property at Giscaro in the Gers. Pourquéry Dubourg, with his swashbuckling manner, soon became the leader of the rather timid group who hoped to organize royalism in Toulouse. After ten months of recruiting for the cause, he received an official recognition from Louis XVIII in February, 1796. With the help of Sambucy and using his cousin as secretary, he tried to rally the opposition to the local Jacobins, but his incurable extravagance and foolhardiness, heightened by the jealousy of other royalists in Bordeaux who sent unfavorable reports to the exile court, caused him to be replaced as the leader of the Toulouse royalist organization in late 1798.[33]

---

[33] J. Lacouture, *Le mouvement royaliste dans le sud-ouest (1797–1800)* (Hosségor, 1932), pp. 29–30; L. de Santi, "Notes et documents sur les in-

THE REVOLUTION: Sans Religiou

The effect of the increase in royalist self-confidence was soon evident in the street fights which took place in Toulouse, stimulated by the traditional rivalries of different districts.[34] There were clashes between townspeople and the elegant *muscadin* thugs on the one hand, and the garrison and former Jacobins on the other. In early May, 1795, several cannoneers, always noted as enthusiastic revolutionaries, were badly beaten up in the municipal gardens.[35] On June 30, 1795, the gates of the St. Catherine prison were broken in and some priests released. On July 28, women demonstrated at the cathedral against the observance of the *décadi*, the day of rest according to the new calendar. Mass was celebrated openly by nonjuror priests in such notoriously royalist households as that of the Dubourgs. Shopkeepers who observed the *décadi* were insulted.[36] The *mange-nation*, one among many insulting terms used to describe ex-Jacobins, were widely and bitterly denounced.[37] *L'Anti-Terroriste*, a royalist newspaper (as the title implies), called openly for the release of refractory clergy from jail and the *représentant en mission* did in fact free a number of them.[38] Meanwhile, the abbé Dubourg tried to reorganize the Toulouse clergy, going so far as to abjure, in full pontificals, the revolutionary errors of a crowd of penitents in the St. Etienne cathedral.[39] In July and August, 1795, the *Manifeste de Charette*, a counterrevolutionary tract, was hawked on the streets of Toulouse, and royalist sympathies were often expressed. At the end of August, a Jacobin cannoneer was killed in a brawl outside the Capitole on the Place de la Liberté; the new administration was alarmed at the prospect of more serious disturbances. A number of measures were taken to bring the royalist faction into line. The owners of *L'Anti-Terroriste* were imprisoned, and demonstrators at the city theater, including women with too much green in their dress (green was the royalist

---

trigues royalistes dans le sud-ouest de 1792 à 1815," *Mémoires de l'Academie des sciences, inscriptions et belles lettres de Toulouse*, 12 sér., IV (1916), 37–115.

[34] *Anti-Terroriste*, 26 floréal II (May 20, 1795).

[35] *ADHG*, L 270.

[36] E. Lamouzèle, "La procédure en usage devant le tribunal révolutionnaire de Toulouse," *Recueil de l'Académie de Legislation de Toulouse*, 4 sér., IX (1930–31), 152–56.

[37] *Anti-Terroriste*, 6 floréal III (April 25, 1795).

[38] *Anti-Terroriste*, 29 prairial III (June 17, 1795).

[39] *Anti-Terroriste*, 7 thermidor III (July 25, 1795).

THE REVOLUTION: *Sans Religiou*

color) were arrested. This reaction became abruptly more severe with news of the anti-royalist coup in Paris of 13 Vendémiaire.[40]

The indefatigable abbé Dubourg called upon the faithful to bear persecution with equanimity and to be charitable. Royalist agitation continued, as in the demands for annulment of the elections of the Year IV. The republican *Journal de Toulouse* lamely stated the royalists went as far as four leagues into the countryside to collect signatures for a petition.[41] It may well be that royalist effort was concentrated largely on the countryside. At Aleth, a religious ceremony of "purification" of revolutionary error had a great success with the country women. The peasants were to express these rural resentments against the Revolution by their participation in the Insurrection of the Year VII (August, 1799). This does not imply that the urban lower classes were necessarily in favor of the less radical regime brought to power after the fall of Robespierre. There were many signs of the same royalist and clerical agitation in Toulouse as in the country. Working women were turning against the Revolution as elsewhere in France; conservative and older artisans had many grievances; the poor were very sensitive to the deprivations brought about by inflation. The funeral ceremonies of a Cordelier friar noted for piety, which took place in December, 1796, were described as the work of an alliance of royalists and working-class women: "Joined to the town's *honnêtes gens* were all the servant women, fishwives, women fruitsellers, and shopkeepers, who had howled the *Réveil du Peuple* [an anti-Jacobin song] during the Terror launched by the supporters of Laurence...."[42] The possibilities of royalists capitalizing on the resentments of working-class women and the poor were many. The Directory's *commissaire* to the Haute-Garonne made this plain in December 1797 when he reported to the Minister of the Interior:

It would be politic, Citizen Minister, for the Nation to carry out its obligations to the poor. The aristocracy profits from their deplorable situation

---

[40] *ADHG*, L 270; L. Dutil, "Un homme de '89. Pierre Roussillon, député de Toulouse à la Constituante," *Mémoires de l'Academie des sciences, inscriptions et belles-lettres de Toulouse*, 13 sér., II (1940), 274. J. Gros, "L'esprit public à Toulouse après la Terreur," *Mémoires de l'Académie des sciences, inscriptions et belles lettres de Toulouse*, 12 sér., VIII (1920), 65–83; AN, F1cIII (Garonne, Haute-) 8.

[41] *Journal de Toulouse*, 6 vendémiaire V (September 30, 1796).

[42] *Journal de Toulouse*, 10 nivôse V (December 30, 1796).

in order to excite them against the Republic. Their sufferings are attributed to the Revolution so that they will detest it. Moreover the poor man is naturally led to complain against a government which refuses him bread. . . .[43]

Royalist propaganda harped on economic and religious grievances with substantial effect.

The events of 18 Fructidor in Paris saw Toulouse under a stricter municipal control by former Jacobins, but the views of those in the town hall did not represent those current in the streets. Throughout most of 1798 and 1799, the grievances of the royalists and their sympathizers smouldered, until the resentments against requisitions, conscription, and the Jacobins finally burst out in August, 1799. This was the rising known as the Insurrection of the Year VII.

The insurrection had been planned by a royalist organization centered on Lyon and called the *Institut Philanthropique*, in which charitable activities provided a "front." The Midi was divided into four regions for the purposes of organizing a royalist rising; each of these four "*arrondissements*" had a leader named by Louis XVIII from his exile court. Toulouse was the headquarters of one of the four. The usual problems of counterrevolutionary organizations affected this body; its members were in constant risk of arrest, government informers like the abbé Montgaillard infiltrated into positions of trust, communication between the components of the organization was sporadic, and, above all, the mixture of timidity and recklessness which characterized the leaders meant that much time was expended on sterile discussions or the desire to make foolhardy gestures. The *Institut Philanthropique* had planned a rising for mid-August, 1799, with simultaneous risings in a number of French cities, especially Bordeaux, Lyon, and Toulouse. Once these cities were in royalist hands, it was hoped to reconquer, with the help of the insurgents and foreign troops, the North and Paris for Louis XVIII.

The nature of royalist support varied widely from one part of France to another. In the area of Toulouse, the Insurrection of the Year VII was given its own local impetus. Two and a half months before the rising, the Black Madonna of La Daurade, a wooden

---

[43] *AN*, F^{1c}III (Garonne, Haute-) 8; F^{1b} (Garonne, Haute-) 2.

figurine in one of the larger churches in Toulouse that was revered as being of miraculous origins (it had come floating down the Garonne) was destroyed by order of the Jacobin municipality. At the time of the Terror, the Madonna had simply been impounded with other religious articles, but it was released to the clergy after the return to legal Catholic religious observance. The police noted that the Black Madonna quickly became "a toy of which the murderous arm of fanaticism made use." The Daurade church attracted many who came to venerate the statue and these were seen as potential subversives: "We noticed that the majority of persons in these gatherings were country people who made the most idiotic as well as the most fanatical statements. . . ."[44] One night the city police commissioners seized and burned the wooden Madonna to end the pretext for these gatherings, an action which outraged devout Catholics in town and country alike. It provided ready-made ammunition against the religious policy of the Directory for the priests working under the direction of the abbé Dubourg.

The rising in the vicinity of Toulouse started a week before the date fixed by the national leaders of the royalist organization. The two young men who commanded in the Toulousain had military experience; the Comte de Paulo had been in the royal army and Baron de Rougé fought in the American War of Independence before serving for the Republic in France. They were jealous of each other's authority in the royalist organization and showed little aptitude for cooperation. The royalist committee in Toulouse held its last meeting on the night of 17/18 Thermidor VII at the home of du Vaure, a returned émigré whose family property had been confiscated. Among those present were de Rougé and others who were to be prominent ultraroyalists under the Restoration: de Villeneuve-Crouzilhac, de Guintraud, de Quinquéry d'Olive, and St. Félix. It was agreed by these conspirators that the movement should begin in Muret canton where it enjoyed much popular support; once the royalist force had assembled they should advance on Toulouse, supported by a movement inside the city gates. The element of surprise was to be vital. Once the royalists would have taken Toulouse, they would control the Southwest also.

The white flag was unfurled in Muret canton on 19 Thermidor VII, and the administrators of Toulouse were appalled to receive

[44] *AN*, F[19]427 procès-verbal 4 prairial VII.

the news that Lanta, Caraman, Montgiscard, Auterrive, Muret, and St. Lys had risen against the Republic. Communications with Paris were still open, although it was feared they would shortly be cut, and there were blockades to the south of the city and along the Canal du Midi. The departmental and municipal administrations went into emergency session and decreed the arrest as hostages of the members of the noble and parlementary families of Toulouse. The energetic response to the crisis frightened the royalists inside the city and they took no action to force one of the city gates, as had been arranged, in order to admit their friends without. The Insurrection was in fact the work of country people, peasants and artisans, lead by military men.

Recruitment among the peasantry had been widespread. A man from Brugières, to the north of Toulouse, reported a month before the rising that he was asked by a peasant at the Toulouse market to join in the Restoration of the monarchy. The departmental administration disregarded what appeared to be another extravagant story, but it seems likely that this was a genuine echo of the effort to win support for the rising.[45] Judging from the list of suspects and those punished in the subsequent repression the majority of participants were illiterate day laborers from the country (*brassiers*) together with carpenters, blacksmiths, weavers, masons, coopers, and other artisans, lead by country noblemen like the de Serre brothers from the Ariège, and a few officials, like the *juge de paix* of Muret. Of those participants who lived in Toulouse proper, a third were engaged in agriculture, men like Joseph Poiresson, who in the shrinking modesty of the prisoner described himself as owning a small property. There were also day-laborers from the countryside, *brassiers*, men like the reluctant conscript from Pouvourville, three miles to the south of Toulouse, together with some artisans. Agricultural workers actually lived in the city and daily went to work in the *gardiage*, the area surrounding the walls; for example, Borret, a gardener who described himself as belonging to "la classe des travailleurs de la terre," or a twenty-year-old orphan apprentice-gardener, or yet another gardener who feared that he was to loose his job during his imprisonment. The latter was like a number of others who came from villages within a ten-kilometer radius around Toulouse, from a transitional zone of rural and urban

[45] *ADHG*, L 270.

concerns. Other prisoners who lived in Toulouse had come originally from further afield, like the tailor Etienne Garrigues from St. Sulpice-sur-Lèze 20 kilometers to the south of the city, who claimed that he was arrested because he was in the insurgent area where he went every year to help his father harvest. François Mandement, a native of Seysses near Muret, who lived in Toulouse as an apprentice-shoemaker, had been arrested close to his home village. The evidence is slight, but particularly in a time of migration, many city dwellers can identify with country concerns in that struggle between town and country which, as de Tocqueville tells us, is fundamental to the history of the Revolution. They shared the countryman's sense of having been cheated, if only indirectly, from what has been called a legitimate and traditional profit in the context of year III.

The largest group of prisoners from Toulouse was drawn from commercial, clothing, food, and artisan trades. They included the widower Dulac, an upholsterer from "the class of artisans without a fortune who have a numerous family which needs his hands in order to feed itself." A cook, an oven-keeper, and a café owner were from the food trades. The oven-keeper was accused of entertaining aristocrats to snacks and meals. He replied that his ovens needed to be watched while the bread was baking, and that "some artisans who were his friends and close neighbors . . . used to come to his place in the afternoon to drink a bottle, just as they had always done, even before the Revolution." Personal spite came out in this repressive situation. A thirty-six-year-old former brigadier of military transports claimed that two of his sworn enemies, without any sign of legal authority, with drawn swords, took him to jail in the former Carmelites convent. On the way, they stopped outside of the bars and attempted to provoke the fury of the customers against him. Foreigners were arrested more because they were suspiciously alien than because they were royalist. A native of Lucca in Tuscany with the gallicized name Valentine lived in St. Michel; he was an apprentice in making plaster figurines, perhaps undecided between a better trade in Madonnas and a slower trade in busts of Rousseau. He was accused of making false passports. Another Italian, a wigmaker from Turin, passing through Toulouse at the time of the Insurrection, was arrested. Spaniards were the common foreign residents in the city and we find among the arrested Jean Benedicto from Saragossa. He lived in Toulouse, ostensibly engaged in the horse trade: he was described as a *tondeur des chevaux*. In jail he might have met the mysterious individual captured at Béziers and sent back to Toulouse where he claimed successively to be a native of New England and an escaped Hungarian prisoner of war. Many of those who fought were young. Among the wounded was Jean Boubène, twenty-five years old, and put out for nursing from the La Grave foundling hospital in 1774 at the rate of three livres monthly.[46]

The energy of the revolutionary authorities and the military in-experience of the peasants caused the rapid collapse of the rising when regular troops confronted the rebels. Battles were fought at l'Isle Jourdain, Muret, Mauvésin, and Montréjeau; the royalists marching down from the mountains of the Ariège were intercepted and routed between Bonnac and Vernet, and the royalists from the small-holdings of the Gers and the area to the north of Toulouse were dismissed at Mas-Grenier and St. Sardos. In none of these encounters was the issue in doubt when the peasants, untrained and poorly armed, faced regular troops.

As many as 30,000 men had taken part in the rising and the casualties ran into thousands. The subsequent official repression was mild. Of those captured, ten men were shot for their part in the rising, two sentenced to deportation, and six sentenced to fines and imprisonment. Apart from making a few examples the authori-ties accepted the argument that the peasants had been mislead by unscrupulous ex-nobles and priests who pushed them into revolt in the hope of regaining their privileges. The deaths caused in the fighting, and during the pursuit, of the panic-stricken peasants flee-ing from regular troops, and in the crowded prison at Toulouse where more died from wounds and sickness, were object lesson enough.[47]

The parlementaire families, the local notables, and sympathizers with hopes for a royalist success were also chastened. Inside the city, there were large-scale arrests of suspects. In the countryside in the insurrectionary areas, many had suffered property damage, like the elder Villèle at Mourvilles-Basses, whose château was looted by republican troops that drove off prize stock, terrified his

---

[46] *ADHG*, L 2294; 2268–74, 2277, 2282; *AMT*, 2 H 39.
[47] *ADHG*, L 2264. Damages arising from the insurrection were evaluated in the department at 282, 267F and in Toulouse proper at 14,992F.

daughters, and irreparably damaged an extensive collection of agricultural books and specimens:

The said Villèle is strongly suspected of being one of the principal agents or partisans of the royalist rebellion. . . . the country house of the said Villèle was an asylum for the ill-intentioned who wished to hide themselves from official surveillance. . . . the canton of Caraman where citizen Villèle usually lived was one of the first and most strongly insurgent. . . . citizen Villèle was not only a farmer but a former noble and a close relative of two émigrés. . . .[48]

The inaction within Toulouse, the lack of military ability among the peasants, and the limited participation of the parlementary families in anything save the planning stage of the rising caused a sense of betrayal among the rank and file. The long-awaited counter-blow against the Revolution was, in the event, little more than a feeble slap. The municipality announced proudly to the Directory that thanks to their energetic action within the city not a drop of blood had been spilled inside the city walls during the two weeks of the Insurrection.[49] The official lawyer for the defense of the 1,500 prisoners who were held in a Toulouse church while they awaited trial asked for mercy to be extended to his clients. He described the city as having the aspect of a besieged town, full of the noise of drums, the clatter of arms, the marching of soldiers, and the maneuvers of cavalry, its shops closed, commerce disrupted and the inhabitants in the grip of mutual suspicion and the fear of arrest.[50] The municipality, shaken by recent events, permitted anti-royalist demonstrations on the part of former Jacobins, in order to humble the *honnêtes gens*. The coaches and sedan chairs of the nobles and the well-to-do were jeered at, and according to the first prefect to arrive in the city, personal cleanliness was seen as a sign of counterrevolutionary fastidiousness.[51] The city was full of rumors, and it was whispered that another rising would take place on All Saint's Day. There were, in fact, sporadic incidents of royalist intimidation in the countryside, particularly around Le Fousseret in the south of the department.

[48] Lamagdelaine to Minister of Police 2 vendemiaire VIII, *AN* F⁷7602.
[49] Rapport, 5 fructidor VII, *AN*, F⁷7602.
[50] Lieussac to Minister of Police, 5 compl. VII, *AN* F⁷7602.
[51] Jugements: 1er et 2e conseils de guerre, Xe Division Militaire; Rapport, 10 floréal VIII. *AN*, F⁷7602.

As was usual in Toulouse, alarmist talk was not a prelude to action. In any event, the Eighteenth of Brumaire curtailed the municipality which had particularly harassed the royalists. There was a general desire for moderation. The new mayor, Philippe Picot de Lapeyrouse, a liberal nobleman, botanist and agronomist, called for an end to political dissensions in Toulouse in his inaugural speech: "For too long the Republic has been confused with excesses of one faction; the time of passions and of storms ought to be already far from us. . . ."[52] After a decade of constant reverses, the royalists of Toulouse were inclined to agree. The experience of the Revolution and the conclusions they drew from it were to be deep-rooted in the ultraroyalism of the Restoration.

[52] *AMT*, Register of municipal deliberations, 18 floréal VIII.

III

FROM BONAPARTE TO THE BOURBONS

URING THE NAPOLEONIC PERIOD, southern royalists were, as one noble beauty put it, "a caste which made up for its lack of numbers by the religious cult it dedicated to its political faith, and by its pitiless rigor towards apostasies or even towards lesser failings."[1] She saw this group as essentially made of the nobility and a few commoners. This political faith of the royalists was little more than a vaguely legitimist set of sympathies or, more exactly, a feeling that the contemporary world was less satisfactory than that before 1789. News of the Bourbons was in very short supply. The Imperial censorship carefully deleted references to the former dynasty which might encourage royalist hopes. The publications which did circulate were full of panegyric about Napoleon and his military exploits. Even a royalist family like the Villèles lacked accurate information about the Bourbons. A quaint example of this lack of news was provided by abbé Trenqualié who preached enthusiastically at Saint Etienne in 1814 on the good fortune of France in regaining its legitimate sovereigns and praised the Queen, obviously unaware that she had been dead for four years.[2] As Chateaubriand observed, the Bourbons were as little known in Restoration France as the children of the Chinese Emperor. Royalist political associations of a sort existed at Toulouse,

[1] Léontine de Castelbajac, *Mémoires de l'Occitanienne* (Paris, 1927), pp. 225–26.
[2] Guillaume-Isidore de Montbel, *Souvenirs ... 1787–1831* (Paris, 1913), p. 115.

50

such as the clique of the octogenarian Villeneuve de Beauville, who by virtue of a discreet retirement to the country during the Revolution had passed without trouble through the Terror. During the Empire he met with elderly cronies of similar royalist ideas who were known derisively as the *Conseil des Anciens*. They were too senile and inept to be considered dangerous by the authorities.[3] There is no evidence of royalist-motivated discontent other than trivial incidents, like the minor official of the Parlement who had been an émigré with French royalist forces in Spain before his return to Toulouse where he lived on the Rue du Salin in .the parlementary district. Poor and proud, he lived by his wits as a general sollicitor and was accused of spreading rumors against the Emperor and encouraging young conscripts to avoid military service. The reports on him made clear that he was an unhappy neurotic rather than a menace to public order.[4]

The economic security of the nobility was increasing; Ramet's claim that the majority of the Toulouse nobility was ruined by the Revolution is clearly unfounded.[5] Examination of the lists of the *Six Cents Plus Imposés*, the men who paid the highest tax in the department, makes this evident.[6] Even those who had been touched by the Revolution were still largely able to keep their wealth, despite exceptions like Dupac de Bellegarde. Of the 354 names on a list of suspects in 1799, all save five were *ci-devants*; eighty-five of these figured either in person or by family in the six cantons around Toulouse during the Restoration, and fifty-five of these paid over 1,000 francs in tax and were men of substantial wealth.[7] It is a curiosity to note that nobles had bought *biens nationaux*: a chevalier de Saint-Louis, Cazals; a former *trésorier de France* Voisins-Lavernière; and the son of a high official of the Provincial Estates, Marcassus-Puymaurin, were all among big buyers. A Toulouse mer-

---

[3] Poitevin-Peitavi, "Eloge de M. de Villeneuve de Beauville," *Recueil de . . . Jeux Floraux . . . 1814–1815–1816* (Toulouse, 1816), p. 109.

[4] *AN*, F⁷ 8437. Report on Ledoux: "Cet homme, qui est dans la misère, était huissier au parlement; il se lamente souvent sur la perte d'un état qui le faisait vivre."

[5] H. Ramet, *Histoire de Toulouse* (Toulouse, 1935), p. 812.

[6] P. Bouyoux, "Les six-cents plus imposés du département de la Haute-Garonne, an X," *Annales du Midi*, LXX (1958), 317–27.

[7] *ADHG*, L 2277, list of hostages; *ADHG*, 2 M 19–24, electoral lists of 1820, cantons: Cadours, Verfeil, Fronton, Toulouse-nord, Toulouse-ouest, Toulouse-sud.

chant in 1799 quite rightly thought the nobility the wealthiest group in local society.[8]

The economic crisis of 1811 revealed the fragility of the few innovations in manufacturing. Boyer-Fonfrède went bankrupt and the Bosc armaments works scarcely outlived the death of its director. In 1806 the prefect had reported a drop in land values because of poor revenues and also a fall in the price of urban properties.[9] It was not surprising that so many looked to the past for the model of prosperity. One local worthy expressed it in a petition which requested Napoleon to set up an Imperial Palace at Toulouse. The presence of a court would give the city some of its former prestige and would generate expenditures lost as a result of the Revolution: "Toulouse has lost everything: its universities, its academies, its churches, its colleges, its courts, its hospitals: surrounded by ruins she is not at all Toulouse the Holy or Toulouse the Learned: she is no longer the capital of the Midi. . . ."[10]

The Empire seemed initially to have brought religious peace to the city by the Concordat. An archbishop had been appointed who was detested by the Old Regime nobility because he had been a juring priest and, still worse, because he was born a commoner. Archbishop Primat had to be accepted in the name of the renewal of the French Church after the trials of the revolutionary period. He worked patiently to reorganise the clergy, to stop the spiteful recriminations to which many of his priests were addicted, and to work out an acceptable arrangement with the Napoleonic regime. He personally considered that his flock was a trial sent to him by God for his sins.[11] Certainly the renewed conflict of Empire and Papacy and the imprisonment of the pope, Pius VII, in the summer of 1809 made this hope for harmony less likely to be fulfilled.

Elsewhere in France, the Empire was under scrutiny for its flaws, and a new royalist organization emerged in Paris to coordinate propaganda and to establish cells throughout France. Mathieu de Montmorency visited Toulouse in 1812 to organize a local section, drawing on the nobility and veterans of earlier groups which had

[8] AN, F1cIII (Garonne, Haute-) 3, Girard to Minister of Interior, 20 pluviôse VII.

[9] H. Martin, Départment de la Haute-Garonne, . . . Toulouse, lxviii.

[10] AN, F1bII (Garonne, Haute-) 4; J. Bataillié-Madron, Voeu présenté, n.d.

[11] J. Birot, Biographie lyonnaise: Claude-François-Marie Primat 1746–1816 (Lyon, 1909).

been hostile to the regime. Many well-known names among the Toulouse ultras appear here: Pons de Villeneuve, d'Hargicourt, d'Escouloubre, de Limairac, de Villèle, Baron de Montbel. They did not engage in any very dangerous sabotage activities or contribute materially to the success of the invasion when it came. However, they stimulated discontent with conscription and heavy taxes and circulated propaganda and some pins in the form of fleur de lys, but this campaign did not have any widespread significance until the very eve of Wellington's entry into the city. Joseph Caffarelli, a councilor of state, had been sent as a special envoy to the tenth military division to coordinate resistance. He was, in fact, related to the wife of a member of the *chevaliers de la foi*, Mme d'Hargicourt du Barry. He reported on the activity of the royalist associations: they were "winning hearts by the practice of charity," the same technique as used during the Revolution. The enthusiastic and devout welcome given to Pius VII on February 2, 1814, on his return to Italy from Fontainebleau showed the temper of the city. There was no surge of patriotic resistance as the enemy armies approached. When Wellington entered the city after the battle of April, 1814, the royalists showed their hand: the White Flag was flying, officials and many inhabitants wore white cockades and sashes, and the enemy troops were given a warm welcome in the city streets.[12]

The First Restoration was joyfully welcomed by clergy and nobility in Toulouse. However, in their exuberance after more than twenty years of greater or lesser restrictions, they struck a lot of very impolitic attitudes. Besides violent recriminations against the most active servants of the Revolution and the Empire, there was a lot of loose talk about returning the *biens nationaux* to their rightful owners. The rumor circulated in the countryside that tithes were to be reimposed, and the peasantry also feared that the unpopular conscription and various exactions of the Empire might be continued. There was rancor over the maintenance of the *droits réunis*. At the same time, there was pleasure at the change in

---

[12] L. Bénaërts, *Les commissaires extraordinaires de Napoléon 1er en 1814*, Bibliothèque d'histoire moderne, 15 (Paris, 1915), pp. 44–46. P. Genevray, *L'administration et la vie écclésiastiques dans le grand diocèse de Toulouse* (Toulouse, 1941), p. 96. Arthur Wellesley, *Duke of Wellington, Dispatches* (London, 1837), XI, 639; XII, 14–15. M. Albert, *La première restauration dans la Haute-Garonne* (Paris, 1931), pp. 39–40.

government, and for the poorest part of the population it had long been clear they could hope for more from catholico-royalists than from other sources. There were clear signs, however, that this fund of good will was spent quite recklessly.[13] Then, in the spring of 1815, the bombshell burst: Napoleon was once again Emperor of the French.

The Hundred Days at Toulouse was marked neither by clear enthusiasm for nor by hostility toward the Empire. All parties eyed each other suspiciously. The supporters of the regime were the most likely to show their hand, but they commanded little popular support. The anti-clerical secretary of the prefecture, Dantigny, tartly described the most influential faction in the city as composed of a lot of women, especially from the upper classes, various decrepit chevaliers de Saint Louis, and the members of the clergy. He concluded by writing that "persons of the noble class, or those who pretend to be such, together with those who are entirely under priestly influence, are perhaps more numerous at Toulouse than in any other city of the Empire."[14] On the other hand, the Empire could look to the support of a volunteer force called the fédérés, who were backed up by the troops stationed in the city. The fédérés had been formed on May 27, 1815, in a way similar to that followed in Brittany, Lyons, and Paris, by maréchal-de-camp Julien, a protestant related to the revolutionary pastor of the same name, and the manufacturer Boyer-Fonfrède, known as an owner of biens nationaux and a bankrupt. Neither the Fédération nor popular Bonapartism have yet received the study which they merit, but the Toulouse fédérés seem to have attracted former revolutionary officials, protestants, some retired officers, and adventurers. They were united by an aversion to royalist arrogance and intimidation.

During the Hundred Days, rich royalists were pressured to pay a Forced Loan, and lower-class supporters of the Bourbons jostled their opponents on the boulevards. Vicar-general Cambon was arrested when he refused to hand over the keys of the Carmelite church to the fédérés; his arrest and exile caused consternation among the devout. In June, possibly as many as twelve hundred fédérés paraded in the streets, but no effective resistance was opposed to the regime.[15]

[13] Ibid., passim.
[14] AN, F⁷9055, Dantigny to Minister of Police, April 8, 1815.
[15] ADHG, 4 M 34; Genevray, L'Administration, pp. 145–83.

Even on June 26, 1815, when news of Napoleon's abdication reached Toulouse, the most serious royalist demonstration was relatively restrained. One man was killed on the Place Saint Etienne. The *fédérés* were led by men like Philippe Louis Savés, *dit* Sempé, a septuagenarian retired officer who lived on the Rue des Chapeliers. He paraded through the streets, carrying the tricolor flag at the head of noisy processions, and he menaced residents of the place Rouaix, the center of royalist activity, with a drawn saber. He railed against clients at the café Cresp, known for an ultra clientele, and he abused a pharmacist whose shop was close by. The pharmacist's son described Sempé as accompanied by the Saint-Cyprien *fédérés*, from the working-class suburb across the Garonne. A businessman and money-changer who lived on the Place had his door struck by Sempé's saber; two porters who served ultra masters in the district, the gatekeeper of a large house on the street where Sempé lived, as well as a woman nearby, all were threatened with violence.[16] Certainly the actual casualties of the transitional period appear to have been fairly light, but the talk of murder and revenge, the threat of violence, and the summary imprisonment of suspects caused panic and hardship. News of the disturbances elsewhere in the Midi elaborated in the telling, heightened the panic among those who were implicated with the Hundred Days. It is not our task to recount the course of events in Toulouse such as the local manifestation of the White Terror, the end of imperial authority, the assassination of General Ramel on August 15, 1815, the attacks on known Bonapartists, and the demand for jobs on the part of the royalists. Dr. Resnick has devoted a chapter of his recent study to these events.[17] It is important to note, however, the existence in the city of a royalist committee, drawn from members of the *chevaliers de la foi*, royalist militants who had been involved in one of the various para-military organizations formed since March, 1815, and local nobles. The committee, sometimes called the "royal commission" or the "royal council," met at the Hôtel MacCarthy in the parlementary district. It had twelve members, although more were consulted on important matters. The most prominent noble families of the city were involved: Reversat de Marsac, Palarin, Quinquéry d'Olive, Chalvet de Roche-

---

[16] *ADHG*, 223 U 7.

[17] D. Resnick, *The White Terror and the Political Reaction after Waterloo* (Cambridge, Mass., 1966).

FROM BONAPARTE TO THE BOURBONS

monteix, Lordat, d'Aguin, Lasborde, and Davisard.[18] They called
for rigor against subversion and unfavorably contrasted the pardons
given to Bonapartists by Louis XVIII with the "firmness" of the
Duc d'Angoulême.[19]

Villèle deplored the welter of charges and counter-charges which
were so common in the city.[20] The excesses of the *verdets* (royalist
terrorists), were sometimes a two-edged sword and soon alarmed
many local notables who were more than a little shocked by the
brutal assassination of General Ramel.[21] In 1814, the English officers with Wellington's army had been puzzled by the dichotomy
between the real interests of the propertied classes, obviously dependent on civil order, and the apparent desire of these same men
to use extremism for their purposes.[22] They failed to see the distinction between words and reality in a culture of rhetoric, and were
shocked to hear men whom they equated with English justices of
the peace expressing their frustrations in a flood of verbal violence.
The noble d'Arbou Castillon echoes the tone in his bitter lament
that the Decazes Ministry was destroying all the good achieved by
those appointed by the Duc d'Angoulême. Officials sent from Paris
did not understand the south, he said, they were mistaken about
public opinion, and did not understand that raucous joy was different from lust for vengeance. People had to be allowed to sing and
shout a lot, and to serve the Bourbons faithfully.[23] He might have
added that northern bureaucrats had to understand a society of
epic speech, with its own rules of hyperbole, symbolic aggression,
and declamation, on its own terms. Henri Lefebvre has written
brilliantly about the linguistic implications of the historic defeat of
southerners by "silent barbarians, efficacious, and organised."[24]

It is important to bear this in mind if the White Terror is to be

[18] Aldéguier, *Histoire de Toulouse* (Toulouse, 1834–35).
[19] *AG*, D³ 3.
[20] *ADHG*, 4 M 35.
[21] *AN*, F⁷9659.
[22] A. Weymss, "L'Angleterre et la terreur blanche de 1815 dans le Midi,"
Annales du Midi, LXXIII (1961), 296.
[23] E. de Guichen, *Le duc d'Angoulême, 1774–1844*, 2nd ed. (Paris, 1909).
[24] Henri Lefebvre, *Pyrénées* (Lausanne, 1965), pp. 150–55. Lefebvre points
out the méridional desire to escape a "Procrustian bed of reality" through
speech and verbal symbolism—and this was what northern revolutionaries described as the *gasconnades* and the *faconde intarissable* of the Midi. The
speaker exaggerates knowingly and is known to "exaggerate" but this provides
a liberty in language aided by the complicity of the listener.

truly understood. Recent studies of the counterrevolution identify men like d'Antraigues and Montlosier as typical and tend to present an imaginative picture of white Jacobins, *frondeur* petty noblemen, avid for a bloody revenge. Yet Bonald and Villèle are equally credible examples from that same nobility. Moreover, verbal forms of violence often went wholesale into the records kept by local administrations, but must be contrasted with the real effects it generated. The ultra police of Savy-Gardeilh, established in Toulouse after the fall of Napoleon, provided an excellent example. On July 23, 1815, they arrested a man named Gabriel Sorto, who was wearing a tricolor rosette. Lest this not be considered sufficiently heinous, he was accused of killing two travellers near Launaguet. He was further described as an extremely dangerous man, "carried through the streets of Toulouse during the Revolution wearing a civic crown for having, with his own hands, killed Mr. de Roquebrune, émigré."[25] In the literal sense this was a web of fabrications, but to the ultra police it meant that the man was a convinced partisan of the Revolution. The rest was emphasis.

The summer of 1815 was frightening enough, and with good cause, but much less so than some historians of violence have pictured it. Tempers cooled quite quickly. The parlementary nobility and the landed notables of the area of Toulouse had only occasionally even thought of becoming a "Marat of the Counter-Revolution." These legalistic, property-owning, cautious men were on the side of order rather than on the side of renovations in the style of peasant violence. The ultra notables endlessly repeated the complaints for which they were so pilloried by their political opponents: their vocabulary ran to words like groan, pain, lament, deplore, and repent. Pons de Villeneuve, closely associated with Angoulême, saw Paris engaged in a sinister attempt to dampen the ardor of the heartland of French royalism. He wrote indignantly that "some have desired to calm this opinion which it was so important to support, this opinion which, buttressed by Marseille and Bordeaux and having noble Spain in reserve, could overawe the Parisian conspirators and even the allies."[26] He deplored the dangerous results of a centralized administration in the capital that sent southwards prefects who talked nicely about Saint Louis in their speeches, but

[25] *ADHG*, 4 M 35.
[26] AV, Pons de Villeneuve to Joseph de Villèle, 26 [November?], 1816.

did nothing practical to strengthen public opinion against future revolutions. The antidote was terror, and what more simple to provide than terrifying talk?

Men like the prefect Rémusat, an Old-Regime noble who had served the Empire, denounced by the royalists as a *girouette* (turncoat), found the declamation of local ultras exasperating, but he was unable to calm them. In a report, submitted when he took over the Toulouse prefecture, he pointed to the nobility as to clearly the most influential section of local society, able to use its socioeconomic dominance in the city to muster popular support for ultraroyalism.[27] A prominent ultra from a family of robe nobility and a close neighbor of Villèle in the country, Reversat de Marsac, described in November, 1815, the salutary effects of popular royalism in Toulouse on rural subversion.

... we are still very royalist, and even intolerantly royalist, at Toulouse. Our secrets, directed by M. Barthélemy, carry out various expeditions in the countryside, sometimes against Clauzel [a Napoleonic general from the Ariège department] who has been seen everywhere but is never found, sometimes against tricolor scarves [i.e., against minor officials appointed by preceding regimes]. These expeditions, irregular as they are, do good. They teach the revolutionaries and the country people that there is a force which can reach them, and thus they are less insolent.[28]

In an effort to halt intimidation, the prefect tried to use the prestige of the Duke of Angoulême to produce obedience, but with little success. Local ultras were well aware of the political divergencies which existed between Louis XVIII and his brother Artois, and they saw through the effort of using the Duke's name against them.[29] However, their opposition to the prefecture was always covert and subdued—as an *adjoint* to the mayor remarked, when measures to integrate the National Guard and the *verdets* failed.[30] The prefect received little cooperation from local officials. His own staff was untrustworthy, at least in his opinion.[31] At the Capitole,

[27] *AN*, F⁷ 9659.

[28] *AV*, P. de Marsac to Joseph de Villèle, November 15, 1815. Other correspondents with Villèle, like Gounon and Aguilar, called for strong repressive measures.

[29] *AN*, F⁷ 9659, November 11, 1815.

[30] *AV*, Félix Gounon to Villèle, December 9, 1815.

[31] C. F. M. Rémusat, *Correspondance ... pendant ... la Restauration* (Paris, 1883–84), II, 242–43.

the father of Villèle exercised authority as his son's proxy after his offspring had been elected a deputy. The elder Villèle, an extremely opinionated man, aided by the *adjoints*, presided over a kind of ultra *junta*. They made it clear they distrusted the prefect and this hostility was extended into the salon. Mme. de Rémusat, who rather despised the pretensions of the noble ladies of Toulouse, wryly remarked on the lack of even social graces among the individuals who came to her *soirées*, which were boycotted by the best circles in the city.[32] Rémusat found himself without local support, while he was constantly instructed by Decazes to suppress extra-legal associations.

By the first months of 1816 the worst excesses of the White Terror were over. The local aristocracy almost unanimously deplored the work of the Revolution, and gilded the story of their own conduct since 1789. In their adulation of the Bourbons, or at least of Monsieur, their self-proclaimed piety, and their abhorrence of the Jacobins, they were joined by some men prominent in commerce. The ultra deputies elected to the *Chambre Introuvable* were naturally the leaders closely seconded and often criticized on the local scene by the clergy. The abbé Ducasse, in particular, was a vocal critic of any kind of accommodation with the Revolution.

The city at large was well pleased with the deputies who returned home in May, 1816, after the first parliamentary session of the Restoration. There was so enthusiastic and lavish a welcome that some notables were scandalised at the almost royal scale of these demonstrations.[33] This adulation, however, gave them a local authority, which Villèle used in suppressing the most extravagant of rumors circulated. For example, when a fire broke out in the tobacco factory, a state monopoly which provided employment for many royalists, the director promptly blamed as its cause the intrigues of the *fédérés* rather than negligence. Villèle quashed these rumors.[34] This was difficult to do when General Partouneaux, commander of the tenth military district, felt that this "plot" warranted declaring a state of siege. The prefect, who had complained

[32] *Ibid.*, I, 196–200; II, 320; AV, Villèle *père* to Mme. de Villèle, January 20, 1816.
[33] AN, F⁷9659, Rémusat to Minister of the Interior, May 16, 1816; E. de Perceval, *Un adversaire de Napoléon; le vicomte Lainé* (Paris, 1926), II, 68; AR, May 16, 1816.
[34] AN, F⁷9659.

two months earlier that military intelligence was too gullible, now had to add that the *procureur du roi* was equally convinced of a conspiracy.[35] Some time later, an accidental explosion at the gunpowder factory caused more talk of a *fédéré* plot.

The prefect saw that Villèle disassociated himself from that political extravagance that was to mark the most extreme group of royalists, those known as the *pointe.* He was in agreement with those who opposed the government but within orderly limits. In September, 1816, there was a flurry of excitement in Toulouse over the seizure of Chateaubriand's book *De la monarchie selon la charte.* The city was covered with a rash of portraits of the author, and the nobility helped to distribute the banned book.[36] If Villèle approved of this kind of demonstration he remained prudent and measured in comparison to ultra hotheads. A man of this temperament and with a notable technical ability in finance debates was an asset and his star rose rapidly in the ultra salons of the capital. Local personalities also showed increasing trust in his future.

Lower-class support for this ascendancy was shaken by the grain shortages of 1816–17, which threw great strain on the self-projection of the royalists as the true friends of the people. The famine provided the opportunity for a paternalist regime to show its concern with the public good, but the actual course of events revealed that those principles were weak. The price of grain was already far higher than average in June, 1816, when grain was being exported from the city, as the news of a poor harvest spread. The ultra Chalvet-Gaujouse, writing to his crochety friend Daignan d'Empaillon at Auch, declared that wheat was selling much cheaper at Bordeaux than at Toulouse, where the monopolistic grain merchants fixed artificial levels.[37] The new wheat which arrived in August caused only a temporary drop in prices, and by early September good grain was sold at 24 francs, and *mitadins* (mixed grains) were at 22.50 the hectolitre. Commercial interests bought heavily at Toulouse to supply the Bas-Languedoc and Provence, causing unseasonably high prices. Chalvet-Gaujouse said that wheat

[35] *AN*, F⁷9659, Prefectural Correspondence with Minister of the Interior, July and August, 1816.
[36] *ADHG*, 4 M 36, letters of Decazes to Rémusat, September 19 and 20, 1816. Rémusat, *Correspondance*, II, 265.
[37] J. Barada, "Toulouse et la vie toulousaine," *Annales du Midi*, XLIV (October, 1932), 443.

was being sent to Paris at the beginning of November, and that it was twenty years since such a thing had been known.[38] Between October 30 and November 6, 1816, wheat prices continued to rise from just under 28 francs to almost 32 francs (the price considered normal for the time of year was 24 francs the hectolitre for good wheat). When grain carts were seen leaving the city, demonstrators stopped them at the gates. The police claimed that the municipality itself condoned this. On November 8, a very serious disturbance broke out, surpassing all others that had taken place in France during that autumn. Demonstrators shouting "Vive le roi, le blé à vingt-quatre francs!" forced the grain merchants to sell at this price. Three days later, demonstrators tried again to fix the price, and dragoons had to be called out to restore order on the La Pierre market and to suppress an illegal market on the Place Dauphine (Place Dupuy), adjacent to the Canal du Midi. On the other side of the city, in the Saint Cyprien quarter, barricades had been raised (although deserted when the troops arrived), and some wheat carts pillaged. Only on November 13 did calm return to the city.[39]

This crisis threw light on the ultraroyalist response to a social crisis which called for real financial sacrifice. Bureaucrats did not have a heart of stone, declared Prefect Rémusat when he asked local landowners to supply the city with food. He also gave the population a lesson in *laissez-faire* economics, stating that if the free course of commerce had not been disturbed by violence, prices would be lower.[40] General Partouneaux was not sure of how reliable his troops would be if asked to fire upon those with whom they sympathized. In fact, some national guardsmen joined with the rioters in the marketplace.[41] Clearly, the great landowners and the municipality had to take a definite initiative in calming widespread resentment against the rising food prices. Villèle wrote to his wife that, if the population would only show the necessary patience with

[38] AV, letters from Bruno Dubourg and Paul Thoron to mayor Villèle, November 9, 1816. AN, F⁷9888; Robert Marjolin, "Troubles provoqués en France par la disette de 1816–1817," *Revue d'histoire moderne* (November, December, 1933), pp. 423–60.

[39] AV, correspondence of adjoints with Villèle.

[40] AN, F⁷9659, Rémusat, "Proclamation," November 12, 1816.

[41] Dubourg and Thoron, in a joint letter to Villèle of November 19, 1816, made the same claim: "... une grande partie de la garde nationale étant composée d'ouvriers artisans qui vivent au jour le jour se disposan à faire cause commune avec les mutins. ..." (AV).

the temporary necessity of paying high wheat prices, the land-owners would assume their responsibility to use increased profits to provide jobs for the common people.[42] Quite apart from the question whether profits made in the country could generate expenditure in the town, this was a feeble answer to an immediate and pressing problem. However, it was better than that given by a rich marquis who, when asked to sell his wheat in Toulouse at a reasonable price, laughed off the request, as he told Mme de Rémusat that

"everybody has to think of his own business and that one was certainly disgusted with doing anything for the common people who would, in any case, knock down the nobles if they could." Still others said the same to me, and when I replied, "if it not be for the people, at least let it be for the King whom you love or say you do and whose provinces must be kept in peace," do you know the answer? "Ah! The King has his ministers whom he loves: it is up to them to get him out of his mess!"[43]

These ultras showed the limitations of their windy declamations about social theory when the *adjoint* Thoron called for setting up *ateliers de charité*. Adrien Rességuier, subsequently to be a mayor of the city, offered to alleviate the grain shortage, but the bulk of the landowners proved themselves to be profiteers.

On November 22, 1816, there was more tension over wheat prices, which fluctuated between 32 and 33 francs the hectolitre. Thoron wrote to Villèle that the cry "Vive le roi, le blé à vingt-quatre francs!" had again been heard, and also a more sinister one: "Guerre aux nobles et aux riches!" The pessimistic *adjoint* imagined himself on the brink of a revolutionary abyss.[44] This was clear in a nervous proclamation which he published, calling upon landowners to help supply the city. Subsequently, a commission was set up to organize the effective working of a *Grenier d'Abondance*, an institution whose inception dated from September, 1815, when Villèle requested help from the Minister of the Interior to set it up. The *Grenier* was to be filled with a reserve of two thousand hectolitres

---

[42] Villèle advised his wife to sell wheat from the Mourvilles-Basses estate in small quantities in order to pay off their outstanding debts, and then subsequently in small quantities to provide cash as needed. He suggested millets should be sold last since their price woud probably rise sharply towards the end of the season. AV, Joseph de Villèle to his wife, November 15, 1816.

[43] Rémusat, *Correspondance*, II, 246–47.

[44] AV, Thoron to Villèle, November 23, 1816.

of wheat purchased with funds raised from the *caisse municipale*.[45] It was rumored that the wheat purchased was of poor quality, but at least there was evidence of some foresight here.[46]

The years 1816 and 1817 were dominated first by the White Terror and then, increasingly, by the food crisis. Popular attention wandered from the first to the second. Political news from the city became increasingly trivial. There was speculation on the health of Louis XVIII, his intention of abdicating in favor of Louis-Philippe, or his intention to exile Angoulême to Versailles.[47] Decazes enquired of the prefect whether the green ribbons, ultra favors, which appeared on the white flags of the mayor and other prominent personalities had impressed the population, but was told they were of little importance as a sign of any organized resistance to the government.[48] The food crisis had weakened the faith of many in the royalist unity of Toulouse.

The new prefect of the Haute-Garonne in 1817, St. Chamans, was a much less able man than Rémusat. He was noted for his bad temper, a family history of lunacy, and an inflexible character; he soon became acceptable to the ultras of the city, although he was received initially with much suspicion. When he assumed the office, he complained of the lack of cooperation from local officials who were, on the surface, docile and malleable but who, in fact, did not give any help to carrying out his policy:

... the measures ordered by the government which do not fit with the views of the dominant party are rejected and pushed aside by thousands of invisible hands; it is not a question here of an open war, there is no manifest resistance to break ... nobody resists and nobody obeys ... and in all the branches of the public service the party of exaggeration has several of its faithful, each involved in his own area to thwart all my measures. ...

He went on to say that this should be corrected for the simple

[45] Prospectus of a method of providing Toulouse with grain, dated 1816. See: Jean Gros, "Un maire de Toulouse sous la Restauration: de Villèle," *Mémoire de l'Académie des Sciences de Toulouse*, 12e, sér., I (1923), 93–110.

[46] Grain merchants provided the information upon which mercurials were based, and this was probably inaccurate. AN, F⁷9659; AMT, Register, June 17, 1816; Georges Frêche, *Le prix des grains, des vins et des légumes à Toulouse, (1486–1868)*, (Paris, 1967).

[47] AG, D³36; Rémusat, *Correspondance*, III, 4–5.

[48] ADHG, 4 M 46, Decazes to Saint Chamans, August 8, 1817.

reason that Toulouse set the tone of public opinion in the southern departments of France, for despite the fact it had less population and commerce than Marseille and Bordeaux, it exercised much greater moral and political influence over the whole of the Midi, where it was regarded as a respected metropolis.[49]

Villèle's father enjoyed the part of the mayor of the city he played as a stand-in for his absent son, proud of his role in the insurrection of the year VII, and of his family's connections with many noble families. He wrote happily to his son that everybody "qui pense bien" in Toulouse came to see him: Dubourg, a nephew of the bishop of Limoges who organized clerical resistance to the Revolution in Toulouse; Dupac de Bellegarde, who had been ruined by the Revolution; Gounon, the ultra merchant whose father had been a *capitoul*; the *procureur général* Bastoulh; and de Rigaud and Savy-Gardeilh, both of them involved in the *verdets* and the royalist committee.[50] When Villèle resigned as mayor in 1818, the prefect rightly said that nobody else could so well command "the affection and hopes of the most influential class in society."[51] His successor in the office, the former mayor of Toulouse during the Empire Baron Bellegarde, enjoyed no such esteem.

It was the clergy which was to provide the focus for the ultras' resentment of a changing France. In November, 1816, archbishop Primat, pious and gentle and bitterly reproached by the ultras for too much Christian resignation in politics, died while carrying out his annual tour of inspection. He was replaced by Bovet, who never appeared in his archepiscopal see, on grounds of ill-health, and who resigned in 1820. In effect, this left clerical administration in the hands of the vicars general, and they had very close connections with the noble and ultra circles in the city. One of them, abbé Cambon, had been arrested during the Hundred Days. The prefect did not mince his words in describing this clergy as "apostle of intolerance, it seeks only to spread it; the pulpit never echoes to words of peace: it is the den from which party-spirit spreads its venom; all the new institutions are attacked furiously, there is deplored unceasingly the fall of religion and subsequently that of

[49] AN, F⁷9659, St. Chamans to Minister of Interior, May 28, 1817.

[50] AV, Villèle père to Joseph de Villèle, February 2, 1818.

[51] AN, F⁷9659, St. Chamans to Minister of Interior, March 31, 1818. E. Connac, "La réaction royaliste à Toulouse . . .," *Revue des Pyrénées*, X (1898), 448.

the state."⁵² The haughty Clermont-Tonnerre, who ascended the chair of Saint-Sernin in 1820, was himself in favor of these sentiments of the clergy. He made no secret of his ultra principles, and on various occasions displayed a vindictive desire to humiliate former juring priests. He was also very vain about his nobility and the antiquity and good blood of his family. For almost the entire period of the Restoration, the catholic hierarchy in Toulouse was closely associated with ultraroyalism.

The secular forces also exhibited excellent principles; the soldiers frequently attended mass in the city. General Partouneaux was well thought of by the nobility.⁵³ The para-military group called the *verdets*, well-known for their catholicism, still met and could be summoned if need arose.⁵⁴ The Decazes ministry of 1819 was greeted with contempt in Toulouse in such circles; it was proper social form to consider the Paris government so deplorable that it could not be discussed.⁵⁵ The ultras, disappointed earlier that year by a false prediction that the favorite would fall, were all the more delighted to hear in 1820 that he had been dismissed after the assassination of the Duc de Berry.⁵⁶ The murder itself was seen as a striking vindication of their conspiracy thesis. The police reported a mournful calm in the city, apart from a few in the streets "qui se regardaient en faisant une grimace qui paraissait un signe d'approbation."⁵⁷ Not everybody lamented in the lachrymose style of newspapers and official proclamations; the memorial mass celebrated at St. Etienne drew a poor response from the student body, although held under the auspices of the law school. Just over a quarter of those enrolled attended. Mme. de Villèle was shocked at the joy which many "monstres" in the lycée had shown.⁵⁸ Various prominent ultras called for censorship, like so many did elsewhere in France, to stop a flood of vicious and irreligious publications.⁵⁹

The electoral law of 1820, better known as the Law of Double

⁵² St. Chamans to Minister of Interior, September 22, 1818, AN F⁷9659.
⁵³ AN, F⁷9659, police report, December 1, 1817.
⁵⁴ AN, F⁷9659; ADHG, 4 M 36. AV, Mme. de Villèle to Joseph de Villèle, end of February, 1820.
⁵⁵ AV, Mme. de Villèle to Joseph de Villèle, November 29, 1819.
⁵⁶ AN, F⁷9659.
⁵⁷ ADHG, 4 M 45, police commissaire to prefect, February 19, 1820.
⁵⁸ AV, Mme. de Villèle to Joseph de Villèle, February 21 and March 6, 1820. See AN, F⁷4006, police report, January 12, 1823.
⁵⁹ JPLT, March 20, 1820.

Vote, gave two votes to the most wealthy quarter of the departmental electoral college and produced a swing toward the ultraroyalists analogous to other movements in French history, such as the June elections of 1968. Fear of subversion and economic instability caused a return to that political group which espoused the conservative views of landed proprietors, the dominant economic elite of the time. In 1820, the department voted the ultras in, as it had almost exclusively since 1815 with the exception of electing Cardonnel in 1815, and Cambon subsequently. What differences existed among these men were personal and cliquish; all were ultra. In a classification of departments on the basis of the number of left and center-left deputies returned between September, 1815, and the end of 1829, the Haute-Garonne was classified as eighty-second in the list, bettered only by the Haute-Alpes, the Vaucluse, the Loire, and the Bouches-du-Rhône in having more ultra deputies.[60] The Haute-Garonne was as solidly reactionary then as it was to be radical in the twentieth century.[61]

The year of 1820 also caused the ultras of Toulouse to look to Spain. Many of the ultras had visited Spain as *émigrés* or as tourists, and they saw the struggle of Ferdinand VII with the rebels of Colonel Riego as analogous to their own political ideas on the dispute between the Crown and the Charter. The *Echo du Midi*, the ultra newspaper in Toulouse, attentively followed the campaign of the French expeditionary force commanded by the Duke of Angoulême, and exulted at the victory of Trocadero on August 31, 1823, as a triumph for legitimacy and religion. The Bourbons had conquered where Bonaparte had failed. The Spanish royalists, the "Defenders of the Faith," used Toulouse as a supply center, and they were given assistance by noble *dévots* in the parlementary quarter of the city.[62] The curé of the Dalbade Ortic, who had lived through the Terror of 1793–94, hiding at Toulouse as a clandestine assistant to the abbé Dubourg, was especially generous to these Spaniards.

When Joseph de Villèle became *président du conseil* in Paris, it

[60] J.-B.-M. Braun, *Nouvelle biographie des députés ou statistiques de la Chambre de 1814 à 1829* (Paris, 1830), pp. 53–54.
[61] AN, F⁷4006. The general tenor of reports from the Thirteenth Legion of gendarmerie commented on the "bon esprit" which reigned in the city and its surroundings.
[62] Adolphe Thiers, *The Pyrénées and the South of France* ... (London, 1823), pp. 161–62.

seemed only proper to recognize the high principles expressed by the electorate of Toulouse. The ultra counter-opposition had never been significant and relied on ecclesiastics like the abbé Ducasse and the abbé MacCarthy, who backed Castelbajac as a representative of the *pointe*. Castelbajac had been bought off in his opposition to Villèle by office and favor from the ministry, and few dissenting voices were to be heard in the fief of Villèle. The colonel of the gendarmerie reported in 1823 that political misdemeanors were so rare that, in effect, they did not exist.[63]

What disturbances did take place were usually in the form of student brawls. On March 29, 1822, some fifty students demonstrated to cries of "Vive la Charte!" and were dispersed from the Place du Capitole, site of the most popular student cafés, by a detachment of cavalry. In January, 1823, on the same square, a peasant wearing a white cockade in his hat was attacked with mud and stones by four people: the guilty ones were arrested. In May, 1823, a seventeen-year-old boy was beaten up, when he replied "M. . . .!" to an invitation from some ultra youths to shout "Vive le roi!"[64] These sporadic incidents were more part of the ongoing pattern of drunken fistfights over prostitutes and grisettes and the rivalry between students and apprentices than symptoms of significant political resistance.

On a more respectable level was a sedate group of liberals, of whom the most prominent was the advocate Romiguière who had edited the *Anti-Terroriste* during the Revolution before deportation at the time of Fructidor but who was less royalist subsequently. He had been in charge of the city police during the Hundred Days, as a result of which his career was in shadow during the Restoration. He pleaded various "progressive" cases, notably in defending the Spanish refugees and the *Revue Méridionale* which was prosecuted for a libel on the archbishop. Frédéric Malpel, professor of civil law at the Faculty in Toulouse, was another figure of importance: he had protested against *verdet* terrorism in 1815–16. J. G. D. Porte, son of an advocate of the Parlement and himself holding the same office before 1789, had held various posts in the revolutionary administration until he was elected *représentant du peuple* in 1797. Under Napoleon, he became a sub-inspector of

[63] *AN*, F⁷4006.
[64] *Ibid*.

revenues, of whom he was the oldest in 1805, but he was never promoted. His career was hardly subversive, but he was denounced
as a *fédéré* chief in 1815: even a moderate past could haunt a man
for many years. During the Restoration he was also considered a
prominent liberal. These men were to be found in reading rooms
which made liberal newspapers available, among the habitués of
the masonic lodge (closed in December, 1815, as a result of pressure
and threats, but reopened in 1818), and at the homes of lesser legal
figures like the advocate and minor writer Tajan.

Thus liberals as well as ultras had strong antecedents among the
men of law, although at different levels of the judicial system.
Lawyers provided the intellectual and political framework of public
opinion in the city, and in a real sense they still formed the transitional group between nobles and commoners during the Restoration. The personnel of the Royal Court in 1830 counted many with
noble connections. Half the councilors, for example, had titles.[65]
This caused friction with those whose avenues of advance were
blocked by these groups.

The mass of the city's population was indifferent to politics. The
persistent rhythm of markets, administration, jobs, feast days and
births, marriages, and deaths were of greater momentum. There
was little diversity of outlook. The Protestants in the city did not
contest the Catholic supremacy and were on the defensive: there
was only one consistory in the city and a small congregation. The
Jewish community was small, poor, and unobtrusive. Jews and
Protestants were buried in the cemetery outside the walls, near the
Canal de Brienne. The elaborate processions which the inhabitants
so enjoyed, in a confusion of banners and candles and religious
reliquaries, the coming of a new play to the theatre with new
songs for the *grisets* to learn and sing, and the price of bread, were
all more important than politics to the occitain-speaking people of
the streets. In language and outlook, Toulouse seemed isolated from
the other France, a land of grey skies and revolutionary disposition
in the north. "Toulouse és lé Paris del Miéjou!"

This sense of apartness from the nation was noted by the authorities. When St. Chamans retired in 1823 because of mental ill-
ness, he was replaced by a former prefect of the Cher, count

[65] J. Fourcassié, *Une ville à l'époque romantique; Toulouse, trente ans de
vie française* (Paris, 1953), p. 46.

Juigné, a man whose principles delighted the ultras. Baron Belle-garde, thwarted within the municipal council by the ultra clique which surrounded Félix Gounon, finally resigned in 1823, to be replaced by Hargenvilliers. The prefecture was also affected by ultra pressures, and Cambon denounced the prefect Juigné as being the creature of "a vexatious and bigotted coterie," influenced by an administrative assistant who was a fanatic supporter of Villèle, and only able to see religious probity among partisans of the Jesuits.[66]

The dusty rhetoric of an 1827 electoral pamphlet exactly struck the prevailing note in the city:

Inhabitants of Toulouse, faithful city above all, the whole of France relies upon you: the *honnêtes-gens* have always been important there, and the enemies of the social order have long known without a doubt that among you they have always lost their money and their efforts . . . in order to live and die peacefully with our possessions, arts, and commerce, we need in France more than anywhere else men who have everything to lose in the revolutions and nothing to gain from them; in a word, deputies like those whom you have always sent to the King, and like those whom you are again going to send him. . . .[67]

"To live and die peacefully" seemed to be the main aim of the ultras. They hated all that disturbed social and intellectual certainties, and there seemed little likelihood of such upsets in Toulouse. Perhaps the intelligentsia were aware of the debates over romanticism and liberal politics in the capital. Perhaps the French economic crisis which followed the 1825 bank failures in England and which was compounded by the bad harvest of 1827 produced a widespread psychological climate of desire for change in the north, but the year preceding the Revolution of 1830 seemed calm enough in upper Languedoc; but in Toulouse there were few signs of that political unrest. Neither the electorate nor the police records showed any strong opposition to the ultra dominance of the city. The new prefect, Camus de Martroy, appointed in 1829 by Martignac's ministry to replace Juigné, described Toulouse as being like other French cities a decade earlier. It existed in a time lag.

[66] *AN,* F1bII (Garonne, Haute-) 8, Cambon to Minister of Interior, September 26, 1828.
[67] *Où en sommes-nous? Où allons-nous?* (Toulouse, 1827), pp. 19–20.

Even the opposition to the Martignac ministry by the great landowners who regretted the fall of Villèle was feeble and took the
form of nodding approval of the ultra papers, the *Gazette* and
Quotidienne, and of believing that the Revolution might return.
At the same time, they found it possible to be a royalist and to
accept an official position.[68]

The Revolution of 1830 was completely unexpected in Toulouse.
None of the local deputies had signed the Declaration of the 221
which criticized the Throne Speech of March 2, 1830. There was
not the same fear of mysterious fires that agitated Normandy and
Picardy. The readers of the liberal papers in the various reading
rooms anticipated student rowdiness perhaps in the face of the
reactionary policy of Polignac, but it all seemed rather distant to
them. On Saturday, July 24, 1830, the municipal council discussed
some building projects, pension schemes, and the beautification of
the flower gardens. On Monday morning, the *Moniteur* was on sale
in Paris with the announcement of modifications of the electoral
law, suspension of the constitutional regime, suppression of the
liberty of the press, and dissolution of the Chamber of Deputies.
The news caused surprise at Toulouse, and reports of the disturbances produced anxiety. Royalist prudence was not, however, overcome by emotion. The prefect called Villèle to Toulouse on August 2, 1830, in order to get his advice, but the former minister
declined saying that it was not "proper" for him to appear. On
August 3, the prefect called on the banker Viguerie to be mayor.
The ultras let power slip through their fingers without resistance.[69]

[68] *AN*, F⁷6769, Prefect to Minister of Interior, January 11, 1829.
[69] *ADHG*, 4 M 49, Barennes to Minister of Interior, August 30, 1831.

IV

RESTORATION TOULOUSE
AND THE ULTRAS

THE ULTRAROYALISTS held to a paternalist and religious theory of man-in-society which supposedly placed social and political aims in natural harmony. They believed that a corporate social organization best represented the interests of all, and that the nobility had special obligations to rule and protect the population at large from the predatory selfishness of less altruistic minorities. They assumed their ideology was acceptable to other social groups in an agrarian society based on the quasi-feudal interdependence of lord and peasant; but they were vague about the role to be played by the merchant, independent artisan, royal official, and the unruly urban poor. The nature of ultraroyalist ideology is discussed in more detail in a later chapter, but before this can be done, some light should be thrown on social changes which had taken place in Toulouse during the quarter century following 1789.

The population of the city seems to have declined at one time during the Revolution, recovered during the Empire and Restoration, and risen very rapidly under the Monarchy of July. Characteristically, the royalists ascribed this to moral causes: the decline was the result of the Jacobin terrorists' wickedness, while the rapid growth was the product of rampant vice and immorality that led to urban overpopulation. Toulouse population increased between 1809 and 1831 through migration of refugees from rural overcrowding; the city death-rate exceeded births for much of the period. The proportion of departmental population living in the city steadily rose, until it was almost 14 percent in 1831. However, the socio-economic composition of Toulouse during these years of growth changed little in comparison to the census of 1809, when more than a quarter of the working population was engaged in agriculture, almost one half were artisans, and there were more servants than transport and manufacturing workers combined. The city developed no new industrial base since 1789.[1]

The political attitudes of the different social groups are not easy to describe, and this is especially true of those artisans, servants, agricultural laborers, small merchants, and the poorer members of urban society excluded from the franchise by the electoral regulations of the Charter. The French language which the northerners and upper classes used in political discussion was imperfectly understood by many of the lower classes. In a time of economic stagnation, low wages, and food crises like those of 1812 and 1816–17, it was understandable that their political outlook was narrow. The workers agreed with the author of an 1807 almanac (even if they could not read it) in observing that the number of servants, carriages, and sedan chairs in Toulouse diminished sharply since 1789 and, in consequence, the employment of many men and women disappeared.[2] The cotton filiature of Boyer-Fonfrède had gone bankrupt in 1811, throwing as many as five hundred out of work. The conditions of those who were employed provided little opportunity for political theorizing, as the description of a local doctor, Saint-André, attests so vividly. The gilders, earthenware and tin-workers, painters of Saint-Etienne, bakers, fullers, and millers often suffered from respiratory illnesses, "violent colics, tremblings, nervous tics," while the thirty-odd workers at the gunpowder manufactory were afflicted by tuberculosis and black phlegm. Women at the tobacco works often coughed until they spat blood, and if the "vapeurs méphitiques" of accumulated excretions were not the cause of mortality among sanitary workers, as the doctor believed, doubtless inadequate protection took its toll among the carters who removed the insalubrious cargo from the city. Those who worked with varnishes risked explosions which blinded. Embroiderers,

---

[1] Jean Coppolani, *Toulouse, étude de géographie urbaine* (Toulouse, 1954), pp. 125–30; M.-T. Plégat, "L'évolution démographique d'une ville française au XIXe siècle: l'exemple de Toulouse," *Annales du Midi*, n.s., LXIV (1952), 237.

[2] L. Faillon, *Annuaire du département de la Haute-Garonne* (Toulouse, 1807), p. 123.

watchmakers, lapidaries, and jewellers frequently damaged their sight with long hours of close work. Among the porters of the Canal du Midi hernias, spinal damage, and exhaustion were common. St. André commented they were rarely so healthy or strong as held by popular myth; he found them pale and thin from a diet in which "generally, they drink more than they eat."[3] Toulouse workers had little success in any attempt to improve their lot. The handful of shoemaker journeymen who tried to stir up their fellow workers to demand better prices from the masters in 1808 were promptly arrested.[4] If the worker was ill or unemployed, he might have received assistance from the La Grave hospital, partially converted into a *dépôt de mendicité* in 1812. Private charity was less available than during the last years of the Old Regime, as an official told St. André; this was a theme familiar to the poor who heard it from the clergy. It was another aspect of the constant unfavorable comparison of the new with the old.

During the later years of the Empire and during the Restoration, the common people of Toulouse—particularly the women—tended to give their political sympathies to nostalgic royalism. With the end of the Empire in 1814–15, they heard fewer tall tales of fabulous lands and loot won by the Emperor and his armies. The apprentices might dream of adventures over their work-benches, but the women were glad to have the men at home, albeit minus a limb in many cases. Although there are continuing evidences of popular bonapartism during the Restoration—a subject as yet unexplored in depth—the sentiments of the ordinary people of Toulouse were turned towards the traditional order. The causes of popular royalism in Toulouse went much further than simple reaction against the military exactions of Napoleon. The picture of loyalty which ultraroyalist propagandists loved to paint, evoking industrious peasant patriarchs saying their rosaries, telling moral tales, and repeating the adages of Henry IV to an attentive family circle, was grotesque. Nostalgia for the past rested on more than images of peasantry seen through the eyes of Greuze. Certainly

---

[3] J.-A.-D. Saint André, *Topographie médicale du département de la Haute-Garonne ... ouvrage basé sur les rapports qu'ont les diverses circonstances locales avec la santé des habitans de Toulouse ...* (Toulouse, 1813), pp. 406–17.

[4] P.-F. Dantigny, *Annuaire administratif et statistique du département de la Haute-Garonne pour l'an 1811 ...* (Toulouse, 1811), pp. 132–33.

many inhabitants of Toulouse saw the Revolution primarily as an attack on Christianity, and they were affronted by Napoleon's religious policy after the imprisonment of Pope Pius VII. There was resentment of new owners of *biens nationaux* and of economic disruption brought by the Revolution. All of these components were to be found in the popular affection for an idealized past, an affection to be found throughout southern France.

Villèle recognized that this popular royalism was a curious feature of the city in a letter he wrote to Lâiné in May, 1816, describing the local situation.[5] Other contemporaries were struck by the same fact. One historian writing in the 1830's claimed that the city bourgeoisie and workers were at odds over this characteristic, which he attributed to the resentment felt by the poor against the Napoleonic appointees who kept their positions throughout the Restoration. Loyal and noisy royalism, it was hoped, might be rewarded.[6] Charles de Rémusat thought that the spontaneous singing, dancing, and house decorations of August, 1815, as well as the exuberance of Toulouse *grisets* gave a highly distinctive quality to local royalism.[7] Villèle noted in his diary that Toulouse was "full of farandoles" in that month. Popular royalism was also strong at Bordeaux, Montpellier, Nîmes, Avignon, and Marseilles; however, it was exceptionally enthusiastic, it seems, in the *ville rose*. The florid newspaper description of popular joy at the news of the Second Restoration was not entirely hyperbole:

I saw all the citizens of a great city, from the most elegant class to the most obscure, join together, meet, become one in expressing the same sentiment. I saw in each district the inhabitants of the same street and place search each other out, harmonize their efforts, distribute the parts to play in order to quickly finish their smiling, fresh decorations. I saw, by a kind of tacit understanding, all the individuals brought together by chance in the same place, known and unknown, friends and enemies, establish suddenly between themselves the most agreeable and joyful familiarity; at the sound of the same music—and what music!—the old man, the young girl, the woman of fashion, the nursemaid, the robust fruitseller, the sparkling high-fashion seamstress, the scholar, the war-

[5] J. de Villèle to Lainé, May 21, 1816, in: *La nouvelle revue retrospective*, VII (1897), 311–20.
[6] J.-B.-A. d'Aldéguier, *Histoire de Toulouse* (Toulouse, 1834–35), IV, 630–31.
[7] C.-F. de Rémusat, *Mémoires de ma vie* (Paris, 1958), I, 215–16.

rior, the artisan, and the dandy. I saw the hardworking laborer, who hardly is able to make a living by his difficult trade, interrupt his work and happily lose a day in order to decorate his hovel; surround with boughs his door and window, afix to the end of a reed the handsomest of his wife's handkerchiefs on which, in gold paper, he had stuck without good spelling these sacred words: Vive le Roi! Vive le Duc d'Angoulême![8]

Popular politics were based on the affiliations which began in the streets (where, as everywhere in the Midi, neighbors spent so much time), in the suburbs, on the job, and in families. The Rue Escoussières was noted for its royalists, like the Rue de la Fonderie, the Rue du Vieux Raisin, the Rue de l'Inquisition and all streets in the old parlementary district with the Place des Carmes, the Place Rouaix, and the Place du Salin as their forums of discussion. The Rue des Trente-Six Ponts was *fédéré* in sympathy in 1815, as were other streets around the Place St. Michel, located outside the historic walls of the city and with a reputation as a thieves' kitchen, with its receivers, old-clothes merchants and the semi-destitute newly-arrived immigrants from the countryside. The Arnuad Bernard district in the west of the city was another area of more recent migration and less wealth, as was St. Cyprien across the river, where the hospitals, *dépôt de mendicité*, and garbage dumps were located. There were few wealthy or noble residents in these districts, and jealous bitterness against the rich and the noble found here a wider expression. The central districts of Daurade, St. Etienne, Dalbade were more mixed in their political sympathies, but the shopkeepers, servants and long-established artisans with a sense of themselves as the true backbone of local civic pride and worth were strongly represented. Within the framework of street and district, loyalty to the family circle and to close friends was the rule, although the odd black sheep could be found. Professional connections were almost as important, and indeed were often reinforced by marriage, especially in the *métiers d'art*. There are only scattered hints on the political outlook of the poorer parts of the Toulouse population during the Restoration but it seems clear that it was city artisans who played the largest part in political action.

[8] *AR*, July 28, 1815. Villèle noted in his diary on July 18, 1815 (*AV*): "Au jour les pavillons blancs ont été mis à toutes les fenêtres . . ." and a day later, that Toulouse was ". . . pleine de farandoles, de feux de joie et de danses royalistes."

The evidence of lower-class support for the ultras is scattered. However, from two cases against royalist terrorists heard during the Hundred Days, from the voluminous documentation assembled by the investigation into the murder of Ramel, and from reports of those who hunted down *fédérés* after Waterloo, we can extract some information about these royalists. Most of them were members of the para-military *verdets*, royalist militants to be discussed further below, but some were drawn from occupations which had a stake in the economic system of the past, especially those that provided clothes and furniture for a more opulent era. Banners of the old corporations appeared in the procession which welcomed the Duc d'Angoulème into Toulouse with great enthusiasm in 1814; this symbolized the extent to which the former rulers were hoping to restore the traditional economy. The men who took active part in the confused days of the White Terror of 1815 and who are known to us are the visible sections of a much larger group of Toulouse citizens who danced and sang in the streets to celebrate the fall of Napoleon. They seemed to be more like thugs than aspirant chevaliers. We find among them a returned émigré café-owner who was accused of robbing a stagecoach in 1801; a former baker with a criminal record; a saddler who was noted for a violent and criminal past; and a turner who had the sinister nickname *Loupenjat* (the hanged). Most notable of all these men so different in their interests from the local nobility was a tailor, known as Anglaret, whose real name was Pierre-Louis Carivent. He was thirty-four years old in 1815 and lived on the Rue du Taur, close to the heart of the city. He was a native Toulousain and was deeply implicated in the Ramel murder. During July and August, he was to be found swaggering through the cafés, cursing and threatening those suspected of Napoleonic sympathies, and looking for former *fédérés*. Yet the politics of these men may have been more opportunist than would appear. We find François Magnac, aged 57 in 1827, illiterate and a bachelor, formerly a member of the national guard and a *verdet*, arrested for shouting "Vive l'Empereur!" His sight was weakened so that he could no longer work as a shoemaker, and he was reduced to begging and sleeping wherever he could find a shelter. Evidently his career as a royalist terrorist failed to bring him prosperity. Table IV-1 below shows occupational affiliations of those lower-class terrorists known to us from 1815–16, but can tell us nothing of the complex web of motivations or personality which explained their political sympathies of that time.

The lower-class *verdets*, like the non-noble suspects of the Revolutionary period, were more likely to be older men and well-established residents of Toulouse. While there was no active royalism during the Restoration in the form of a political organization, the conservative cast of mind continued.

Commercial and professional circles in the city were more sophisticated in their politics. Purchasers of *biens nationaux*, lawyers, officials in the prefecture and administrative bodies, doctors, engineers, cloth merchants, grain dealers, manufacturers, innkeepers—in short, the prosperous commoners of Toulouse—still did not compare with the nobility in the extent of their wealth, in their political ambitions, and most importantly, in their local self-assurance. There were only rare exceptions to this general economic superiority of the nobility, for example, Jean-Paul Lafont-Cazeing, the wealthiest man in the department, whose fortune was amassed by sharp dealings during the Revolution. He was in his middle seventies in 1815 and inactive in local politics. Before 1789, he was a merchant, but subsequently took the lucrative post of district tax-collector in the Saint Lys cantonal administration in the Muret *arrondissement* and had his respectability consecrated by appointment to the departmental *conseil général*. He was involved in extensive wool and cattle trade with Spain and with the Army of the Pyrenees, the profits of which he invested in land. In 1820 the prefect thought him to be an influential liberal, although it was more as example than because of any political activity, as Lafont-

TABLE IV-1. LOWER-CLASS ROYALISTS IN TOULOUSE, 1815–16

Professions	No.	Age Distribution	Percent
Agriculture	1	36 and older	48
Commerce	3	26 to 35	22
Food Services	4	25 and younger	30
Clothing	10		
Artisans	5		
Métiers d'art	2		
Servants	2		
State Employees	4		
Total	31		

Source: *ADHG* 233U5; wU620

Cazeing rarely appeared in Toulouse. Few other fortunes, however, were so dramatic an affirmation of the benefits which could be ascribed to the Revolution, although a number of soldiers gained fortune along with fame during the Empire.

The 1809 census showed almost fifteen percent of the working population to be engaged in commerce, that is, 3,188 persons. This, however, conceals the range of social standing involved, from a barrow-boy to a textile wholesaler. Obviously, a street-vendor had more in common with his market-day peasant and artisan customers than he had with the merchant members of the Chamber of Commerce or the *tribunal de commerce*, the court which settled disputes between businessmen. Merchants who paid the tax on commerce and industry (the *patente*) were assigned a definite place in the official hierarchy of society. The Empire, with its mania for lists of the respectable and important as well as those of conscripts, criminals, and deserters, fixed into an institutional form the list of *notables patentés*.[9] The wealthiest of these appeared on Restoration electoral lists: among the annual average of 2,412 *notables patentés* between 1805–15, less than ten percent were wealthy merchants classified as the first or second class. More than half of the total were drawn from the poorer artisans who sold their goods in workshops and from the itinerant hawkers. Just as before the Revolution, the wealthiest merchants were textile dealers. Some of them—for example, Azais, Carrayon, the influential royalist Ville-Teynier, and the liberal Sarrus—added banking to their other business concerns. The 240 men in the top two classes included wholesalers, highly skilled artisans, and brokers; they reported an annual revenue above 10,000 francs, but rarely in excess of 20,000 francs.[10] At the bottom of the scale, the poorest of the city merchants had an income which was only barely sufficient and which, as the records show, often dipped below the bankruptcy line.

[9] The *patente* was the tax on commerce introduced by the law of 2–17 May, 1791, to replace the *vingtième d'industrie*. The *patente* was paid according to a scale of professions. This legislation was modified by the law of Brumaire VII, which provided for a proportional tax rather than a fixed amount, payable on two bases: first the *droit fixe*, levied according to profession and the size of the commune in which it was exercised, and second, the *droit proportionnel* which generally represented one tenth of the rental of the business premises.

[10] J.-C. Duphil, "Les notables patentés de Toulouse sous le premier Empire," Mémoire pour le diplôme d'études supérieures, Toulouse University, 1959, *B.U.T.*

Toulouse had by far the strongest concentration of wealthy commercial voters in the department. This was very apparent on the 1820 electoral lists of the *Grand Collège*,[11] the members of which comprised that wealthiest quarter of the electorate given a second vote by the law of May/June 1820. Only five men in the fourth electoral *arrondissement*, composed of the combined administrative areas of Muret and Saint-Gaudens, paid the *patente*. In the electoral *arrondissement* of Villefranche, which had the same area as the administrative one, only three men in the *Grand Collège* paid the commercial tax. The first and second electoral *arrondissements* (made up of the cantons of the administrative area of Toulouse) had far more citizens who paid it, especially in the cantons where the urban area lay. In Toulouse-Centre, 27 men out of 80 voters paid the *patente*; and in Toulouse-Sud, further 28 voters did, three of whom paid over 500 francs. This is relatively unimportant when compared with the lowest amount of total tax paid among the electors of the *Grand Collège*: 1,066 francs. The electoral lists and elections clearly show how slight was the challenge provided by commercial activity to that of the landowner. The author of a 1824 almanac for the Haute-Garonne was justified in regretting that local merchants did not take part in the "vast speculations" seen elsewhere in France.[12]

What was the political opinion of business circles in Toulouse? In 1815, they opposed the Empire because they suffered from its commercial policies and taxation. A primitive opinion poll, compiled by the prefect in 1820 from the voters listed on the complete electoral rolls, classified them under four headings: royalist, doubtful royalist, liberal, and doubtful liberal. (These are presented in a

---

[11] These lists are at *ADHG*, 2 M 19-24. The limits of the four electoral arrondissements did not correspond to the administrative areas in the department. The ratio of electors to population is revealing both of the relative wealth and representation.

Name of Electoral Arrondissement	Population of Administrative Arrondissement	Ratio of Elector to Population
Toulouse I		
Toulouse II	125,854	1 : 147
Villefranche	57,953	1 : 204
Muret	77,032	1 : 387
Saint Gaudens	117,990	1 : 1,053

[12] *Almanach de Toulouse . . .* 1824, p. 223.

79

table in the appendices.[13]) While voters engaged in commerce or manufacturing made up a larger proportion of liberal support than royalist, the actual numbers of men involved were quite similar in both camps. The businessmen's affiliation with liberalism was more marked in the countryside than in Toulouse. The prefect wrote to Villèle in September, 1821, that the commercial group in Toulouse was generally characterized by tepid royalism rather than truly ultra persuasion.[14] On the other hand, Barthélemy de Castelbajac, the flamboyant Gascon ultra elected in Toulouse in 1819, particularly thanked his supporters engaged in commerce:

> The man of moderation, regardless of the social class to which he belongs, seeks without discrimination and prejudice in all the other classes him whose principles offer him a guarantee for the defense of the monarchy and of the interests of the country. The most complete proof of this assertion is to be found in the benevolence with which the commerce of Toulouse has so kindly favored me.[15]

There does not seem to be any simple correlation between the commercial classes and liberalism. If we compare the four most prominent ultra merchants with their six liberal counterparts (all of whom appear in one of the departmental electoral colleges in 1820), the wealthiest merchant in the department was opposed to the ultras. The approximate revenues of these merchants were quite similar, although the liberals paid a higher *patente*, showing they were the more active of the two groups.

Easily the most notable ultra merchant was the bachelor Jacques-Léon-Félix Gounon, son of the richest merchant in Toulouse during the last years of the Old Regime. The family, originally from Auch, had shown much success in accommodating itself to the social system of eighteenth-century France. Included among its members in Toulouse were several *capitouls*, hospital administrators engaged in charity work, and other prestigious offices. Gounon's father married the daughter of a seigneur, and bought the ennobling office of *secrétaire du roi* in the Toulouse *chancellerie* in 1786; he was imprisoned during the terror as a sympathizer with the *ci-devants*.

---

[13] *AN*, F¹ᶜIII (Garonne, Haute-) 6, "Travail demandé par la lettre de Son Excellence le Ministre de l'Intérieur du 23 juin 1820."

[14] *AV*, Saint-Chamans to J. de Villèle, September 19, 1821.

[15] *Le Conservateur*, 53 livraison (1819), pp. 4–5.

TABLE IV-2. TEN MERCHANTS OF TOULOUSE COMPARED BY POLITICS
AND REVENUE, 1820

Names	Patente Francs	Total Tax Francs	Approximate Revenue (tax = 15%) Francs
Ultra			
Felix Gounon	457.36	1,733.76	11,540
Joseph Duchan	174.24	2,299.12	15,320
Fs. St. Raymond	152.46	458.31	2,040
Etienne Ville-Teynier	—	1,904.18	12,680
Liberal			
Antoine Chaptive	206.90	1,242.55	8,280
Jean Authier	544.48	1,146.65	7,640
JLM Viguerie	—	497.79	3,320
Bernard Lignières	588.04	2,018.70	13,460
G-J Barre	588.04	3,591.26	23,940
Joseph Cassaing	479.14	1,390.66	9,260

Source: *ADHG*, 2 M 23

One of his daughters married a councilor at the Parlement, de Barbasan, and a son became a *curé* in Toulouse while Félix followed the commercially successful career of his father, as indicated by the fact that he paid the highest *droit proportionnel* among the *patentés* as a successful cloth merchant during the Empire.[16] However, at the second Restoration, his energies turned to local politics, and he was a candidate for the *chambre introuvable*. Although not elected, he became an *adjoint* to mayor Villèle in 1816, was in constant attendance in the *capitole*, and took his position very seriously. He was vociferous against new-fangled ideas, and during the year 1820, he expressed this hostility in daily meetings with his supporters at his home. Among those present there were the advocate and writer Pinaud (thought influential as a result of the "habit of glib talk picked up in the courtroom"); Demouis, a former *adjoint* and ultra; a police *commissaire*; and the two Decampe brothers, both school teachers, one of whom had written a tract on the moral corruption of French youth.[17] This group of cronies puzzled the *procureur*, for Pinaud and Demouis owned *biens nationaux*, and in general none of them had suffered serious

[16] G. Marinière, "Les marchands d'étoffes de Toulouse à la fin du XVIIIe siècle," *Annales du Midi*, LXX (1958), 251–308; Duphil, *"Les notables patentés"*; *ADHG*, 1, 313, "Tableau de la vie politique de Jacques Gounon."
[17] *AN*, BB[238]dossier 4, Gary to Garde des Sceaux, October 5, 1820.

81

hardship as a result of the Revolution; yet, they agitated against mayor Bellegarde and against all who seemed suspiciously moderate.[18] Perhaps they wanted to bring themselves to the attention of Villèle. Gounon's efforts were rewarded in 1823, when he became a chevalier of the Legion of Honor; Pinaud received a promotion to *procureur général* at Metz in 1824; and Decampe became Rector of the Academy of Lyon towards the end of the Restoration. Only Gounon remained in Toulouse; while he was respected, he remained a marginal figure in ultra circles.

At his death in January, 1833, Félix Gounon left a considerable estate comprising an annual pension of 1,000 francs for ten years to a resident of Toulouse, another pension of 1,200 francs to Mlle. Jeannette Vinaud, and a pension and donation to her daughter, presumably Gounon's bastard, of 5,000 francs, payable at age eighteen. He left 1,000 francs to the curé of the Daurade, his brother, to be distributed to the poor. The legacies amounted to 58,000 francs. The remainder of the estate was left to his brother Prosper Gounon. The summary listing of his possessions in the Toulouse registers showed his fondness for real estate and stocks of merchandise, while outstanding debts accounted for less than twelve percent:[19]

Furniture		1,813.90F
Merchandise on hand, *créances*		26,669.76
One share in the Bazacle Mill		6,000.00
Rental of a wheat warehouse		4,105.70
A house, 6 rue de la Bourse, revenue	4,000F	
A house, rue des Couteliers, revenue	750F	
A house, Place d'Assézat, revenue	1,000F	
A half-share in a house, 6 Place de la Trinité, revenue	1,500F	
A half-share in a house, 2 rue de la Madelaine, revenue	100F	
A *métairie*, called Dabadie, with a farmhouse, meadow, vineyard, pigeon-cote, approximate area 34 hectares 14 acres, revenue	2,100F	
au denier vingt		189,000.00F
Total		227,589.36F

[18] *AV*, Bellegarde to Joseph de Villèle, January 1, 1822.
[19] *ADHG*, WQ 5594, Mutation par décès, July 6, 1833.

The mother of Félix who died in October, 1824, had left a total capital of 356,311 francs, the shares of which were distributed to her children.[20]

Another merchant who had been an ultra sympathizer and an *adjoint* to Villèle was Paul Thoron who had formerly traded at Constantinople for many years. At his death in April, 1838, his estate of the Toulouse area was declared as:[21]

Furniture, ready-cash, *créances*		217,828.30F
A house, 1 rue Dalbade, revenue	1,500F	30,000.00
Total		247,828.30F

On August 24, 1814, Thoron sold for 140,000 francs an estate of three *métairies* to the wife of a teacher in the Artillery School.[22] His wife, Angélique Testa, whom he had married at Marseilles in the winter of 1804, died in June, 1815, leaving an estate of:[23]

Furniture, jewels, etc.	14,526.00F
Créances	73,911.93
Total	88,437.93F

Thus Thoron had owned real estate earlier in his career, but seems to have converted the majority of his funds into other assets later in life. Both Thoron and Gounon had estates worth over 200,000 francs, which places them among wealthy landed society.

Liberal professions were often to be found among city voters: the most common were, in some ways, connected with legal training, from officials to advocates and notaries. These have been classified among members of the civil service on the grounds that their interests as a group were largely dependent upon the government which granted places in the courts and which provided patronage. Certainly they were as much affected by an "official" outlook as they were representatives of an independent social force. Members of the Royal Court were the wealthiest group in local society like the parlementary nobility before the Revolution; almost half of

---

[20] *ADHG*, WQ 5585, Mutation par décès, March 20, 1825.
[21] *ADHG*, WQ 5599, Mutation par décès, April 26, 1838.
[22] *ADHG*, 3E-27422, sale to dame Marie-Céleste Collet.
[23] *ADHG*, WQ 5579, Mutation par décès, July 31, 1815.

them paid over 1,500 francs in tax. The poorest professional group was the doctors. An example of the wealth of an ultra with parlementary antecedents is offered by Armand Dubourg, ex-deputy and landowner, who died in the family château at Seilh in September, 1831. His estate in the area of Toulouse proper was small:[24]

Furniture and effects	1,629.00F
Créances and rents	3,330.00
A house, 32 place St. Scarbes, and stables, with a revenue of 1,350F constituting capital of	27,000.00
Stables and remittances, revenue 150F, capital of	3,000.00
A house at Belbèze, revenue of 150F, capital of	3,000.00
A parcel of land: 3 hectares 48 ares 30 ca arable: pigeon-cote, loft, etc., revenue 90F	1,800.00
Total	39,759.00F

The majority of Armand Dubourg's properties were located in Aussonne, Merville, and Seilh cantons, and their evaluation by the *enregistrement* no longer exists. Armand's will gives further information about the inheritance he left to his children, described as "although not very considerable, can be sufficient to those moderate tastes with which I have inspired you." He left to his eldest son the house in Toulouse, the park and Chateau at Rochemonteix, buildings and gardens of an area of almost fifteen *hectares*, the driveway leading to the main road, orange trees and wine-making equipment for the vines. The eldest son thus received the noble château and the town house as the *préciput légal*. The rest of the estate was divided between the other six children and his wife, Eugénie d'Escouloubre. While these records are incomplete, there seems no indication of investment in anything other than land.[25]

The politics of these men in some branch of the legal professions are indicated in the appendix. Throughout the Restoration, lawyers and judges were mainly in the royalist camp, and it may be added that the law students also counted many young ultras. Naturally there were exceptions, especially among the advocates, the most prominent of whom was Dominique-Louis Romiguières who gained notoriety for his defense in court of Spanish refugees after the

[24] *ADHG*, WQ 5592, Mutation par décès, March 28, 1832.
[25] *ADHG*, WQ 5595, Mutation par décès, February 19, 1834; *ADHG*, 3E-27061, Testament, April 3, 1818.

Triennio and for his anti-clerical opinions. He was citing Montlosier in April, 1826, on the Jesuit conspiracy to take over French government in what was clearly an attempt to revive the breech between the descendants of Jansenist parlementarians and the Society of Jesus.[26] Another advocate, J. P. C. Amilhau, son of an advocate to the Parlement who had also served in the Seneschalsy, was a brilliant student who won the approval of the king for a eulogy of Louis XVI early in the Restoration. Despite these promising beginnings, he was not able to enter the inner ultra circle. He became increasingly liberal in his views and, like Romiguières, he pleaded for the accused in the case of the Spanish refugees. By 1830, he was one of the foremost liberals in the city.

More typical of the road to success for Toulouse lawyers was the career of Pierre-Salvy-Félix de Cardonnel, who had sent a petition to Louis XVI in the early months of the Revolution, asking him not to relinquish his royal prerogatives. He lived most at Albi where he became advocate after graduation, moving then to become judge in the local *tribunal civil*, and living in rural seclusion during the difficult period of the Terror. In October, 1795, he was elected to the Five Hundred, with the enthusiastic support of the moderates in local society. His political views were evident in his denunciations of divorce and of the Jacobin municipality of Toulouse, and in his call for the return of *biens nationaux* to their rightful owners. He also suggested that *émigrés* who studied useful arts abroad should be given an amnesty. He narrowly escaped deportation after Fructidor, but then returned to Albi where he held judicial posts until elected by the Tarn to the *Corps Législatif*. The Restoration made him a President of the Toulouse Royal Court and ennobled him in February, 1815. He remained the deputy for the Tarn throughout the Restoration, fulminating against the liberty of the press and asking that unsold *biens nationaux* be given back to their rightful owners. Although he had given up his presidency as a result of being a deputy, he still kept the position of councilor at the court until 1821. His connections with legal and ultra circles in Toulouse reached back to his days as a law student before the Revolution. In 1819, he was made a chevalier of St. Jean de Jéru-

[26] A. Madrolle, *Défense de l'ordre social, attaqué dans ses fondements . . .* (Paris, 1827).

salem; in 1825, he became a commander of the Legion of Honor. He was a Villèlist at the Chamber of Deputies.[27]

Officials were concentrated at Toulouse, the *chef-lieu* of the department. The government left them in no doubt that they were to support the regime. In 1820, the Minister of the Interior Simenon wrote to the prefect that he should display his own "excellent principles" and spread them among the electorate. Officials should be reminded of this duty not by letter, but rather by obvious insinuations.[28] It is not surprising that at a time when the number of individuals in the bureaucracy was actually declining, as it did during the Restoration, very few officials had liberal ideas which might cost them their livelihood.

Various other professions were represented at Toulouse, much more so than in the surrounding small towns and villages where there was little opportunity for a wide range of professional activity. Doctors had perhaps less social prestige than at present; they were certainly not a very wealthy group, compared to the others. A royalist with this type of background was François d'Aubuisson de Voisins, an émigré who served in Condé's army in the artillery. He was educated at Sorèze, the model school of the area before the Revolution. When in exile, he turned his leisure to good use in acquiring knowledge of metallurgical techniques at Freiburg. Upon his return to France, he joined the *corps des mines* during the Empire, wrote a number of technical books, and was responsible for useful innovations in his new profession. His ability was recognized, and he became director of the *corps des mines*, a correspondent of the *Institut de France*, and an officer of the Legion of Honor. He also became a member of the municipal council of Toulouse from 1816 to 1830, and wrote a book on political theory. He was among the most distinguished of the professional men in Toulouse. After 1830, he retired from public life.[29]

It is in a sense artificial to separate landowners from the other professional groups, since the mania for landownership (which Stendhal thought the great vice of southern France), was particu-

[27] G.-A. Cavaille, "Eloge historique de M. de Cardonnel . . . 14 fevrier 1830," *Recueil des Jeux Floraux* (Toulouse, 1830), pp. 223–45. AN, BB⁵68.
[28] *ADHG*, 2 M 24.
[29] D.-S.-J.-P. de Panat, "Eloge de M. d'Aubuisson de Voisins . . .," *Receuil des Jeux Floraux* . . . (Toulouse, 1843). E. Brassine, "Eloge de M. d'Aubuisson de Voisins," *Histoire et Mémoires de l'Académie de Législation de Toulouse*, 3rd sér., I (1844).

larly marked in all levels of society. The reluctance to indulge in other investment forms was perhaps a result of the desire to "live like a noble." This was an explanation current during the Restoration. The liberal journalist Etienne de Jouy described Toulouse as

one of the largest French cities, and among the best-placed for commerce but today, perhaps, one of the poorest and most depopulated. Formerly possessing a presidial, a seneschalsy, a mint, a *généralité*, a Parlement, and a *Capitole*, the inhabitants of Toulouse never saw anything above municipal or judicial office which bestowed nobility. They used to disdain commercial and manufacturing activity where they saw merely money to be made. It is easier to carry out a revolution in a country's laws than its manners. The changes in the laws of Toulouse have not effaced this distinctive characteristic.[30]

In Toulouse, little capital was available for industrial, commercial, or speculative purposes, because so large a proportion of wealth was immobilized in land and real estate. On the electoral lists, the landowners (propriétaires) made up the largest single "occupational" group; if men described as mayors or *adjoints* of the communities in the four cantons which included urban Toulouse are taken into account, 40 percent of the enfranchised were landowners. Moreover, they included a high proportion of the wealthiest members of local society.[31]

Taxation was based largely on the land in the form of the *foncière*, the land tax established early in the Revolution as being one-fifth of the value of the produce of the land. The English friend and translator of Picot de Lapeyrouse noted that, after deductions for the costs of improvements the amount of land-tax averaged from one-sixth to one-seventh of the value of the produce, or about 15 percent. Picot de Lapeyrouse preferred to make calculations over a five-year cycle, to avoid the effect of years of glut, and thought the tax came to an average of 19 percent. In consequence, "over the whole of the southern part of France, there is a striking want of capital in agriculture which will ever act against its rising into any high degree of perfection."[32] The father of Joseph de Villèle had a keen interest in taxation law. In 1817, he

[30] Etienne de Jouy, *L'ermite en province* (Paris, 1818–27), II, 76–77.
[31] *ADHG*, 2 M 24.
[32] P. Picot de Lapeyrouse, *The Agriculture of a District in the South of France* (London, 1819), notes 87–88.

pointed out that in fact only two departments paid a *foncière* which was calculated as one-fifth of land revenue: the Seine and the Aveyron. Eleven departments paid one-sixth, including the Haute-Garonne, which makes his estimate roughly congruent with Picot.[33] Since these opinions were put forward for polemical purposes, it is reasonable to take 15 percent as an approximate basis for estimating income from the *foncière* paid.

Among the landowners there were many nobles. Boyer-Fonfrède, one of the *fédéré* leaders in 1815, described the Toulouse nobility as remaining in the front rank of the wealthiest landowners, despite their troubles in the Revolution. In consequence, they were the main dispensers of work for the lower classes.[34] In 1820, the wealthiest quarter of the combined electorate of the department (the *grand collège*) included 40.9 percent nobles. In the electoral colleges of the *arrondissements*, nobles accounted for 38 percent of the 465 voters of the first, 24 percent of the 474 voters of the second, 35.2 percent of the 306 in the third, and 27.9 percent of the 401 in the fourth college. The nobility comprised 31.2 percent of the total electorate. Within Toulouse society in 1820, the nobility was still the wealthiest group on a per capita basis, as they had been before 1789. The second wealthiest man in the department was the marquis d'Escouloubre and the third was of parlementary antecedents, Lassus-Camon. Not a single commoner was elected in the department during the course of the Restoration.

In a sluggish economy like that of Toulouse, a Restoration nobleman could live comfortably enough on a carefully managed estate of fifty *hectares*.[35] The main object of his existence was to maintain the family social standing. Restoration nobles were more united in their aspirations than before 1789: the Revolution made them close ranks. Although difficult to pin down, social unity of the nobility clearly had its social symbolism: much family behavior of the typical nobleman was a constant and startlingly self-conscious

[33] Henri de Villèle, "Moyens simples de rectifier la répartition foncière," *Journal des Propriétaires Ruraux pour les Départements du Midi*, XIII (1817), 261–74.

[34] J.-J. Hemardinquer, "Affaires et politique ... un libéral: F.-B. Boyer-Fonfrède (1767–1845)," *Annales du Midi*, LXXIII (1961), 175.

[35] Mary Boddington, *Some sketches in the Pyrenees* (London, 1837), II, 253, was told that thirty hectares sufficed. For a full analysis of the noble estate, see R. Forster, *The nobility of Toulouse in the Eighteenth Century* (Baltimore, 1960).

rehearsal of common standards. It is reminiscent of Tocqueville's description of the almost "instinctual" recognition of one man of good blood for another: keen examination of his speech, clothes, comportment, manners, allusions, and acquaintances revealed a subtle code recognized by other members of the minority group. Like all such systems, it had to be sufficiently complex or strange to exclude outsiders. Allusions to ancestors and noble 'naturel' constituted a latter-day version of Boulainvillier's theories. This pride was put by one minor nobleman of the Toulousain in a letter of November, 1801:

"I know very well that it is hoped to make us forget the prejudice of nobility, but they can do as they please, we shall hold to it. We are born to it."[36]

The basic way of keeping long-term group solidarity going was marriage. The network of relatives, assiduously cultivated, provided not merely social but financial and political backing. In 1811, the prefect reported that the Old-Regime nobility of Toulouse showed aversion to intermarriage with the new Imperial nobility on the grounds that this would mongrelize and degrade their own heritage.[37] The correspondence over a quarter of a century of two ultra noblemen, Jean-Baptiste-Louis Chalvet-Gaujouse and Clément d'Aignan d'Empaillon, contained a constant survey of the possible marriages among their acquaintances. As Chalvet-Gaujouse put it in the letter cited above: "I am of the good old times: I am for the good marriages [in the sense of noble endogamy]." This was understandable, since loans and political alliances were heavily dependent on family links. The dowry was a matter of keen interest, but even more important was the subject of status. In February, 1820, he described the marriage of a noble into "a well-off bourgeois family, thinking properly, and to which the King gave letters of nobility ... it is said there are 600,000 francs in the family. The mania of bourgeois women is to marry nobles. Do they do well? I see frequent examples to the contrary."[38] It was very rare for local nobles to marry outside of their group, particularly among the ultras, as is shown on Table IV-3:

[36] J. Barada, "Toulouse et la vie toulousaine ...," *Annales du Midi*, XLV (1932), 171.
[37] AN, F1cIII (Garonne, Haute-) 9, compte-rendu administratif, 1811.
[38] Barada, "Toulouse et la vie toulousaine," p. 468.

TABLE IV-3. MARRIAGES IN EIGHT ULTRAROYALIST NOBLE FAMILIES OF TOULOUSE

Name	Type of Nobility	Wife	Eldest Son married:	Younger Sons					Daughters		
						married				married	
				religious	died young	noble	commoner	religious	died young	noble	commoner
Armand Dubourg (1778–1831)	Parlement	sword	Died young	✓		✓✓		✓✓			✓
Adrien de Rességuier (1785– ?)	Parlement	sword	Foreign noble			✓✓					
P-M-C-L-H d'Hautpoul (1796–1847)	sword	noble	commoner		✓✓				✓✓	✓✓✓	
Joseph de Villèle (1773–1854)	seigneurial	commoner	noble							✓✓✓	
G-Isidore de Montbel* (1787–1861)	capitoulat	Parlement	noble			✓				✓✓✓	
J-F-M de Savy-Gardeilh (1761–1833)	capitoulat	noble	Parlement						✓	✓✓	
A-J-M de Saint-Félix (1784– ?)	seigneurial	Parlement	noble			✓				✓✓	
A-M-A de Sambucy (1756–1832)	sword	Parlement	noble				✓		✓		

* The five children of second and third marriages, born in emigration at the court of Henri V, are not included

A typical noble family in this respect was that of Jean-François de Savy-Gardeilh, son of a lieutenant of dragoons in the Harcourt regiment. He had military, municipal, and parlementarian ancestry; his mother was of the parlementary Pérès family, while his brother was one of the councilors executed in 1794 at Paris. He himself began his career as a *cadet-gentilhomme* in the Beaujolais regiment, resigning his commission on August 18, 1792. He did not emigrate after the fall of the monarchy, and although he was to appear on the list of royalist hostages at the time of the Insurrection of the year VII, he remained quietly on his Verfeil estates throughout the Jacobin and Directorial periods of the Revolution. Despite a large bribe given to the adjudicator, he was prevented from bidding on the lease of his brother's confiscated property in the way used by so many nobles to keep their family lands intact. He married a noblewoman, was appointed to the municipal council of Toulouse in 1809, and became municipal *adjoint* in 1811. At the first Restoration, however, he declared himself vehemently for the Bourbons; he was member of a deputation sent to salute the duke of Angoulême in Bordeaux, and of another one which presented a petition to Louis XVIII. After the Hundred Days, he temporarily held the post of special police lieutenant and put his knowledge of the city to good use in directing royalist terrorism under the cover of legality; his son led attacks on the home of the former mayor of the city, the bonapartist Baron de Malaret.[39]

The marriage patterns of the Savy-Gardeilh illustrate how the ultra nobility was linked. One of his daughters married a wealthy landowner from the Tarn, Comte d'Hautpoul, who was somewhat implicated in the events surrounding the assassination of General Ramel in 1815. Witnesses at the wedding included Chalvet de Rochemonteix and Sambucy, also involved in royalist resistance, and Latour-Mauriac, St. Félix, and Comtesse de Lafitte-Pelleport.[40] Another daughter married Baron Capriol-Payra of the Aude, and the ceremony was graced by the presence of Dupac de Bellegarde, Despluts, Chalvet de Rochemonteix, and Sambucy.[41] His son Hippolyte, twenty-three years old in 1815, "an elegant blonde much ap-

[39] A. Duboul, *La fin du parlement de Toulouse* (Toulouse, 1890), pp. 161–62; *AMT*, 1 S 47; Jean Loubet, "Le gouvernement toulousain du duc d'Angoulême après les Cent-Jours," *La Révolution française*, LXIV (1913), 356.
[40] *ADHG*, 3E-27435.
[41] *ADHG*, 4E-2775.

preciated by the high-society ladies of the Rue des Nobles and the Place Mage," married in 1820 a younger daughter of Marquis de Campistron de Maniban, former *président à mortier*. His witnesses included the ultra municipal councillor Blanc, his friend Guintraud whom Ferdinand de Bertier described as a resolute and devoted member of the *chevaliers de la foi*, Aldéguier, and Vicomte de Théon.[42]

Other less flamboyant ultra families showed the close social links among the parlementary and ultra nobility. The Dubourgs were related to the Escouloubre and thus to the Savy-Gardeilhs. The nephew of the deputy Castelbajac was married to a Villeneuve. The Vicomte de Panat married the daughter of a parlementary ultra deputy in the presence of Bruno Dubourg and Miègeville.[43] Deputies, judges, and prefects thus found themselves in a web of family ties.

These connections were constantly brought into play in local politics; indeed, to a large extent, these were clan wars. Villèle relied for his influence in both town and country on "many relatives and allies, all very active."[44] His father was his stand-in at the Capitole, his uncle the chevalier his spokesman among the local military. Friendly neighbors like Saint Félix and Reversat de Marsac campaigned for him in the Villefranche *arrondissement* and were themselves to be candidates—Villèlist candidates, it need hardly be said—during the Restoration. He dined frequently with these men and their wives as his diaries reveal. Augustin Manavit spread his views in the ultra press of Toulouse. Secretary Delpy at the prefecture was one of his admirers. The wide hospitality was part of the noble tradition of maintaining extensive family connections; while some contemporaries jibed that the fare was far from elaborate, the meals were plentiful and freely given and provided constant opportunities to meet and talk with supporters. In Paris, Villèle dined often with deputies from the Haute-Garonne and attended the larger salons; in Toulouse, he met the local nobles—MacCarthys, Dubourgs, Montbels, Beauregards, Saint-

---

[42] Jean Gabriel Cappot, *pseud.* Capo de Feuillide, *Le Midi en 1815* (Paris, 1836), I, 123; G. Bertier de Sauvigny, *Un type d'ultra-royaliste: le comte Ferdinand de Bertier* (Paris, 1948), p. 140; *ADHG*, 4E-3040.

[43] *ADHG*, 3E-21481; *ADHG*, 4E-3040.

[44] *AN*, F¹cIII (Garonne, Haute-) 6, Rémusat to Minister of Interior, October 7, 1816.

Gérys, Sabrans, Roquettes and Bastouilhs—in the reception rooms of Mlle de Saint Léon, Mme de Gavaret, Mme d'Orgeix, Mme de Bellissens, and in that of the most beautiful and outspoken of these women, Mme d'Hargicourt. These noblewomen were never slow in proclaiming elegantly extreme ultra views.[45]

Along with the marriages and the close-knit network of relations and friends went the snobbery necessary to censure those inadmissable to ultra circles. A noble who had friends outside of the socially acceptable was described as "tout à fait encanaillé."[46] The elder Villèle approvingly described his grandson as mixing only with good company—"la bonne compagnie."[47] Social climbers who passed off titles to which they had no justified claims were soon discovered. In 1818, the *Ami du Roi* published an article on the subject, denouncing the widespread usurpation of titles.[48] Affirmations of the quintessential difference between the noble and the commoner produced naturally a resentment. One man told the prefect during the famine of 1816–17 that the citizens willingly obeyed the representatives of royal authority, but "if the *gentilshommes* want to revive their former rights and to walk on our bellies, Good God! they had better watch out!"[49] Social snubs by the ultras had added to the liberal ranks in Toulouse. There were the déclassé nobles—the Cambon brothers, Malaret, Martin d'Aiguesvives—who were rejected by the ultra nobles. So was young Romiguières, of a family that was about to enter the nobility in 1789.

Neither wealth, nor rank, nor official position gave access to the local elite. Nor for that matter did piety or charity, as the example of Malaret showed. Whole families became involved in generalized social disapproval. Marquis Alexandre de Cambon, son of the last First President of the Parlement (a high social recommendation indeed), disgraced himself by his behavior during the Hundred Days, when he took the oath of loyalty to the Empire. At the second Restoration, he resigned from his office at the Royal Court but was persuaded by the Ministry of Justice to remain at the court.

[45] C. E. de Rémusat, "Lettres de Province, 1815–1817," *Revue de Paris*, IX, iv (July–September 1902).
[46] AV, H. de Villèle to Joseph de Villèle, August 27, 1822.
[47] AV, L. de Villèle to Joseph de Villèle, n.d.
[48] AR, June 23, 1818.
[49] C. F. M. de Rémusat, *Correspondance*, II, 240.

The stigma attached to his conduct soon affected the whole social context of the de Cambons in ultra Toulouse. Only his elderly uncle, the vicar-general, was excepted from the general oprobrium, redeemed by his royalism. De Cambon compounded his sins when he, in 1818 at the age of forty-eight, married the daughter of a rich Toulouse merchant. Chalvet-Gaujouse, a dependable barometer of ultra opinion, was appalled. He thought Cambon should quit the court having married "the daughter of a wretched little shopkeeper who prides himself in the language of a porter on being the builder of his own very large fortune which, he rightly says, he started here when he arrived with a knapsack on his back. O tempora! O mores!"[50] Cambon's sister, married during the Revolution to the parlementarian Félix Martin d'Aiguesvives who had become a *procureur* at the Toulouse appeal court during the Empire, saw her eldest son married to Camille de Malaret, of another family disgraced in eyes of the ultras by bad political behavior.

The "consideration" so constantly evoked in the documents of the time, implied more than simple criteria of wealth, birth, or office; it also meant the respect for the practice of Catholic conservatism and noble prejudice. It was more censorious than affirmative, and as a stamp of social approval it was easily lost.

Elected deputies represented more than mere political views of the ultras. Elections were orgies of lobbying, visits paid, evocations of various debts of gratitude now to be paid off, and influence mongering. The Haute-Garonne was among the most ultra of French departments as demonstrated by the deputies it elected. The colleagues of Joseph de Villèle, whose brilliant career in local and national politics was partly based on family ties, were his social acquaintances in Toulouse and Paris.

Only two of the sixteen men who represented the Haute-Garonne during the Restoration were not part of his circle, although both came from robe nobility. Perhaps they should be examined as exceptions to the Villèlist ascendancy; at least they provided some contrast to the attitudes of the ultraroyalists.

The Marquis de Catellan, of a family claiming Florentine and robe antecedents, was imprisoned briefly before the Revolution for his vigorous objections to the edicts of Loménie de Brienne. Although he had been in the Parlement, he did not emigrate during the

[50] Barada, "Toulouse et la vie toulousaine," p. 458.

Revolution. On the strength of his parlementary background, he was offered a place in the Toulouse Royal Court at the Restoration, but he refused, feeling that his knowledge of new legislation was inadequate. In 1815, he stood as a candidate and was elected to the *Chambre Introuvable* where he showed himself to be a moderate. The Rémusats were startled by his acid mockery of the Toulouse nobility's pretensions. The local ultras cordially disliked Catellan when they realized the turn of his mind; Villèle's father thought he should be pelted with mud if he showed his face in the city. He was not re-elected in 1816 and did not again live at Toulouse until 1833.[51]

Auguste, marquis de Cambon, was the brother of Alexandre, whose misalliance was mentioned above. His mother had been executed for concealing the whereabouts of her proscribed husband, the First President, and he emigrated a few months after this tragedy. Auguste returned to France after the fall of Robespierre and, like his brother, accepted office during the Empire. Auguste was a member of the *conseil général*. During the Hundred Days, he served with royalist forces in the Drôme. Despite the personal sufferings inflicted on the family by the Revolution, both Cambons disapproved of ultra policies and ideas, and took no part in the terrorism of 1815. When he was elected to the Chamber in 1824, Auguste attacked Villèle's 1823 budget, to the discomfort of the ministry. Villèle strongly opposed the re-election of Cambon, but Cambon was supported by strong family connections. The "Jacobins" of 1823 voted for him: ". . . it was impossible to resist all these intrigues headed by Baudens, father-in-law of Alexandre de Cambon, the sollicitor Malafosse, and President d'Aiguesvives."[52] In May, 1830, Villèle told his wife that Cambon had dubious principles and should not be re-elected.

Both Catellan and Cambon were renegades in the opinion of the ultras. Both had the social background which made them completely acceptable, yet both had betrayed the conventions of the lesser provincial nobility. It was difficult to forgive two "traitors of the class." It was also striking that the two who could be described as of center-left or liberal political opinion among the deputies of Toulouse were noblemen; even the opposition was recruited from the well-born.

[51] C. F. de Rémusat, *Mémoires*, I, 299; AN C 1215.
[52] AV, Naissac to Henri de Villèle, n.d.

Villèle, elected by a very close margin in 1815, soon became the dominant political figure in the city. His colleagues of 1815 at the *Chambre Introuvable*—the President d'Aldéguier, his brother-in-law Limairac, and de Puymaurin—were to remain his faithful supporters throughout his political career. Like Villèle, they were noblemen; like him, they held office during the Empire. All were by definition wealthy, for only men paying a thousand francs or more of tax could stand for election as a deputy. Limairac had lost some family property during the Revolution, sold to the value of 157,000 livres, although he was described as the wealthiest of the deputies of 1815 with a revenue estimated at 18,000 francs. Puymaurin was also affluent, and owned some *biens nationaux*.[53] All three were mediocrities: d'Aldéguier said little at the Chamber, and Limairac said less. After his loyal and uncritical service to the royalist cause, Limairac was very hurt to be excluded from the deputation in 1824, and blamed this on his brother-in-law: "... at least the families which have a rank in society ought not to descend in this electoral rivalry to miserable intrigues, not to speak of good faith cruelly abused by the means which have been used against me."[54] Puymaurin, despite his interest in reviving the local woad industry, which had received some stimulation during the Continental Blockade and despite his technical knowledge of chemistry (not to mention his *biens nationaux*), seemed able to convince the ultra voters of the sincerity of his views. He sat at the Chamber from 1815 to 1830, voted with the right, rarely made speeches, but had a reputation for clever quips at the expense of the opposition.

The other deputies elected during the Restoration had many similar characteristics. They were noble, none had seen their family fortunes ruined albeit diminished by the Revolution, and most of them had experience in public office under the Empire. They all took second place to their distinguished compatriot at the Chamber of deputies; with the exception of Castelbajac (and then only a brief one), they unanimously supported Villèle. Hocquart, Ricard, Montbel, Dubourg, Bastouilh, and Chalvet de Rochemonteix had parlementary antecedents; Roquette-Buisson, Saint-Félix de Mauremont, Castelbajac, and Vézian de Saint-André were of military background.

[53] *ADHG*, 2 M 7.
[54] AV, Limairac to Villèle, March 10, 1824.

These ultra deputies displayed the qualities which typified the ultra life-style. They were men of impeccable morals, pious in at least an external way, austere in dress, and grave in demeanor. Their women had the same rigid morality, perhaps as a conscious repudiation of the looser mores of the eighteenth century. The two sisters of the comte Jean Dubarry, brother-in-law of the famous mistress of Louis XV, were noted in the Restoration for their fervent piety. The noble ladies of Toulouse found much of their social life connected with religious observances and associations, and they encouraged their husbands in good works. Aldéguier was administrator of the hospitals of Toulouse; comte Ricard gave a house to the missionaries from Lyon in 1809. Religious associations like the *Aa*, the revived brotherhoods of penitents, and charitable work offered a wide scope for this kind of activity. The *Aa*, for example, included among its members Bruno Dubourg and Palarin, both ultra deputies during the Restoration; Saint-Raymond from the municipal council, Dalayrac from the Royal Court, and d'Orgeix, a wealthy landowner and royalist militant of 1815. Montbel, who subsequently became mayor of Toulouse, deputy, and minister in the Polignac government, noted other local noblemen who belonged to a religious association—in fact, the *chevaliers de la foi*—which was involved in politics and charitable work. They included the returned *émigré* Dupac de Bellegarde, Robert de MacCarthy, de Saint-Géry, the Cantalauze brothers, and inevitably the Dubourgs. The brother of Robert MacCarthy, Nicolas, became one of the most famous preachers of his generation, in demand in court circles in Paris. His family was related to the Castelbajac. These ultras were in contact with the *abbé* Ducasse, the *abbé* Cambon, and the *abbé* Berger, leading members of the very conservative faction of local clergy. There was strong lay support for the assaults launched by Archbishop Clermont-Tonnerre on the "revolutionary" principles of liberalism. His vicar-general Henri Berger directed the Toulouse congregation and founded the religious association called the *Société des Bonnes Etudes* (to be discussed in more detail in a later chapter), which was strongly ultraroyalist.

Neither all religious bodies nor all pious individuals were ultra. In many of the revived confraternities and religious associations, however, the membership was overwhelmingly royalist and hostile to the irreligion of the Revolution. Of the ten members of the *Mont de Piété*, founded in 1828, with the exception of the president and of the protestant banker Courtois, all were associated with noble, Catholic, and ultra circles.[55]

The ultraroyalist prototype emerges silhouetted against the pink brickwork of the streets in Restoration Toulouse, a censorious figure, if not a noble then wishing to associate with the nobility, mindful of his country property and civic responsibilities. The larger ultra landowners moved from town to country, as did Joseph de Villèle who moved from the large house on the Rue Vélane to the château that looked over the rolling fields of the Lauragais. Noble ultras maintained the web of obligations which bound families together in the complicities of dowries, inheritances, and land deals; even the raising of money was personal and within the bounds of the "bonne compagnie." Armand Dubourg's will at his death in 1831 included references to the 1756 obligations left by his grandmother and to others in the will of his father at the end of the eighteenth century. The ultras lived in the accumulation of the memories and experiences of the past. In Toulouse, where liberal mockery of their anachronistic attitudes had little audience, they felt relatively secure; why should they accept a new social outlook?

[55] *JPLT*, December 23, 1828.

V

LOCAL GOVERNMENT
AND THE ULTRAS

ONCE THE WHITE FLAG of the Bourbons fluttered again over the pink façade of the Toulouse *Capitole* in the summer of 1815, the leading ultraroyalists of the city—Limairac, Joseph de Villèle, Savy-Gardeilh, Gounon, and others—found they were able to apply in practice their views on local government. Throughout France, in the wake of the second humiliation of Waterloo, there was a press of candidates for official posts who stated their desire to purify and strengthen the government that was obviously corrupted by the politics of the past quarter of a century. During the Restoration, there was a much wider participation and interest in government on the part of nobility, from its highest to its lowest echelons. Now that the upper reaches of army, church, and law could no longer be considered essentially noble prerogatives, the nobility wished not merely to recover lost ground, but to re-think its attitudes to other kinds of state service. Toulouse was no exception to this novel development. Service in municipal offices and on advisory councils of *arrondissements* and the department, the committee work that was considered before the Revolution not only vulgar and inelegant but dreary and demeaning, was now highly regarded as politically useful and morally worthy. There was a clear tendency for the former seigneur to become mayor in the place where his family lands had been located before the Revolution—if he still possessed them; Villèle was mayor of Mourvilles-Basses, Chalvet de Rochemonteix at Mervilles, and Baron de Montbel at Beaumont. They saw this as the practical affirmation of a "paternal" interest in their villages. It might well be said that the Restoration prefects who encouraged this practice were often short of suitable candidates for office. In the Haute-Garonne, the mayor was usually literate, while his *adjoints* and members of the council were often unable to read and write adequately; the clearest administrative instructions were frequently misunderstood.[1] Nobles were asked to fill positions for the simple reason that they were often the only person who could read and write that was available in smaller communities. On the other hand, the nobles were now aware of a moral obligation to take on such tedious duties. The son of the last seneschal of Toulouse, Chalvet de Rochemonteix, wrote to the prefect about the difficulty of finding candidates for municipal office who were confirmed royalists and of good morality, displaying zeal, ability, and strong character. He went on to lament the absence of such model men in the gloomy and exaggerated style so typical of the ultras:

You appear to wish that these functions should be filled as much as possible by the former seigneurs. The frightful effects of this destructive Revolution have dispersed some of them, others by its dreadful effects lost their fortune and no longer inhabit those places which were dear to their childhood, and of which they have seen themselves unjustly stripped by the consequence of their fidelity to the King and to legitimate principles.[2]

Nevertheless, the Haute-Garonne had a high proportion of mayors who were Old Regime nobles, and these men took their social responsibilities seriously.

Service in the local government of a large city like Toulouse was obviously different from serving as the mayor of a country community. It was even more vital that the major city in the region should be controlled by men of royalist outlook. Despite the fact that nominations had to be approved by the ministry in Paris, it was evident that many of the city fathers were partisans of "the good cause." They never tired of describing the *capitoulat's* glories and pointing out the need to watch carefully for revolutionaries.

Edmond Lamouzèle wrote in 1910 that, despite the differences between municipal governments in the Old Regime and those that

[1] *AN*, F1bII (Garonne, Haute-) 8.
[2] *AB*, Chalvet de Rochemonteix to Prefect, March 22, 1816.

100

followed, the former contained the "fertile seeds" from which grew the nineteenth-century municipality of Toulouse. Another local historian, Ramet, rejected this, pointing to the abolition of the *capitoulat*, changes in the territorial divisions of the city, and different electoral procedures as signs of a complete break between the old and the new.[3] However, Lamouzèle was certainly right in seeing a significant social continuity. Names like Savy-Gardeilh, d'Olive, Baron de Montbel, Miègeville, and Puymaurin were to be found on the lists of the *capitouls* and on the registers of the nineteenth-century municipality.

On the other hand, the institutional structure had undergone many changes. During the Revolution, there were rapid and successive changes in local government.[4] The Consulate established, in the year VIII, the system of government which remained in force until 1837.[5] Appointments to municipal councils were made for twenty-year periods, with a renewal of half of the membership every decade. Continuity in office was clearly more important than representation; until the Monarchy of July, the Councillors, once appointed, remained in office until they resigned. The desire for stability was stated under the Empire as well as the Restoration; Picot de Lapeyrouse (appointed mayor in 1800), and his successor Bellegarde (appointed in 1806), each emphasized this theme in his inaugural address. When Bellegarde was appointed to the *Corps Legislatif* in 1811, he was replaced by a pious and charitable old regime noble M. de Malaret, known locally as an excellent farmer.

This traditionalism was also to be found among the members of the municipal council, composed of lawyers, landowners, professional men, and some merchants. The men of law were well represented, even disproportionately so, in the years VIII, 1815, and 1830. There was an increasing tendency to call wealthy landowners to office; even the merchants were substantial *propriétaires*, men who at retirement from their business careers had translated their profits into the respectability of fields, woods, *métairies*, and country houses.

[3] E. Lamouzèle, *Essai sur l'administration de la ville de Toulouse . . . 1783–1790* (Paris, 1910); H. Ramet, *Histoire de Toulouse* (Toulouse, 1935), p. 660.

[4] J. Mandoul, *Les municipalités de Toulouse pendant la Révolution* (Toulouse, 1906).

[5] Law of 28 pluviôse VIII. See E. Monet, *Histoire de l'administration* (Paris, 1885).

It is difficult to separate this rural base of wealth, enhanced by property in the city, from the politics of the councillors. Are they countrymen or city dwellers in their outlook? Many students of the pre-industrial city have emphasized the preponderantly urban nature of upper-class elements who were large landowners.[6] The actual running of estates was largely in the hands of managers, and the landowner often had little direct contact with the lands which provided his income. Yet it is equally difficult to suppose that the pre-industrial city differed very much from the surrounding countryside. The city was a place where special skills and a variety of bureaucratic and social functions were concentrated for the benefit of the rural population. The peasant coming to market, school, cathedral, or court, as well as the landowner on a visit to his property, the merchant supplying the cottagers, or the doctor on his rounds were part of a complex symbiosis. In Toulouse, peasants lived within the city walls and went out daily to work in the *gardiage*. In such a situation, it is misleading to see a simplistic contrast between town and country.

The landowners of the municipal council of Toulouse varied in the degree of their civic concern. Some were assiduous and others made only token appearances. The small Protestant community in Toulouse had a spokesman in Courtois of the banking family, while the tiny Jewish community had no representation. In the absence of the mayor, the *adjoints* controlled the city and dealt with much of the daily routine of the municipality. The municipal council provided a forum for discussion of matters of general interest, and set up committees of investigation into problems such as what sort of water fountain was best to be constructed.

The polarization of ultraroyalist views on the council came about not in 1814 (although, to some extent, it had occurred then also), but in 1815, after the Hundred Days. The search for scapegoats upon the return of Bonaparte placed political sympathies of the municipal councillors under scrutiny. During the brief return of the Empire, a number of candidates for municipal office were proposed by the new prefect, among them Picot de Lapeyrouse, the ex-mayor; Ayral, who owned many *biens nationaux*; Saget, an "ami de la liberté" and a big landowner; and the iron-merchant Garrigou, who was described as a partisan of revolutionary principles. These

[6] Gideon Sjoberg, *The Pre-industrial City, Past and Present* (New York, 1960), pp. 110–16.

nominations were a roll-call of men distasteful to the ultras. Only Picot de Lapeyrouse, of a noble family, a leading member of the Society of Agriculture, and the Director of the Botanical Gardens, and Malaret, the turncoat mayor left in office although the Bonapartists considered him irresolute and at heart the protector of priests, *dévots*, and royalists, had an acceptable social background. The others were *parvenus*.

After the news of Waterloo, recriminations began. The local establishment had been inglorious in their easy acceptance of Bonapart's return. Officials outdid themselves in declaring their loyalty to Louis XVIII and their revulsion against the fallen emperor. The municipal council proclaimed they had nothing to do with the "horrid treason" which had taken place, and that "the force of bayonettes and furious oppression by the revolutionary government were used to stifle their expostulations." This was hardly to be taken seriously, and as if to compensate for it, those who had actually declared themselves for the Empire were savagely criticized. The prefect de Rémusat, who had held a number of important posts under the Empire before 1814, saw the need to bring this name-calling to an end. He wanted to make changes on the council to avoid possible grounds for disorder, and the men he put forward were something of a concession to the exasperated ultras. He had suggested a former sub-prefect of Toulouse as one of the new *adjoints*, a man disliked by the ultras, but he could not take the job because he had been given a new sub-prefecture in the neighboring department of Gers. Instead, Félix Gounon, son of the wealthiest merchant in Toulouse on the eve of the Revolution and himself a heated supporter of ultraroyalism took the position. His colleagues were Bruno Dubourg, a brother of the abbé from the noted counterrevolutionary parlementary family; Ricard, later to be a deputy and much noted for his piety; and Paul Thoron, the import-export merchant who had retired as a landowner on the profits of his cloth trade with the Levant. The prefect claimed that he tried to avoid proposing ultra candidates in an attempt to prevent a further increase in the local power of Joseph de Villèle, who had been made mayor by the Duke of Angoulême in August, 1815, and who remained in office despite his prolonged absences as a deputy to the *Chambre Introuvable*. Rémusat failed in this effort.[7]

[7] *AN*, F1bII (Garonne, Haute-) 26.

The list of candidates for municipal councillors included men like Baron de Montbel, a relative of Villèle and a *chevalier de la foi* who was to hold office in the Polignac ministry of 1830. There were no forceful rivals to the ultra ascendancy on the reformed council of 1816.

Between 1820 and 1830, the intake to the council consisted of men of law, three landowners, a banker, a merchant, and the *payeur du departement*. For the rest of the Restoration, the council changed little in its composition and less in its political views, but continued to uphold the traditional outlook of the men of law and the landowners of Toulouse.

What then was the nature of these static municipal politics, and how were they expressed? Certainly they coexisted uneasily with the highly emotional outbursts of the White Terror. Joseph de Villèle, soon to become one of the major figures among the ultra-royalists in the capital, had little sympathy for hotheads. The prefect de Rémusat came to appreciate the quiet administrative talents of the new mayor and to admire his private virtues. The main problem was, in fact, the father of Villèle who showed considerable ability as a farmer and who had a firm grasp of taxation law, both of which he passed on to his son. However, the father had not the same emotional self-control. Even in the Old Regime he published vituperative pamphlets denouncing a local tax official, and with advancing years he became increasingly cantankerous. He often appeared at the town hall as well as in the royalist salons as the deputy of his son, and he took every opportunity to denounce dangerous modern innovations. Joseph de Villèle, while always a respectful and submissive son, seconded the prefect in calming his father's exaggerated denunciations of "Jacobins" and discounted them as mere imaginative outbursts of an inflamed meridional temperament.[8] Rémusat thought that Villèle disdained "the vaporous passions of occitan royalism."[9] At the same time, Villèle was more committed to his excitable friends than to the prefect for obvious reasons, and the path he trod was a narrow one. He had to show opposition to the royal appointments, but provide sensible guidance for local ultras. His *adjoints* in the municipality called for firm measures against subversives while the prefecture insisted that

[8] *AN*, F1bII (Garonne, Haute-) 26.
[9] C. F. de Rémusat, *Mémoires de ma vie* (Paris, 1958), I, 228.

imprisonment should not be arbitrary.[10] Villèle wavered between arresting and releasing the suspects.

The ultraroyalists called constantly for dismissals at all levels of government. The Villèle family archives provide an insight into the grounds for appointments in an undated "List of persons who ought to be brought to the attention of mayor, of recognised ability, being of good life and morals, devoted to the family of the Bourbons by their conduct." Many of these were without doubt, rank-and-file members of the *verdets*. Their qualities were of the order of "very learned in writing," or "good writer," and one, in fact, was described as a "royal volunteer, good for a writing job in an office or at the *octroi*." They were destined to replace men described as a "great *fédéré* brigand," an "owner of *biens nationaux*," or "faking royalism." Minor officials like the dues collectors at the Arnaud Bernard, Montgaillard, and St. Etienne gates, the five employees of the *bureau central*, and the clerks and the inspector of the Canal du Midi were under heavy attack.

The Ministry of the Interior looked on this situation in Toulouse with considerable suspicion. Villèle thought in 1816 that he should resign from the post of mayor because of the hostility shown to him by officials at the ministry. He found that he was of little help to his fellow citizens, since his lobbying in Paris was usually ignored. He resented being accused of complicity in the Ramel assassination, an accusation which he considered intolerable. Mme de Villèle wrote to him that the *adjoints* would probably follow him if he resigned, thus bringing about disorganization of the municipality and, still worse, replacements by unsuitable men. Discouragement and fear would be sown among the common people who had showed devotion to the royal cause and who would feel deprived of any support. She warned that, if the ultras needed popular support in the future, this might not come; the people would remember that they had been "vexed for having served the cause too well."[11] The *adjoints* also felt hindered by political enmities and one, Thoron, did resign in February, 1817, a year before Villèle finally gave up the mayoralty. Throughout the period from the end of the Hundred Days to February, 1818, the municipal government was acutely conscious of the hostility of the central government.

[10] *ADHG*, 4 M 39, correspondence between *procureur du roi* and the municipality of Toulouse.
[11] *AV*, Mme de Villèle to Joseph de Villèle, December 11, 1816.

At the beginning of 1818, the prefect Saint-Chamans reported concern in the city, caused by rumors of Villèle's resignation. The mayor was the most prominent exponent of ultraroyalism in Toulouse and in Paris, and books and pamphlets expressing the ultra point of view were spread in profusion and read avidly in the city.[12] When Saint-Chamans nominated Baron de Bellegarde, a mayor of the city during the Empire who was appointed by Paris, it was to be expected that he would be denounced. Anglaret, one of those who were tried for complicity in the Ramel assassination, wrote to Villèle that all the wicked in the city were delighted with the new official.[13] Bellegarde, for his part, protested that his health, a projected visit to England, and above all the violence of political opinions made his job difficult. Even so, he accepted, and proved to be a talented if tactless administrator. In July, 1818, he clashed in the municipal council with Marquis d'Escouloubre over the hospital budget. The discussion became very heated when Bellegarde stated that it was unclear what had become of the 12,000 francs for which Escouloubre was responsible. The marquis, enraged, challenged him to a duel and, in consequence, was forced to resign.[14] Episodes of this sort made the ultras his enemies. He tried to end the political rancor which was prevalent in the city; for example he organized two "Festivals of Reconciliation and Forgetting the Past"—a banquet, various sports events, dances, and processions—in the districts most Napoleonic in sympathy, Saint Cyprien and Arnaud Bernard.[15]

Political views appeared in addresses and resolutions of the municipal council. The assassination of the Duc de Berry by Louvel as he was leaving the Paris Opera in February, 1820, reinforced local criticism of freedom of the press. The municipality called on royal authority to chain irreligion so that the social order would no longer be menaced with destruction and France could again find the stability that had been enjoyed by it for eight centuries and that could be guaranteed only by the Bourbons. A year later, on the anniversary of the assassination, another address was voted, calling for severe repression of seditious doctrines. The original

[12] AN, F⁷9659.
[13] AV, Anglaret to Villèle, March 17, 1818.
[14] AN, F¹ᵇII (Garonne, Haute-) 26.
[15] Ibid; A. Brémond, Annales du XIXe siècle de la ville de Toulouse de 1800 à 1850 (Toulouse, 1865), p. 111.

106

included the ominous words: "Justice! Justice! The heads of the obscure are insufficient to redeem such a crime." The *procureur général* was able to report, with satisfaction, that the wiser members of the council suppressed this vague threat. In 1822, the council was angered by liberal protests against the new censorship laws and again called for strong action against subversive publications. More than this, it said that although the Chamber of Deputies should be a forum for discussions of the welfare and happiness of the people, too often revolutionary doctrines were to be heard there, with insults to France, apologies for revolt, and seditious appeal to the population. This would have to be halted.[16]

There was an ultra clique in the municipal council that pressed these views with particular passion. It was led by the first *adjoint* Félix Gounon, who has already been discussed in another connection. He met frequently with his friends in a café on the Place Rouaix, the meeting place of the city ultras. There he planned the opposition to mayor Bellegarde. The mayor became very irritated by this constant resistance to his policy on the part of his subordinate, a resistance he put down to Gounon's desire to become mayor and a deputy. The extremists of the Café Rouaix and the *Echo du Midi* encouraged Gounon's ambitions. They wanted war to be declared on the liberal government in Spain, villified those who were moderate towards liberals, and hoped for a vigorous ultra-royalist municipal policy. At the beginning of 1822, Bellegarde sent his own complaints against Gounon and his carping friends to Villèle in the hope that Gounon could be made to retire, but his adversary in fact outlasted him. Bellegarde resigned in 1823, but Gounon, the darling of the ultras, stayed in office until the July Monarchy and provided for a decade a focus for ultra views inside the Toulouse municipality.

Gounon could direct his disapproval against Bellegarde's moderate successor, Comte Joseph-Thimoléon d'Hargenvilliers, a nobleman of military origin who had fought in the American War of Independence. He returned to France and served in the army during the Revolution in the general staff of the army of the Pyrenees with the rank of a *général de brigade*, but he was suspended in December, 1793, and sentenced to imprisonment by the revolu-

[16] *AMT*, registers of municipal deliberations, February 21, 1820; February 8, 1821; April 20, 1822.

tionary tribunal of Peripignan. Released after the 9th of Thermidor, his career advanced; he attended the coronation of Napoleon and was made a Baron of the Empire. Despite this, after the Hundred Days, the Duc d'Angoulême appointed him commander of the Tarn and Aveyron. He was not confirmed in this position, but was named to preside over the *cour prévôtale* of the Aveyron. He lived in Toulouse. The prefect Saint-Chamans thought well of him, but his successor, Comte de Juigné, strongly recommended Baron de Montbel, a kinsman of Villèle, to replace Hargenvilliers.

Guillaume-Isidore, Baron de Montbel, was named mayor of Toulouse in January, 1826. His *adjoints* were the indestructible Félix Gounon, Bernadet, Duchan, and St. Raymond. The *Echo du Midi* was delighted with this nomination. It considered him to be a virtuous citizen, an enlightened magistrate, and a faithful royalist who would give royalists the guarantees necessary for the interests of religion, monarchy, and the city. Montbel, in short, was an ultra candidate, the first one clearly so since the mayoralty of Villèle from 1815 to 1818. He also favored economic progress and technical education in a city particularly dear to the heart of Charles X.[17] Indeed, his administration was marked by a number of successful innovations, and he was elected to the Chamber of Deputies in 1830. He was replaced by a noble of parlementary origins, de Rességuier.

Rességuier did not hold office for long. His appointment of November, 1829, was soon to be terminated by the Revolution of 1830. On August 3, 1830, the prefect broke with the past, and called on the local banker Joseph Viguerie to be mayor of the city. The Viguerie family was better known for its doctors than for its businessmen, and Joseph, while rich, was of a conciliatory character. He had been an unsuccessful liberal candidate in the elections. Thus he was not prepossessing as a vigorous representative of a new order, but he was put forward since nobody more suitable could be found. In turn he was proposed for the post by two deputies who lived in the city but were not elected by the department, "for the reason that the Haute-Garonne has no *constitutionnel* deputy."[18]

The new mayor set about replacing members of the municipal

[17] *Echo du Midi*, February 14, 1826.
[18] *AMT*, registers of the deliberations of the municipal council, August 3, 1830; *AN*, F1bII (Garonne, Haute-) 26.

council who were clearly ill-disposed to the government of Louis Philippe. A new council was called, the flower of local liberal opinion, composed of seven landowners, seven lawyers, and sixteen men of commercial interests (including five bankers, a stock-broker, and others ranging from a sculptor to a physics professor). This was clearly a new emphasis on recruitment, different from that which prevailed under the Empire and Restoration. In France at large, Guizot's ordinances dismissed over six thousand municipal officials, half of whom were mayors.[19]

After 1830, the legitimists were divided between the policy of continuing in municipal politics or holding aloof. In the later years of the decade, a number of them rejoined the struggle to express their ideas, but they were never to regain the ascendancy of the Restoration years.

A place on the *conseil général* of the department or on one of the *conseil d'arrondissement* was even more attractive to ambitious ultras than service in municipal government. Such councils not only demanded less time of the members, but they seemed to be a con-tinuation of those regional assemblies of the Old Regime which were so often cited as the models for effective local administration. Comte Louis de Villeneuve, a very active member of the Society of Agriculture, declared in 1816 that a prosperous agriculture would result from the creation of departmental administration which was a strengthened *conseil général*. This was the way to establish the type of government that produced the prosperity of the *pays d'états* before 1789.[20] Many of his fellow ultras shared this favorable view of the councils. The membership of these bodies became increasingly aristocratic during the Empire and the Resto-ration. Napoleon encouraged the recruitment of noblemen and, as a liberal author noted in 1827, the address of the councils showed how narrowly the public interest was identified with that of the local nobility. The councils were "aristocratic in essence and by nomination," and this did not escape the notice of the Toulouse ultras.[21]

[19] Charles Pouthas, "La réorganisation du ministère de l'intérieur et la re-constitution de l'administration préfectorale par Guizot en 1830," *Revue d'his-toire moderne et contemporaine*, IX (October–December 1962), 241–63.

[20] *Journal des propriétaires ruraux des departements du Midi*, XII (1816), 134–53.

[21] Eyraud, *De l'administration de la justice* (Paris, 1825), I, 251–70.

The departmental *conseil général* convened annually for no longer than fifteen days at the *chef-lieu* in order to advise the prefect, and ultimately the government, on matters of local administration and finance. At the time of its creation under the dispositions of the law of 28 Pluviôse VIII (February 17, 1800), the council represented five *arrondissements* in the Haute-Garonne, one of which was subsequently transferred to the Tarn-et-Garonne at the creation of that department in 1809. The prefect could, and did, attend meetings in order to contribute to the discussion among those of the twenty-four members who were present. These men were supposedly appointed for a fixed time; the *Sénatus-Consulte* of 16 Thermidor X laid down that the council should be renewed by a third every five years. Not until after the law of June 22, 1833, were these regulations on renewal observed precisely.[22] As a result, until this date, the members of the council enjoyed long tenure and became well acquainted with the details of the allocation of the tax load among the *arrondissements*, public welfare, and the need for road works, changes in agriculture, and encouragement of industry. They made adjustments in tax allocations after hearing appeals, and they decided on the number of *centimes additionnels facultatifs* to be levied to cover purely local expenses. These men had the task of dealing with public issues of some consequence; and while the time limit on the annual meeting was deliberately intended to prevent a political body emerging, it was inevitable that this group of big landowners evolved into a corporate entity. During the Empire and the Restoration, the council frequently expressed an opinion on political and economic subjects, and on occasion criticized the government.

The recruitment to the council before 1814 reflected the Napoleonic attempt to enlist the support of local notables for the Empire. The council included members who had substantial holdings in *biens nationaux*. It boasted a number of Old Regime nobles. Joseph de Villèle, a member of the council, said all the notable landowners of the department belonged to the council under the Empire. There was no serious shake-up under the First Restoration of 1814. A local nobleman of slightly tarnished reputation, Baron

[22] A. Godoffre, *Conseil général du département de la Haute-Garonne, délibérations de l'an VIII à 1838* (Toulouse, 1869–70), I, 22; Félix Ponteil, *Les institutions de la France de 1814 à 1870* (Paris, 1966), chapter III.

of the Empire Charles de Caffarelli, former prefect of the Ardèche, Calvados, and Aube whose career had begun in the canonicate of the cathedral of Tours, was forced to join in 1814, after being threatened with the loss of his pension. He followed a dignified course at the Hundred Days, however, and refused the oath to Napoleon.[23] A number of his colleagues followed a less proper line. After having signed an address of loyalty to Louis XVIII which promised their fealty to the death, they neither fought nor died as the Emperor retook control of France. The council was convened during the Hundred Days, and three members of the former council actually took the oath; the rest simply did not appear; and Lasplanes and Caffarelli deliberately refused. The new appointments included a number of *juges* and *avocats*, like the young Romiguières, who were to be associated with the liberals thereafter.

Just as in the case of the municipal council of Toulouse, the restoration of Louis XVIII to his throne produced recriminations against the weak behavior of the council. Rémusat thought a number of councillors who were particularly compromised should be changed, but the government in Paris, already alarmed by reports of the "government" of the Duc d'Angoulême and his ultra entourage, by the murder of General Ramel, and by the terrorizing of Protestants and various officials, thought no useful purpose would be served by appearing to sanction the White Terror by such dismissals. The prefect replied that the municipal council was almost deserted, and the same thing could happen to the *conseil général*; the majority of members would not attend, rather than compromise themselves by sitting with men of "bad" political views. In any case, old and sick members should be replaced, and he suggested collective appointments to avoid unpleasant distinctions.[24] When his first letter went unanswered, he put the same argument a second time: "Please believe also that in an area (*pays*) where heads are incandescent, the methods of keeping peace must be changed constantly; very little cause can furnish the pretext of breaking it."[25] The replacements he was proposing were prudent and judicious men, he assured the minister, and constituted in every respect the

[23] *ADHG*, 2 M bis 2.
[24] *AN*, F1bII (Garonne, Haute-) 8, Rémusat to Minister of Interior, March 15, 1816.
[25] *AN*, F1bII (Garonne, Haute-) 8, Rémusat to Minister of Interior, June 14, 1816.

elite of the department. When the reply came, however, it contained a sharp reprimand for vague condemnations and insidious distinctions. Should not the merchant Hémet, for example, who was proposed for replacement on the grounds that his business affairs were disordered (although he was neither dishonest nor in danger of bankruptcy), be retained for the reason that he was the only member engaged actively in commerce? The prefect responded by saying there were two very enlightened merchants on the council, Lafont-Cazeing and Thoron, whom he had only designated as landowners on his list of candidates because they owned very considerable property. As for Hémet, "without speaking of his disordered business affairs as a merchant (négociant), which is important because he has almost no property," he had also been involved in fraudulent bookkeeping. In fact, the prefect placed a heavy emphasis on the absolute necessity of removing a number of present members from the departmental and arrondissement councils if a really serious scandal was not to be caused when they met.[26]

For a variety of reasons, some political and some related to health and age, nineteen members of the old council were not reappointed in 1816. Significantly, several of those retained in office had sworn the oath to the Emperor, like Lafont-Cazeing who made a fortune during the Revolution by selling sheep and cattle, particularly in the Saint-Lys region and at Toulouse. He was the wealthiest man in the department, apparently honest, with numerous business interests and an annual revenue estimated at about 200,000 francs. His total fortune, calculated on the contemporary assumption that revenue equalled five percent of the total capital was at least one million francs.[27] Lassus-Camon, son of a councilor to the Parlement, was one of the rare individuals from that milieu who adapted to the new political situation during the period of Revolution. He had made a fortune in the lucrative, if disreputable, post of commissaire des guerres. He also took the oath during the Hundred Days, was mayor of his community, and had extensive holdings in biens nationaux.[28] The nine new members were all land-

[26] Ibid., Minister of Interior to Rémusat, June 22, 1816.

[27] J.-C. Duphil, "Les notables patentés de Toulouse sous le premier empire," Mémoire pour le diplôme d'études supérieures, Toulouse University, 1959, B.U.T.

[28] ADHG, 2 M 7.

owners, but included Paul Thoron, a retired merchant who could be assumed to have an appreciation of commercial interests, the notary Amilhau, and Alexandre de Cambon. In short, the *conseil général* underwent a shake-up, but not a real purge of those who had not behaved well during the Hundred Days. The general tone of the council became decidedly ultra, for Villèle, Escouloubre, Marsac, and Palarin now spoke out on most public issues without the discretion of earlier times.

Although the council became increasingly noble during the Restoration as new members were recruited, there were variations in the range of wealth. Lafont-Cazeing had a very large annual revenue of 200,000 francs, while the only active merchant, Hémet, had only a modest sum of 3,000 francs.[29]

Toulouse and its *arrondissement* had a disproportionate representation on the council. In November, 1824, fifteen members of the council were from Toulouse, three from Muret, three from St. Gaudens, and three from Villefranche. A table drawn up to establish the ratios of population and tax paid by the *arrondissements* showed that, while the three districts other than Toulouse were less wealthy, their representation should be increased in the interests of equity. At the same time, it was noted that several members of the council noted as residing in Toulouse had "in all probability, a large part of their property in other arrondissements."[30]

During the period of 1816–30, there was only a slight turnover in the membership, caused by deaths and resignations. Nine new members joined the council, only one of whom was a commoner, and all of whom were ultras. All these appointments were dismissed after the July Revolution. Their names are a roster of influential ultra landowners: the Vicomte Marcel de Marin, Baron Mathieu-Louis Hocquart, Baron Anne-Antoine de Roquette-Buisson, Baron de Saintegème, Chevalier Armand Dubourg, Comte de Brettes-Thurin, Morier, Prévost, and Duran. Four of them were deputies and foreshadowed the typical deputy-mayor of the Third Republic. Armand Dubourg said that he could explain local issues at the Chamber of Deputies, and told his fellow councilors of the

[29] See Table 1, p. 189. Information taken from AN, F1bII (Garonne, Haute-) 7, 8; ADHG, 2 M bis 1, 2, 3. These figures are conservative, and show rough official estimates of the wealth of members.
[30] AN, F1bII (Garonne, Haute-) 8.

difficulties which faced the government in an attempt to satisfy all requests.[31]

Sixteen councilors, including the most distinguished ultras, left the *conseil général* after the July Revolution. It was the year of 1830 that marked a decided reverse for the landowners of conservative views who had used this organization for expressing their views since the First Empire. The excellent results of the administrative practice of the Estates of Languedoc were being cited in July, 1800, during the first session. Napoleon wrote from Milan in December, 1807, asking the Minister of the Interior to report on the impudent views expressed in the council by some members: "It appears that the worst frame of mind is displayed there: that comparison has been made between the Old Regime and the New, that regrets have even been expressed for the former Estates of Languedoc."[32] During a discussion of the *droits réunis*, the most unpopular of Napoleonic taxes, Lasplanes, Monna, Escouloubre, de Villeneuve-Vernon, and Romiguières the elder, were heard,

all employed by the former government either as barons of the Estates of Languedoc, or as members of the Parlement. These gentlemen did not restrict themselves to speaking against the tax on wine, a subject on which they had the least to say, but they attacked all the institutions created by His Majesty. They demanded the abolition of the prefectures, the re-establishment of the provincial estates, and of the religious teaching orders, they attacked the establishment of lycées, observing that the military instruction given in them could only corrupt morals and that the vices which had been introduced into these schools could only exhaust youth: they even allowed themselves to slander odiously the chiefs of the Toulouse lycée. They attacked the gendarmerie and the gamekeepers [*gardes champêtres*]. They spoke out against the administrations of water and forests, taxation, and the division of expenditures. They carried their delirium to the extent of saying that the re-establishment of the Estates of the Province was the only remedy to bring to an end the deplorable state in which the department found itself. Such extravagances demonstrate the character of the membership.[33]

This vigorous criticism, somewhat exaggerated by the report, shows that the council saw itself as more than an intermediary between

[31] See Table 2, p. 190.
[32] *AN*, F¹ᶜV (Garonne, Haute-) 2.
[33] *Ibid.*

114

the government and the taxpayers of the department. The views of new institutions, in an unfavorable contrast with the old ones, adumbrate ultra views that were so often put forth during the Restoration.

The departmental councils tended, inevitably, to be anti-centralist, like the earlier provincial assemblies set up before the Revolution, which they resembled in some important respects. In 1814, Villèle published a pamphlet that attacked not only representative government, but the centralized administration as well. He signed his diatribe as "a member of the departmental council" and called for a return to local liberties which existed before 1789, when the nobility was protected in its material independence by provincial privileges.

In 1816, these views were expressed in a major attack on centralism, produced by the council and probably largely the work of Villèle. The statement was preceded by the maxim that in political administration, as in mechanics, unnecessary complexity was to be avoided. They wanted to navigate between the concentration of power in a national center and too much dispersion of local representation, which would result in ineffectual institutions. France in the Old Regime had thirty-three intendancies [sic] which had been inflated into eighty-three departments: Languedoc alone had been divided into eight departments, despite the dubious administrative advantage and the certain economic damage which this produced. The council declared that the old province of Languedoc cost annually 340,000 francs to administer, but that the new administrations which replaced the former one cost 995,159 francs. At a time when prisons, hospitals, roads, and the clergy of the area desperately needed extra funds, the *conseil général* was disturbed to consider 665,146 francs unnecessarily spent on maintaining a greedy bureaucracy. Moreover, the poorer departments could not collect sufficient *centimes additionnels* to pay the cost of their prefects, sub-prefects, councillors at the prefecture, and the rentals of courts, prisons, prefectures, etc. On the other hand, the council said any regrouping of administrative units must consider the rights of the community, which were like those of an individual, contrary to the departments which were essentially artificial modern innovations. The reason was that communes were the sole remaining traces of the former monarchy that even the Revolution had been unable to smash, presumably because they were coterminous with the former

115

parishes and thus made up the basic unit of local life. The council envisaged a reorganised administrative system in which there would be larger blocs within France, controlled by wealthy landowners. Men holding local offices, "of necessity unpaid," provided the stability needed to govern. Certainly the existing system of mayors in communes was unsatisfactory, for it was difficult to find men in each commune suitable for the office and willing to discharge it. Many of the mayors were peasants who worked land with their own hands, and were illiterate; yet they were entrusted with tasks more difficult than those given to the former consuls. Many communities had ineffectual municipal government, where councillors could not even make out a budget. The public interest, and what was described as a return to healthy ideas, made it necessary to appoint officials who were above the people, and by the greater social distance free from the suspicion and attacks of those administered.

The council also called for reform of the Napoleonic legacy in the matter of regional appeal courts; for Toulouse, they felt, was abused by the Empire. In 1789, the city had held the second Parlement of France, whereas in 1816 it was merely the seat of an appeal court. Agen, Rioms, and Poitiers—all smaller cities—boasted larger courts. The council also criticized the proliferation of courts of First Instance, not only because it was unreasonable to expect an able man to live in some remote village on a poor salary, but more importantly because it was unwise to provide the peasants with the opportunity to start litigation. Members of the council which represented essentially the great landowners of the department thought it unwise to give the rural families close contact with "men whose interest is to encourage intestine strife."[34]

Not content with the sweeping recommendations contained in this report of 1816, the council obliquely criticized royal moderation in politics. In an address which it voted to be presented to the throne, there was an arch allusion to the enthusiastic reception given to the ultra deputies of Toulouse upon their return from Paris, by implication a criticism of the policy which the Chambre Introuvable so vigorously combatted. When the relevant sections

[34] AN, F1cV (Garonne, Haute-) 2. Report of commission requested to give opinion on new limits to be given administrative and judicial bodies of the kingdom. Procès-verbal, July 26, 1816.

of the address were read to Louis XVIII, he ordered that no synopsis should appear in the *Moniteur*.[35]

The ultras constantly criticized the centralization of French administration, which they correctly saw as the most striking governmental consequence of the Revolution. In 1824, the council made a major statement of this important royalist theme of hostility to the extension of bureaucratic power. The prefects were particularly obnoxious, and the prefectoral system was called a "product of imperial despotism resulting from the distrustful and rapacious spirit of that dictatorship." (The similarities to the system of intendants were not mentioned.) The paternal authority of the Bourbons rested on the foundation of popular affection; therefore, the excessive strain of decisions placed on the ministers could well be given over to the charge of local notables most intimately concerned with them. An intermediary body between Paris and the communal level, inspired by the experience of the departments, the Estates of Languedoc and the Provincial Assemblies, and the *conseils généraux* would be invaluable. As the council put it, the government could draw from the rich treasure of experience and traditions all that was compatible with the circumstances after the major changes of recent times. The reorganization would also have the effect of effacing the memories of "agitations politiques" and would increase popular gratitude for the Restoration. The wisdom and generosity of the King would thus prevent demagoguery or political excesses.[36]

The statements of 1816 and 1824 were representative of the views of landowners who wanted to counterbalance the attraction of national politics and influence which flourished in Paris around the ministers and which menaced their own local ascendancy. At the same time, they saw themselves as well above the common people of their own area, whom they wished less to represent than to rule. Their wealth and family status meant little if unbuttressed by real power; and while some of the group had been able to become deputies in the capital, it was also necessary to provide a local stage for the satisfaction of the ambitions of their fellows. The former provincial estates offered themselves to the minds of the members as the vehicle for directing an essentially federal state,

---

[35] *AN*, F1cV (Garonne, Haute-) 2.
[36] *ADHG*, 1 M 11; *AN*, F1cV (Garonne, Haute-) 3.

117

based on historic and hence "organic" regions. They saw these bodies as the necessary counterpart to centralized authority. Local notables, by exercising political power, broke that simplified line of authority which led to despotism. These views were commonplace in nineteenth-century France long before de Tocqueville's brilliant expositions of the theme. Camus de Martroy, the prefect of the Haute-Garonne who took office in 1829, took up this idea in his inaugural address. He flattered the council as being a direct continuation of the Estates of Languedoc and of the provincial assemblies. He spoke warmly about the value of their advice, the power of moral persuasion which they exercised. The council was, he said, an element of stability in the unstable lives of representative governments; while ministers and prefects come and go, the annual meetings of this group of worthies are fixed and regular. Was not the Haute-Garonne (excepting the *arrondissement* of Saint Gaudens, specifically singled out for reproach) among the most faithful, most law-abiding, most prompt ones in paying tax of all the departments of France?[37]

Local liberties were the main political concern of the council; the price of grain was the major practical concern in a wheat-producing area. The famine of 1816–17 brought about very high prices, from which many of the council members had profitted; but it was followed by a steady decline in the level of wheat prices throughout France, a decline which was felt particularly keenly in the valley of the Garonne. During the famine, Russian wheat, shipped from Odessa, appeared on the Marseilles market, and during the following decade of good harvests and low prices caused by overproduction, the growers of the South-west, South, and Burgundy consistently blamed falling prices on the presence of foreign wheat. While this "blé exotique" made up an insignificant fraction of the supply, various laws were passed to mollify angry wheat producers; in July, 1819, a sliding scale of duties was imposed on imported wheat, reminiscent of the Corn Laws in Britain. The Haute-Garonne *conseil général* declared the measure inadequate even before it had been put into effect, claiming that, with only a small duty levied, the brokers of Marseille could market Russian wheat at a price which undercut French prices. Quite apart from the absurd exaggeration of the figures cited—it was claimed that Mar-

[37] *Ibid.*

seilles, after duty, could sell wheat at 14.75 francs the hectolitre while the national price was 22 francs—there was inconsistency in the council's views. In their petition of 1819 they said that, in the year XI, wheat prices fell to 9 francs the hectolitre during the blockade, at a time when French producers were supplying armies in the field and foreign regions of the Empire. This made nonsense of the protectionist system they wished to introduce, but the council attacked the theory of free exchange as illusory in a situation where it was unevenly applied by governments. The council was indignant at the impractical chatter of economists of the liberal school: "... there, however, is the result of these pretty theories which are good in the study to occupy idlers who don't have much to do with the world; they ought to stay there and never come out, because facts contradict them and we ought to have been cured a long time ago."[38] When it became widely apparent that the 1819 law was having no effect on the downward trend of prices, a call went up for more stringent legislation, especially in an area where the sale of wheat was the vital nerve of economic activity. A law of 1821 again raised duties on imported wheat, and by an artifice in the choice of markets, the official price of wheat was consistently cited as lower than the level which actually prevailed. Toulouse, a center of wheat production, won completely over the port of Marseilles, which was a centre of consumption and importation. Despite the protective legislation, prices continued to fall, to the complete exasperation of the landowners. The council noted in 1824 that the economic stagnation of an agricultural department was causing public opinion to turn against the government. If further measures were taken to stop the import of foreign grain, the people would be able to bear their sufferings with more equanimity. The council went on to say that if the poor were interested only in cheap food (a proposition which conflicted with earlier statements), the interests of the producers should also be considered.[39] Unwilling to drop Russian wheat as the explanation for all difficulties, many *conseils généraux* suggested that the *entrepôt* of Marseilles was used as a contraband device. Finally, in 1825, the *entrepôt* was suppressed. This gave satisfaction to the ultra landowners, who never tired of

[38] *AN*, F1cV (Garonne, Haute-) 2.
[39] *AN*, BB30238; see G. Frêche, *Le prix des grains, des vins et des légumes à Toulouse, (1486–1868)*, Travaux et recherches de la faculté de droit et des sciences économiques de Paris, 10. (Paris, 1967.)

proclaiming that agriculture should not be sacrificed to trade: "Does liberty, or to say better, speculative lucre, need to grow until it destroys the constitutive principle of France?"[40]

Decentralization and wheat prices were much on the minds of the councilors, but other issues of social control were also considered in their discussions of education, prisons, roads, and public life. The touchstone for all these principles was religion. Wanting to encourage a strong clerical influence in education and public life, the council praised religious orders providing public service within the department. The *Dames de Refuge*, many of whom were from the upper classes, were commended for running a reformatory for penitent prostitutes. This was not only a religious establishment, but one which would have had to be established by secular authorities if it did not exist (although, as the council put it, only piety and charity could effectively provide such a service. Incidentally, the council observed that only one-tenth of the prostitutes came from Toulouse, although almost all were from the department). Although this allowance had already been vetoed once by the ministry on the grounds that it was not within the council's jurisdiction to bestow, it voted a grant of 4,000 francs to the reformatory. The Brothers of the Christian Doctrine, the *ignorantins*, were commended in 1811 for spreading virtue among the lower classes of society that would be depraved without these good offices, and in 1823, the council offered 6,000 francs to the first community to provide lodgings and support for this order. In 1826, a call was made for more aid to teaching orders, for the suppression of lotteries, and for a check on the license of the press that corrupted the towns and countryside of France with anti-monarchist works. The council called for higher clerical salaries and more priests in the department, and generally expressed the support for accelerated training and recruitment plans of the Church, underway during the Restoration.

This loud devotion to the interests of the Catholic Church had limits, however, as was shown rather quaintly by the reply given by the council to the Archbishop of Toulouse Clermont-Tonnerre, who requested the return of the former episcopal palace that had been confiscated during the Revolution and subsequently became the prefecture. The council, while heartily protesting its esteem for

[40] *AN*, F1cV (Garonne, Haute-) 3; *ADHG*, 1 M 11.

the archbishop, refused to take on the expense involved in finding new quarters for the prefect. The councillors made the snide observation that the Christian charity of Archbishop Clermont-Tonnerre would make him suffer in face of hardships to taxpayers involved in the enabling taxation: "... how can such sacrifices be required of taxpayers when revenue sources dry up because of low cereal prices and the almost total obliteration of commerce makes necessary the most severe economy?"[41] Clermont-Tonnerre did not take refusals of any kind lightly and renewed his request in the following year, but the council then stated categorically that it could not redress the situation of the "ci-devant clergé." As was so often the case, the ultras of Toulouse showed that they did not confuse their practice with their preaching.

The council in each *arrondissement* was a lesser version of the *conseil général*, with similar advisory powers on matters of local concern, especially roads and distribution of the tax load. In 1805, the prefect nominated to the council of Toulouse *arrondissement* a former advocate to the Parlement, a former engineer of the royal *Ponts et Chaussées*, and a retired *enregistrement* inspector.[42] All of these were substantial landowners. At the time of the Hundred Days, there was a division of political opinion about the Napoleonic regime. Six members of the council took the oath of allegiance, three men refused it, and one man abstained or, more precisely, was never heard from.[43] Two of the men who refused to take the oath were hospital administrators (Barrué and Sabatié) and were in close touch with pious ultras.[44]

The major shake-up of membership in 1816 followed the same general trend as indicated by the *conseil général*. The new council was composed of seven important landowners, a former councilor to the Parlement (de Fajolle-Giscaro), a lawyer, a former *trésorier de France*, and an émigré officer who had become expert in mining. Eight years later, most of these men were still in office. As in the *conseil général*, the regulations about renewing the membership were virtually a dead letter under the Restoration. Those replacements who did take their seats were ultras: Félix Gounon (*adjoint* to the mayor of Toulouse discussed above) and de Marcorelle.

[41] *Ibid.*
[42] AN, F[1b]II (Garonne, Haute-) 8.
[43] *ADHG*, 2 M bis 2.
[44] AN, F[1b]II (Garonne, Haute-) 8.

This lesser council showed its similarity to the *conseil général* in more than the patterns of recruitment and service. It held also the same political views. In 1816, the authority of the Bourbons was invoked whenever political dissension was to be halted. Under the Old Regime, France had seen less bloodshed than in the twenty-five years following 1789, it was observed. Besides praising the exercise of a conservative royal power, the council dealt with a petition, discussed the prisons, and encouraged the efforts of the Society for Agriculture.[45] In all of this, there was the same covert disapproval of the central government's moderate policy as was expressed by the departmental council. The mining inspector Aubuisson de Voisins wrote to Lainé in 1816 that opposition to government policy was to be found on both the municipal and *arrondissement* councils of Toulouse.[46] Later in the Restoration, the council was particularly insistent on the need for more religion in French life. They also campaigned against low wheat prices, blamed on the import of cheap foreign wheat at uncompetitive prices.[47] In short, the views of the *conseil d'arrondissement* were a reflexion of the views of the *conseil général*.

Public service of this sort at the communal, city, arrondissement, and departmental level attracted the most important ultras. Villèle was a mayor and a *conseiller général*; Gounon was an *adjoint* to the municipality; and Dubourg a *conseiller général*. The opportunities for really effective political action on these bodies was limited, but they provided a range of offices and status for the ultras. Their absorption in the minutiae of local government and their constant reiteration of authoritarian and religious principles became in large measure an end in itself that had little relation to developments in the rest of the country. If such activity was its own reward, this was not the case of the administration of justice, the traditional concomitant of landed wealth in the Toulousain. The continuity of the parlementarians in the judicial system and the way in which the ultras saw the organization of social control are the subject of the following chapter.

[45] *ADHG*, 2 M 34; July 8, 1816.
[46] E. de Perceval, *Un adversaire de Napoléon, le vicomte de Lainé . . .* (Paris, 1926), II, 68.
[47] *ADHG*, 2 M 36.

VI

LAW, ORDER, AND THE ULTRAS
IN TOULOUSE, 1815–30

THE REVOLUTION offered many opportunities in the new judicial and administrative system to members of the lesser city courts. Most of the parlementarians refused this accommodation, but the members of the intermediary courts like the *présidial-sénéchaussée* of Toulouse cautiously accepted the new order. The advocates, solicitors, notaries, and minor officials of the former legal system accepted positions in the new system with enthusiasm. In general terms, it is correct to say that those who entered the French legal system in the years of the Constituent Assembly were never subsequently expelled from it, although this was not the case of the appointments made by the National Convention. During the Directory, the courts had shown themselves generally sympathetic to the royalists and the *honnêtes gens*. By the time Bonaparte was First Consul, a system of justice had emerged as conservative and hierarchic as that of the Parlements. One result of this evolution was that Toulouse parlementarian families gradually accepted service in the courts as an acceptable outlet for their talents. Napoleon welcomed them back into the administration of justice.

The legal system of the Empire was represented, on the lowest level, by police courts that dealt with minor infractions of police regulations, punishable by up to three working days of imprisonment. These police courts were presided over by justices of the peace in rotation. These justices also had their own courts, one for each canton of Toulouse, North, Center, South, and West. Appeals against the verdicts of these lesser courts went to the Court of First Instance in each *arrondissement*, which also judged civil and criminal cases of greater consequence. Appeals and major criminal and civil cases were heard by the Court of Appeals with its assize chamber. In 1811, this system of justice provided employment for approximately 240 to 260 families in Toulouse, fewer than during the Old Regime, but still the major single feature of the city economy.

The Court of Appeals owed its basic structure to the reorganization of the judicial system of the year VIII. These courts had the approximate jurisdictional area of the former seneschalsies and were established with a rough ratio of one court to three departments. The Toulouse Court of Appeals exercised authority over the Ariège, the Haute-Garonne, and the Tarn, together with the Tarn-et-Garonne after the creation of that department in 1809. This was much less than the jurisdiction of the Parlement which functioned as the court of appeal for three million people in 1789; nevertheless, it was the major court in the region in 1800. Its personnel was mainly recruited from the *tribunal civil* of Toulouse, headed by a président and the *commissaire du gouvernement* with judicial personnel drawn from the ranks of former advocates of the Parlement, officials of the seneschalsy, and other members of the lower ranks of the pre-revolutionary judicial system. Numbers gradually increased: in 1808, a number of *juges-auditeurs* (who might be described as "apprentice judges") were added. In the following two years, the advocates were reorganized and provided with new possibilities of taking seats on the bench. Throughout France, the legal system was expanding, perhaps faster than the population, and offered employment to educated youths.

The Courts of Appeals, renamed Imperial Courts in 1804, seemed a social pinchbeck to Napoleon when he compared them with the Parlements. In 1811, prefects were told to list former magistrates in the pre-revolutionary high courts who lived in their departments; the government hoped to find suitable candidates for office from these lists. The prefect of the Haute-Garonne observed that few of the councilors of the Parlement were still alive, and those who were could only be described as either too old or unsuitable for new responsibilities. However, the children of parlementarians were more numerous, and the prefect noted that a number of such indi-

TABLE VI-1. Age and Estimated Fortune of Parlementarians and Descendants in the Region of Toulouse, 1811

Age (years)	Name	Office or Ancestry	Estimated Fortune (in thousands of Francs)						
			100	200	300	400	500	600	700
17	J.-A.-H. Pégueyrolle	Son of Conseiller	....						
18	A.-F. Gaillard de Frousins	Son of Conseiller	....						
20	B.-C.-M.-J. Montégut	Son of Conseiller	....						
20	P.-L.-M.-A. Lespinasse de Florentin	Son of Conseiller	....						
20	F.-L. Combettes-Labourrelle	Son of Conseiller	....						
21	G.-I. Baron de Montbel	Son of Conseiller	....						
21	S. de Panat	Grandson of Président "robe"	....						
21	A.-J.-H. Fleyres		....						
30	V.-J.-M. Aussagel de Lasbordes	Son, Grandson, and Great-Grandson of Conseiller	....						
35	J.-A. Miègeville	Son of Conseiller	....						
36	A. Rigaud	Son of Conseiller	....						
37	A. Mazade	Grandson of Président	....						
38	G.-A.-T. Belloc	Son of Président	....						
42	H. d'Aldéguier	Conseiller	....						
46	Raynal de Saint Michel	Conseiller	....						
56	P.-M.-A.-L. Fraissines	Procureur	....						
55	C.-L. Latour-Mauriac	Procureur	....						
56	Fajolles-Giscaro	Conseiller	....						
57	Fajolles-Pordeac	Conseiller	....						
61	J.-B. Cérat	Conseiller	....						
66	Lalo	Conseiller	....						
70	L.-E. de Cambon	Premier Président	......						
80	Cassaignau de St. Félix	Conseiller	......						

Source: *ADHG*, 2 M 24

viduals in Paris had been given appointments.[1] Moreover, these men needed little persuasion to accept. They had no focus for the social power of their families outside of charity work and estate management. Aussagel de Lasbordes, son, grandson, and great-grandson of parlementarians, and others like him, were prepared to take the new title of Councilor of His Majesty in the Imperial Court of Toulouse. After all, they were one generation removed from the abolition of the Parlement, there was little likelihood that it would be re-established, and Napoleon offered a rewarding career to men of property and experience.[2] New judges had to possess an annual revenue of at least three thousand francs, to be over thirty years of age, and to have legal training or experience.

At the same time, younger men who had the revenue required of a councilor were becoming *auditeurs* at the court of appeals which provided them with two-years experience in the working of a high court. Only at the age of twenty-seven could the *conseiller-auditeur* actively participate in the dispensing of justice. They were selected from among those who were nominated as *juge-auditeurs* at the age of twenty-one and over and who had a year of legal training. These two categories of *auditeurs* supplied officials to the prefectoral council and other lesser regional courts, providing a "bloodbank" for the recruitment of subprefects, and other officials. Like the *maîtres des requêtes* of the Old Regime, they became civil servants not only trained in law but conversant with social conventions of the upper classes.[3] The whole system heavily and systematically favored men of private means and family traditions of service. Only under the July Monarchy was this "judicial militia" to be abolished.

Not all of those whose names were put forward as parlementarians returned to office. They were not only too old, like Cassaigneau Saint Félix, or impoverished, like Joseph Cérat, or of unsuitable background, like the former member of the Convention Mazade. Yet a very substantial promotion of old families took place. Raynal de Saint Michel and Aldéguier became presidents, while Louis-Alexandre de Cambon, son of the last First President of the Parlement, Charles-Louis Latour-Mauriac who was formerly *procureur*,

---

[1] *ADHG*, 2 M 24, Prefect to Minister of Justice, March 7, 1811.

[2] Alfred Hiver de Beauvoir, *Histoire critique des institutions judiciaires de la France de 1789 à 1848* (Paris, 1848), pp. 470–71.

[3] Vivian R. Gruder, *The Royal Provincial Intendants* (Ithaca, 1968).

and Aussagel de Lasbordes became councilors. Not all of the new appointees were from the Parlement: Pinel de Truilhas had been a councilor at the Montpellier *Cour des Aides*, while Martin d'Aigues-vives was from a military line. However, by the end of the Empire, the parlementary notables of the city were well on the way to reabsorbing the sixty major judicial offices that existed in the city, and this tendency continued throughout the Restoration. While it would be an exaggeration to say the court held the same socio-economic importance in the city as the Parlement, it acquired an increasing social prestige in the years prior to 1830.

The growth of the judicial system did not proceed at a constant rate but was interrupted periodically by political dissension. Theoretically, the principle of tenure (*inamovabilité*) protected magistrates from dismissal once they were appointed. Articles 58 and 59 of the Charter maintained judicial personnel and organization. Denunciations of magistrates appointed during the Revolution were often heard in 1814, but since the royalist faction in the court had served the Empire no less faithfully, any investigation seemed invidious and embarassing. The events of 1815 and Napoleon's return from Elba, however, broke this compromise. Once reinstalled in the Tuileries, the Emperor dismissed all magistrates named by Louis XVIII; in turn, upon his return from exile, Louis swept aside Napoleonic nominations made during the interregnum.[4]

The ultraroyalists argued, on the basis of article 57 of the Charter, that magistrates were delegates of royal power; consequently, all mandates delivered by the usurping emperor were invalid.[5] They were certainly deeply resentful of the conduct of many court members during the Hundred Days. When the members of the court wished to present their compliments to the duc d'Angoulême upon his arrival from Spain in July, 1815, they were kept waiting for an hour in an anteroom and then told they could not be received. The

[4] The principle of *inamovabilité* sustained a number of attacks after its first modern French statement in the constitution of 22 frimaire X. In 1807 and 1808, the Imperial Government dismissed a large number of magistrates; the law of April 20, 1810, again provided the government with an opportunity to change undesirable personnel. The renewal of *institutions* excluded a number of these.

[5] In France at large 1,694 magistrates were dismissed; 294 of them from the 19 *cours royales*. G. Martin-Sarzeaud, *Recherches sur l'inamovabilité* (Paris, 1883), 457; Marcel Rousselet, *Histoire de la magistrature* (Paris, 1957), pp. 164–65.

following day they were greeted with cries of "A bas les girouettes! A bas les fédérés!" from the waiting crowds.[6] The men surrounding the King's nephew advised him to take firm action in purging the court of subversive and cowardly judges whose acceptance of the *Acte Additionnel* had disgraced the entire company. These feelings went into social life; the Duc d'Angoulême twice ostentatiously snubbed the wife of Martin d'Aiguesvives, a former councilor at the Parlement, at a reception given in the city. She was forced to withdraw in humiliation.

This critical campaign against Bonapartists caused men like Baron Desazars, the First President who owned *biens nationaux* and was a former advocate at the Parlement to confess his "mistaken political conduct during the recent times of oppression, violence, and terrifying threats." He asked to be allowed to keep some minor post at the court, like that of a *conseiller-auditeur*! His career had shown the opportunities opened to the lower ranks of the legal profession by the Revolution. From an advocate he had become a judge at the Villefranche *tribunal civil* in 1792, moved to Toulouse in Vendémiaire IV, and was taken into the Imperial Court at the time of its establishment. In time he was awarded the Legion of Honor, became baron of the Empire in 1810, and a member of the *Jeux Floraux.* He could claim Old Regime nobility: his father, *seigneur* of Montgailhard, had been a *capitoul.*

The royal ordinance of March 25, 1816, was the basic instrument which excluded the major Bonapartist members of the Royal Court of Toulouse. Sixteen individuals lost their positions, including Desazars, Président Dast who had been a lawyer before 1789 and who rose through the ranks during the Revolution, and the *procureur général* Corbière whose judicial career had begun at Guitalens in the Tarn in 1788 and who had also held numerous offices during the Revolution. Among the dismissed councilors was a former *trésorier de France* and several advocates at the Parlement. Rabaly was particularly excoriated for his substantial holdings of *biens nationaux*. Montané de la Roque, a former advocate at the Parlement and a son of a *lieutenant-criminel* of the Toulouse présidial who had risen to the Revolutionary Tribunal in Paris, was detested not only for his father but for having made a personal declaration of loyalty to Napoleon during the Hundred Days. Local

[6] *AN,* BB⁵61, 69.

ultras applauded the dismissal of these men whom they described as "vicious and immoral."[7]

On the other hand, the ultraroyalists took heart from the nobles among the new court members seated between 1815 and 1817. Mathieu Hocquart remained in Desazars's place until his talents took him to Paris as an ultra deputy. Miègeville, son of a councilor at the Parlement, was promoted from *procureur* in the Court of First Instance to the post of a councilor. Like the advocate Pinaud, now appointed a councilor (a rapid promotion indeed), he was known as a fervent royalist. Three noblemen became *avocats généraux*: the *dévot* Montégut, son of an executed conseiller to the Parlement, related to the Limairacs and thus, indirectly, to the Villèles, who became a monk in late 1817; Vialas; and de Naylies who was recommended to this post by the deputies of the department and by the duc de Berry. There was a clear trend to favor heavily the parlementarians, and they were nearly all ultra in politics. In other parts of the Midi, the same development had taken place: Ginest, Juin de Siran, and Clément de Long took office in Royal Courts. The parlementarian resurgence favored by Napoleon continued extensively during the Restoration.

Over forty members of the former court remained in office after the second Restoration, but this did not indicate any homogeneity in politics, for many had given the oath of allegiance to the *Actes Additionnels*. Cambon, son of First Président of the Parlement, had been an enthusiastic supporter of the royal cause during the first Restoration, but surprised many by signing the oath. Meanwhile, his brother had gone to support the Duc d'Angoulême. He was so embarrassed by his position that he resigned after the news of Waterloo, but the prefect persuaded him to resume his seat on the bench. Noel Solomiac, first an advocate who became a judge during the Consulate and a councilor in 1811, was noted for his Bonapartism, and his son was believed to have belonged to the *fédérés*. Nevertheless, he was not dismissed, and his son entered the court as an *auditeur* in 1819. Monssinat, a former deputy of the Third Estate to the Constituante noted for his charity, and Germain Pinel de Truilhas, a councilor at the *cour des aides et finances* of Montpellier and an émigré with Condé who had lost a large fortune from revolutionary confiscations, were among the signatories. In-

---

[7] *AN*, BB⁵69, Hocquart to Garde des Sceaux, October 9, 1815.

cluded in the same opprobrium were lesser officials, like the *greffier en chef* Cabos who was described in one denunciation as a Jacobin, a leader of the *fédérés*, and a desecrator of churches.

With the passing of the White Terror, the judges were able, no doubt with relief, to forget this embarrassing period of political honesty. The government was concerned with obedience, which meant that those who did not unite in the same devotion the ligitimate monarchy and the Charter would find no public career open to them, as an announcement in the *Journal de Toulouse* put it in 1820. Government choices had to be merited by sincere devotion to the monarchy—which meant to the Ministry. The correspondence of the court officials with the *Garde des Sceaux* showed how keen they were to protest their loyalty to the regime.

Family connections within the magistracy soon became as important as they had been in the Old Regime among the parlementarians for reinforcing the sense of a noble minority. When the son of President d'Aldéguier was installed as a *conseiller-auditeur*, the ultraroyalist *Echo du Midi* waxed sentimental over paternal affection and usefulness of setting up a family tradition in support to the throne.[8] Carloman de Bastoulh was recommended for "his integrity which is, moreover, generally considered to be hereditary in his family." He was the son of a law professor and brother to a *premier avocat général* and a councilor at the court. A new substitute to the *procureur du roi*, Adolphe de Castelbajac, was recommended as a nephew of Cazalès, the royalist spokesman in the Constituent Assembly, as brother of the Marquis de Castelbajac who was a colonel of dragoons in the royal household, and as a cousin to the flamboyant deputy and treasurer of the ultra newspaper, *Le Conservateur*: ". . . faithful to these splendid family precedents he was himself a royal volunteer at the March 12 period, and an officer in *chasseurs des Pyrénées* regiment."[9] Article 19 of the Law of April 28, 1816, re-established a form of venality of office. If a properly qualified candidate was available for a post, he could be nominated to the *Garde des Sceaux* by the incumbent.[10] This was done quite frequently, and the parallel with the parlementarians was praised. Villèle encouraged his son to enter the magistracy,

[8] *AR*, July 28, 1818.
[9] *EM*, March 31, 1823.
[10] Gabriel Lepointe, *Histoire des institutions du droit public français au XIXe siècle, 1789–1914* (Paris, 1953), p. 425.

for he thought it a stable profession which provided recognition of innate superiority.[11]

Royalism could be a substitute for good family background, as was shown by Pinaud, a Parisian who had been an unimportant advocate during the Empire. At the second Restoration he was named *avocat-général* and then a councilor. He enjoyed a literary reputation, was the perpetual secretary of the Academy of the *Jeux Floraux*, and had encouraged the adolescent Victor Hugo with his poetry. In February, 1822, he requested a new position, despite the fact that he was neither well-born nor wealthy:

> My fidelity to the legitimate authority has never faltered; when the royalists were condemned to persecution, I was persecuted; when they had the duty and obligation of taking arms, I armed, notably during the Hundred Days when, having contributed to the limits of my ability in raising a corps of royal volunteers, I had the honor of entering their ranks; finally when, more recently, so many faithful servants of the King were submitted to such strange rigors, I also was subjected to open hostility by the agents of that deplorable system.[12]

Mistakes were made in political recommendations; one candidate, Ferradou, was said to have hoodwinked the First President and Archbishop.[13] Experience and the right social background could even efface serious weaknesses. Aldéguier noted in a memorandum signed by Villèle, Puymaurin, and Limairac that despite the bad behavior of Martin d'Aiguesvives during the Hundred Days, they believed it possible now, some years later, to propose him for the place of a President.[14] Even Desazars, a former advocate to the Parlement, and Loubers, whose son had gone with Napoleon to Elba, were to be reinstated by Paris with only a mumble of disapproval from the ultra press. Desazars and Martin d'Aiguesvives paid the highest taxation in the court, over 3,500 francs. Some of the poorest councilors were the most royalist, like Monssinat, Flottes, and Dubernad. While no clear trend is indicated by the wealth reported on the electoral list, it may well be that the poorer

[11] AV, J. Villèle to Henri de Villèle.
[12] AN, BB⁵69, Pinaud to Garde des Sceaux, February 18, 1822. In 1824, he was appointed *procureur général* at Metz.
[13] AV, Michel de Bellomayre to Henri de Villèle, April 21, 1824.
[14] AN, BB⁵65.

the members of the judiciary were, the more they emphasized their respectability and their royalism.

After the Revolution of 1830, the *cours royales* throughout France were once more under attack, this time by liberals who wished to see prominent partisans of the deposed monarch dismissed. But if it was relatively easy to change the composition of the *parquet*, this was more difficult at the higher levels. The liberals who previously defended the special rights of the judiciary now wished to expel senior magistrates who were protected by *inamovabilité*; however, the Chamber upheld the principle by declarations of August 7 and November 26, 1830. The categories of *juges-auditeurs* and *conseillers-auditeurs* were suppressed, since these in particular were the nurseries of legitimist support and were packed with representatives of *parlementaire* families. The oath of allegiance to Louis-Philippe may have been a bone that stuck in the throat of the fastidious, but was not an insuperable difficulty for the judiciary of Toulouse.

None of the appointees of 1816 left the court because of legitimist politics, and one, indeed, was appointed a councilor. Hyacinthe de Bastoulh, ennobled by the Restoration, was dismissed from the political post of *procureur général du roi*. Two councilors and all four *auditeurs* left the court, the latter all coming from ultra families: Limairac, Delacroix, Roquette-Buisson, and de Vaillac. There were other changes, as when *président* de Cambon resigned to become a deputy. Almost forty percent of those sitting after 1830 had taken the oath of loyalty to Bonaparte before pledging loyalty to the Bourbons. Some members of the court were supporters of Carlism, like Miègeville, who had a dissolute youth in which he was ruined by gambling and who stayed in retirement on his estate during the Empire. Early in the Second Restoration he was named police inspector by the duc d'Angoulême, and he and his son were closely connected with the White Terror and the *verdets*. By 1828, he had risen to the post of *président* which he kept until 1834, although the Orléanists considered him to be a dangerous Carlist. He was able to control his strong political emotions and commanded a wide following in Toulouse.[15]

There was a marked continuity in the personnel of the Royal Court of Toulouse. Many legitimist judges kept their places on the bench. In turn, they were very restrained in expressing their politi-

[15] *ADHG*, 4 M 48, Prefect of the Haute-Garonne to Minister of Interior, February 21, 1831.

cal opposition to the regime of which they disapproved. The lesser courts, like the *tribunal de première instance,* displayed the same flexibility.[16]

The negative and sententious side of ultraroyalism emphasized punishment for crime and the need for eternal vigilance against subversives. Perhaps the most notorious expression of this attitude is that passage of *Du Pape* where Joseph de Maistre describes the atrocious process of breaking a man on the wheel, and approvingly cites the public executioner as at once the horror and the bond of the human association. The state must rule by fear, and should boldly repress the writings and assemblies of those who plan to overthrow the legitimate government. These views constantly appeared in the newspapers, speeches, conversation and correspondence of the leading ultraroyalists.

As a result of this outlook, more had to be done than to ensure that only worthy judges sat upon the bench. It was important that the army and the police, the protectors of social stability, should display a temper different from that which they showed when they captured the émigrés and smashed counterrevolutionary risings. Although suspicion of the machinery of repression was natural to an aristocracy which had atavistic memories of a *frondeur* resistance against the royal government, the Revolution had shown decisively how important it was to control the police and the army. Fouché, who so brilliantly organized the police of the Empire and survived so many changes of government, was more sinister to the ultras than Robespierre. The former oratorian and terrorist had shown how effectively France could be ruled by a well-organized and determined police.

The ultraroyalists of Toulouse took a close interest in the organization of the local police, pressed for a number of changes in its composition, and were also concerned with the *gendarmerie,* the national guard, and the army itself. The peasantry shared the noble distrust for the army which was synonymous with requisitions, damage to crops, and the taking of the youths and men for conscription. The rural prejudices and the ultraroyalist theories coincided here as in so many other instances. Many ultras agreed with Saint-Chamans when he said in 1820 that they lived in a century of revolutions that took place because of the defection of

[16] A. J. Tudesq, "L'opposition légitimiste en Languedoc en 1840," *Annales du Midi,* LXVIII (1956), 391–407.

a *corps de garde*.[17] Mme de Villèle was impressed by the part played by the army in subversion:

The example given by the Spanish army could be dangerous here with a minister who is asleep when he ought to be remedying the evil which has been underway for the last four years in the army. It cannot be hidden that in many [departmental] legions opinion is detestable. Instead of putting in the towns only a few troops, on the contrary, a great many have been placed there. Here in Toulouse, for example, we have two artillery regiments when formerly we had one. . . . should the spirit of insubordination spread, Toulouse will be one of the points which the troops will try to seize.[18]

This suspicion of the army resulted not only from the memories of the revolutionary and Napoleonic wars, but more immediately from the events of 1815–16. The Duc d'Angoulême, in an ordinance of August 1, 1815, tried to bring order to the confused mass of deserters, terrorists, volunteers, and others in Toulouse in the aftermath of the allied invasion of France. Each department was to have a legion, commanded by an officer selected from those dismissed, retired, or on half-pay who had shown the most fidelity to the cause of Louis XVIII. In Toulouse, the prefect hoped to integrate the royalist terrorists called *verdets* into this legion and into the national guard, as it was difficult to get the officers of line troops to accept them. In the confusion of August, 1815, the number of troops was decreasing steadily through desertion. Almost three hundred vanished from the barracks in the first ten days of the month.[19] To royalists, officers like Ramel were condemned by their past. They believed the troops were at heart bonapartists, and they feared the depredations of bands of deserters said to be moving about the countryside. The departmental legion system which Gouvion de Saint-Cyr had devised existed until 1819, when the legions were abolished. The new system did not rely on raising troops for a particular regiment or corps from a specific region.

To the ultras this confusion and the reluctance to incorporate the *verdets* seemed proof of the bad intentions of the military. Marshal Pérignon, annoyed that his powers had not been renewed after the cessation of Duc d'Angoulême's command and bitterly

[17] AV, Saint-Chamans to J. de Villèle, September 3, 1820.
[18] AV, Mme de Villèle to J. de Villèle, March 14, 1820.
[19] ADHG, 4 M 35.

aware that the central government was communicating directly with his rival, General Ricard, retired to his estate in the Tarn-et-Garonne. The Ministers of War and of the Interior were bombarded with correspondence laying claims and counter-charges, like that of Commère, who asked to be made commander of Toulouse on the grounds that his private police force was keeping order, and thus thwarting the work of the Orléanist faction which was paying for the *fédérés!*[20] The reports of the general commanding the division, gathered from military intelligence, and the reports of the gendarmerie were often at odds with those of the prefect. In December, 1818, Partouneaux admitted that he found it difficult to give on-going reports on affairs since he had inadequate information; at the same time, he was easily persuaded to believe exaggerated reports.[21] Later he entered into conflict with the prefecture and generally showed himself excitable and incompetent. In the main, however, the army became more stable in its attachment to the Bourbons after the Spanish campaign and after the number of veterans of the Empire and Revolution in the ranks had diminished. The army, like the police, *gendarmerie*, and *garde nationale*, was to an extent affected in its local action by the ultra ascendancy in the town hall, but all of these units ultimately obeyed instructions which emanated from Paris.

Only one armed force was purely local, and it existed briefly. The royalist terrorists of the summer of 1815, called the *secrets* by the ultras and more commonly known as the *verdets*, were named after similar para-military formations which operated in the Midi after the 9 Thermidor and during the Hundred Days. An agent of Louis XVIII sent to organize resistance, the fatuous Vitrolles, tried to raise volunteers in early March, 1815, and while these efforts had no immediate practical result, they gave an impetus to the formation of the force.[22] The historian Loubet claims the *verdets* were organized as a result of a meeting held in the townhouse of the chevalier de Mauran, a local landowner, in mid-April, 1815. By the end of the month, incidents between supporters of the Empire and royalists were taking place in the streets. An eighteen-year-old art student was knocked down, and subsequently struck across the face

[20] *AN*, F⁷9056.
[21] *AG*, D³76.
[22] J. Loubet, "Le gouvernement toulousain du duc d'Angoulême après les Cent-Jours," *La Révolution française*, LXIV (1913), 151–61.

with a whip by a shoemaker after a slanging match between a royalist washerwoman, her daughter, and a group of teenagers coming out of a billiard hall near the Montoulieu gate. On May 1, 1815, there was a gathering of young people on the Esplanade, close to the same gate, in which one man was badly beaten. The *verdets* were behind the shouts and scuffles which went on during the Hundred Days in opposition to the *fédérés*, organized in Toulouse by the Protestant Julien and Boyer-Fonfrède. They gained more recruits in June and July, especially when general Decaën was preparing to leave the city. The *verdets* were fervent Catholics, at least in their own estimation, and while religious dissension was not as significant in Toulouse as in Provence, a number of local Protestants sought refuge in Lyon. The *verdets* were described as "fanatic like thorough-going Spaniards."[23] These royalist terrorists virtually took control of the city, acting in response to commands from the entourage of the Duc d'Angoulême after the collapse of the Empire.

Not all the *verdets* were Toulousain. Rougé, the conspirator of the year VII insurrection, recruited deserters from the Toulouse garrison as well as members of the Marie-Thérèse regiment, made up of volunteers from the army of Angoulême which had been stationed at Figueras, Spain. Many of those associated with these volunteers were local noblemen. The *procureur du roi* described the rank-and-file as ex-terrorists of 1793, artisans without work, petty criminals on the lookout for pillage, and others who hoped to recoup their fortunes by getting the job of someone less visibly a good royalist than they were. The kind of men involved were typified by Barthélemy Bordier, a breeches-maker, illiterate, aged thirty-two, who was a sergeant in the fusileers, or Félix Brousse, a former soldier and now a shoemaker in Toulouse, who claimed he was a member of the second batallion of royalist volunteers because he had been promised the place of master-shoemaker. A sergeant in this second batallion, Jean-Louis Montaubry, was a fencing master. All three had taken part in the riot of May 1st, and had subsequently hidden in the country château of a royalist

---

[23] *AN*, BB[30]254, "Notes particulières sur l'affaire Ramel." Picot de Lapeyrouse was told in November 1815 there were 6,000 "*verds*" in the Toulousain. E. Connac, "La réaction royaliste à Toulouse (1815–1816), trois lettres inédites . . .," *Revue des Pyrénées*, X (1898), 438; J. B. A. de Aldéguier, *Histoire de Toulouse* (Toulouse, 1834–35), notes 63, 642.

sympathizer at Colomiers.[24] In 1827, a former member of the Marie-Thérèse batallion, a shoemaker, had fallen on hard times as a result of a weakening of his sight and was arrested for shouting "Vive l'Empereur!" in front of the Capitole.[25] The suspects in the Ramel case were artisans. Other members of the *verdets* included an "étudiant en commerce" whose lodgings were on the Place Rouaix and a man who subsequently collected chair rentals in St. Etienne. Under the Monarchy of July, a group of some eight workers at the *Tabac* were described as former *verdets*. Malaret, the turncoat mayor forced to flee from Toulouse in fear of his life, described the royalist terrorists as the dregs of the people, but in fact, like the revolutionary militants, they seem to have been mostly artisans and minor independent professions. The *procureur* thought they numbered as many as twelve hundred and that they received funds from the clergy as well as from royalist laymen.[26] However, no documentation exists which confirms this.

Decazes and his colleagues in Paris strongly disapproved of the existence of this turbulent and dangerous formation, and put pressure on the prefect to bring them under control and to disband them. Although the military commanders were reluctant, a number of the *verdets* were transferred to the 17th of the line; others turned to less exciting pursuits as the flow of funds for food, wine, and lodgings dried up. The prominent figures in the city who had initially cheered on the opponents of the *fédérés* now found them an embarrassment. Although there were rumors that the *verdet* organization survived after the winter of 1815–16, in fact it played no part in local politics. Shared experiences of the White Terror were not forgotten, however; a police report of 1832 noted that the house of one well-known *verdet* was a social center for others, now in their fifties, who had been involved in the White Terror of 1815.

[24] *ADHG*, 223 U 5.
[25] *ADHG*, 223 U 9. Aldéguier, *Histoire de Toulouse*, pp. 75–76.
[26] *AN*, F⁷9659, Malaret to Minister of Interior, August 16, 1815.

VII

THE ULTRA MIND

THE RULERS of Restoration Toulouse saw themselves joined in battle with *philosophes*, Jacobins, and anarchists; a battle waged by the powers of Roman Catholicism, royalism, and country virtue. Intransigent rejection of the Revolution was a moral imperative; the Revolution was pure evil. One could not meet it halfway, for it destroyed all social certainty and was, in a communal sense, patricidal. The foreign observer of Restoration Toulouse would have seen few signs of the horrors which the ultras loved to evoke, and might have found the local liberals—the benign lawyer Romiguières, or lieutenant-general Cassagne, or professor Malpel—unlikely candidates for a reformed Committee of Public Safety. Throughout France, the virulence of ultra denunciations of the revolutionary minotaur produced scepticism like the tongue-in-cheek discussions of J.-B. Pérès and Bishop Whately on the question of the existence of Napoleon (perhaps he was a Sun Myth?). Yet simply to dismiss ultraroyalist hyperbole is to underestimate the genuine fear which beset them, not unlike the fear of any minority group that suffered persecution and therefore suspects the intentions of those who subsequently approach them. Ultraroyalist ideology shows why the extreme right in French political life was unable to work out an accommodation with the politics of the nineteenth century.

The local press, pamphlets sold by hawkers and in the bookshops, private letters, and official reports all reveal political attitudes. The ultras were conscious of their ideas as an ideology: in

138

Toulouse they used the word *ultracisme*, although in Paris it was customary to say *ultraïsme*.[1] The basic ultra ideas underwent little change during the Restoration—which was to be expected in a doctrine denouncing change—although contemporaries noted that these ideas were stated less vehemently in the later 1820's. In Toulouse they can be traced most systematically in the two ultra newspapers, the *Ami du Roi* (1815–19) and the *Echo du Midi* (1821–29). Both Fouché and Decazes thought the *Ami* was dangerous because of its extremism in 1815. The editor, Augustin Manavit, had to stop publication in 1819 for financial reasons, and did not resume publication of his views until 1821, after the introduction of new censorship laws, when he was editor of the *Echo*. There was a rival and colorless newspaper, the *Journal de Toulouse*, edited by François Vieusseux, which provided more local news. Besides these publications, Parisian newspapers were distributed in the department. They could be consulted in the various Toulouse reading rooms. In 1830, the legitimist *Gazette de France* was the most widely sold, with 153 copies, then the liberal *Constitutionnel* with 101 copies, and third the *Débats* with 88 copies. In overall figures, there were some 338 liberal subscriptions, 57 moderates, and 224 legitimists. Since many subscribers were café owners and reading rooms, and each copy circulated widely, such figures do not necessarily indicate much about the extent of given opinion.

Electoral results showed the strength of ultraroyalism among the most wealthy groups in the population. Among the common people, literacy was rare; songs were the medium for expressing their views and feelings. The *grisets* and *grisettes* of Toulouse prided themselves on their *mélomanie* and were only too willing to serenade. In 1827, the prefect noted that in an area like the Haute-Garonne, where the people sang a great deal, songs could be used to influence opinion. The ultras made use of this method to popularize their ideas among the common people, and in 1816 distributed the occitain song, "Toulouse Recouneissento: couplets en l'aounou de nostrés brabés députats," among the crowds that gathered to welcome home the ultra deputies from the *Chambre Introuvable*.

---

[1] Letter of January 16, 1817, in C. F. M. de Rémusat, *Correspondance* (Paris, 1883–84), II, 367.

The ultraroyalist attitudes do, in total, make up a socio-religious view of the past based on history, but perhaps it is too much to expect great rigor in the exposition of this ideology on the popular level. A count of the incidence of key words like *philosophe, ordre,* and *gémissement* might reveal the contours of these "social fossils," these persistent obsessions of a group of people who felt insecure in a changing world as they tried to explain the revolutionary holocaust, the confiscation of their property, and the execution of their relatives. Yet a better view is to be had of the nature of their dilemma by looking widely in various sources for a guide to their political attitudes. Fiévée, the ultraroyalist journalist, remarked: "Our century is singular in that it apprehends by memories, as it makes politics with memories."[2] Here I want to examine the results of this retrospection.

The ultra view of society was focused on the tension between the individual and the family, and that between the King and the nobility, in a structure of authority ordered by God. Just as the individual sometimes disregarded and fought against the discipline of the family, so the King could cross the line from monarch to tyrant and exercise an arbitrary power against the nobility—and hence against the national interest. The common people were the childish part of the nation. The basic supposition was that limitations on competitive, selfish, and materialist "social Darwinism" of the liberal ethos were necessary to a truly happy and just society. This limitation was conservative: "Providence placed within us a conservative spirit which causes us to love all that contributes to our moral and physical well-being."[3]

The nature of the state in which this salutary conservatism was to exist concerned them. Initially, the ultras believed that Louis XVIII had made a mistake upon his return to France in 1814, when he accepted the Charter which they saw as an abdication of "paternal" authority. Constitutionalism and revolution seemed synonymous, and they wanted to return, as quickly as possible, to the pre-revolutionary situation. This simplistic and popular view lasted

[2] S. Mellon, *The Political Uses of History* (Stanford, 1958), p. 2. Writing from Toulouse to her son Charles, Mme de Rémusat described Fiévée as the "catechism" of Toulouse high Society. C. F. M. Rémusat, *Correspondence*, I, 262.

[3] *AR*, March 31, 1818.

for a long time; an ultra song which circulated in Toulouse in September, 1815, summed up the sentiment:

La Charte principale
Dans tout notre pays
La loi fondamentale
C'est l'amour de Louis

La tête la première
J'enverrai ces brouillons
Faire dans la rivière
Des chartes aux poissons

Au bon sens de nos pères
Que ne revenons-nous?
Le siècle des lumières
N'a produit que des fous.[4]

The experience of the first Restoration and of parliamentary practice as provided by the *Chambre Introuvable* and the succeeding sessions of the Chamber of Deputies soon modified this simple rejection of any form of constitution. Ultras like Villèle, despite his pamphlet which violently attacked the Charter in 1814, soon reached the conclusion that, since the document had been "octroyé" by Louis XVIII, it was firmly established as a basis for government. Indeed, these ultras hoped that a constitutional framework could be turned to their own advantage, since it was a limitation on absolute power. All royalists agreed with the scientist Aubuisson de Voisins, engineer and municipal councillor of Toulouse. De Voisins wrote a work defending the royal power as the keystone of civil administration, in which he pointed out that the more power rested in the hands of the king, the greater was the degree of popular welfare. As the Revolution had shown,[5] democratic assemblies debating in public had produced much evil and little good. However, many of de Voisins's colleagues on the municipal council would have departed from him in his refusal to allow any counterweight to royal authority. Certainly they would agree that democratic despotism was to be feared, and appeared imminent; but in his work there was also a suspicion of the aristocracy and of other

[4] Manuscript song entitled: *Chant nouveau pour le retour du prince et l'arrivée de la princesse à Toulouse*, written in honor of the visit of the Duc d'Angoulême (AV). "The main Charter/throughout our region/the fundamental law/is the love of Louis./ Head first/ I shall throw these scribblings/to make in the river/Charters for fishes./To the good sense of our fathers/when shall we return?/The Century of Light/ only produced fools.
[5] Jean-Francois d'Aubuisson de Voisins, *Considérations sur l'autorité royale en France depuis la restauration et sur les administrations locales* (Paris, 1825), pp. 23, 69, 87.

intermediate groups which made up that balance which in the Old Regime had so well protected local pockets of privilege. De Voisins considered stability to be the first necessity of government in France, and believed that this could not be attained if fundamental institutions of the state could be overturned at will. Like the advocate Pinaud, he considered representative government to be unnatural and inconsequential. If representative government was generally considered by ultras to be an absurdity since the common people were inherently incapable of governing, the French nobility, according to Voisins "more hated than esteemed by the other classes," did not have the control of the government institutions that produced stability.[6] He was very much aware of the link between social position and opinion, for he saw society in terms of fixed oppositions of economic groups: "There is a struggle, or tendency to struggle, between those who have not and those who have; almost everywhere, the first are the most numerous."[7]

Because of his suspicion of the nobility and his hostility to decentralization which served particular interests at the expense of the public good, de Voisins's views were at variance with the sentiments of most ultras. At the same time, however, some of his attitudes reflected a social outlook which justified the importance of undemocratic elite groups. In a quaint forerunner of the "opinion poll," de Voisins presented an analysis of the attitudes of the component groups in society drawn from a sample of one thousand. Among the *peuple*, whom he considered to be generally docile and passive, he distinguished an active group of town artisans, discontented peasants and workers, and the turbulent youth of the *bas peuple*. Ignorant and physically strong, they were the natural enemies of the social order, and it was from them that the revolutionary clubs and Napoleonic *fédérés* had been recruited. The lower middle classes, by which he meant the *cultivateurs aisés*, the *petits marchands*, wanted peace and were disturbed only by such practical issues as taxation and the likelihood of the sales of the *biens nationaux*, from which they had profitted, being put in question. These individuals favored the Charter which guaranteed their acquisitions. They were against monarchical principles, since only the ideas of the purest democracy were within their grasp. Unable to appreciate the political combinations necessary to ensure the stable

6 *Ibid.*, 91–92.
7 *Ibid.*, 18–19.

working of social institutions, their commercial activity was essentially republican and they were jealous of and hostile to the upper middle class. The intelligentsia, especially lawyers and doctors, had no special interest in maintaining the existing government. De Voisins believed, like Burke, that they had much to gain from change, as they had in 1789. Being men of "litigious disposition," the natural and most dangerous opponents of royal government came from this group. The young, in their violent search for novelty, were innately anti-social, and therefore should not be seriously considered in the government. The top of the social pyramid was composed of the *haute bourgeoisie*, great landowners, and Old Regime nobility. De Voisins thought that even here was a certain superficiality—*variabilité*—which produced democratic inclinations, although he declared that, happily, sentiment was more important than reason in this group's decisions. This former émigré was suspicious of the nobility before the publication of his book. In a letter to Laîné of July 21, 1816, he wrote that the spirit of counter-revolution among the local nobility was based on the desire to increase its influence in the departmental administration, and in order to regain the *biens nationaux*. He thought that they were renewing the course of action they had followed in 1788 and that they would again incur another Revolution, of which once again they would be the first victims. The royal power should not make itself dependent on this group.[8] In short, his ideas were those of an absolutist, rather than those of a corporatist who hoped to maintain group privileges in a stable society.

Men less sensitive than Aubuisson de Voisins were outraged at peasant fears of compulsory tithes, references to the feudal regime, and talk that commoners would again be excluded from office—while in fact they probably wished that all these things could be.[9] The *Ami du Roi* wrote:

One is astonished to find in certain verses declarations against gothick hobbles and baubles of outmoded pride, when nobody thinks of ressuscitating the first nor of being amused by the second. The hobbles of despotism [the Napoleonic period] under which we groaned are what

[8] Aubuisson de Voisins to Laîné, July 21, 1816; September 5, 1816, cited in E. de Perceval, *Un adversaire de Napoléon; le vicomte Laîné* (Paris, 1926), II, 68.
[9] AG, D320, Partouneaux report, February 7, 1816.

ought to be detested. The glory of France under Louis XIV was not a bauble and is not to be described as a ridiculously outdated thing.[10]

The *Echo du Midi* conceded that it was difficult to define what constituted the primacy of the nobility, which was formed naturally in any state by the accumulation of services, talents, virtues, and riches in certain families. The theory of egalitarianism was a vain commentary on the fact that each son is taught by his father to emulate and inherit the virtues of his ancestors.[11] Obviously, the aristocracy could not be restored in its pre-revolutionary state; there could be no question of a noble condition before the law. However, if the government would pay its debts to servants of the pre-1789 monarchy (the émigrés), this would help them keep a secure position in the state. "We shall never believe the state to be stable without a strong and vigorous aristocracy, at one and the same time its ornament and its inner spring."[12]

The moral values of the nobility were contrasted with those of the new commercial groups whose voices were being heard. Wealthy critics of the nobility professed liberalism but not liberality. (The public and private commitment of the ultras to the systematic exercise of charity was one of their proudest boasts.) The same liberals who talked of equality but disdained the poor could be seen as nothing more than irreligious money-worshippers. At the same time, ultras were aware that economic well-being for the common people was the best answer to subversive ideas. They were fond of citing the maxim of Henry IV, which called for a chicken in the Sunday cook-pot for the peasantry; and men like Louis de Villèle and captain Villeneuve, or the advocate Espinasse, all members of the Royal Agricultural Society of Toulouse, were concerned with popular diet. In 1829, a *juge de paix* from Muret gave a paper in which he deplored the country diet of thin wine, rye bread, and no meat, calling for an increase in the consumption of both food and goods on the part of the rural population.[13]

The nobility, then, was to feed and clothe the poor, and was not to suffer competition from "materialists" and liberals. The justifica-

[10] *AR*, August 31, 1816.
[11] *EM*, January 14, 1824.
[12] *Ibid.*; *EM*, July 21, 1823; January 23, 1824.
[13] Louis Théron de Montaugé, *L'agriculture et les classes rurales dans le pays toulousain depuis le milieu du xviii siècle* (Paris, 1869), p. 443.

tion of this special place was presented in theoretical argument: All nations, from the time of savagery to the present, show that the majority of society are ignorant men destined to brutish work which perpetuates their ignorance and makes them unsuitable to exercise political rights. This mass believes that it is in its interest to destroy the property rights of the state, but it is incapable of that intellectual and moral perfection necessary to maintain states. "Can political bodies of which the principal aim is to protect the acquisition of the social advantages be managed by men who have not themselves made such acquisitions?"[14] If the mass of the population display "the absolute and necessary incapacity of the masses," it must be accepted that the rights of individuals are relative, and that nations differ one from another. In some countries it is feasible to entrust a larger proportion of the population with responsibility than in others; for the protection of the "corps social," the government must rely on a privileged minority, the land-owning aristocracy, to rule the state.[15] The revolutionaries had shown themselves incapable of destroying the reality of "superiorités sociales" because these grew out of the historic development of nations; social interdependence might shock latter-day *philosophes* but it is the unchanging law of society. Revolution could only exist in "the absence of all hierarchies and of all social relationships." Even during the Revolution the "People" which figured in the revolutionary pamphlets and speeches were, in fact, an unrepresentative band of thugs and criminals who terrorized the capital.[16] The royalists, on the other hand, were essentially the party of the landed gentry: "Masters of three-quarters of the large landholdings who have in their favor all the memories, esteem, credit, and confidence, and they make use of these in the localities."[17] It was they who had the valid authority to rule in France.

The society which had existed before 1789 was the ideal with which the ultras contrasted the present and found it wanting.

The oldest of our wise men still remember that Golden Age where the people, docile to the voice of religion, was formed to obedience by the

---

[14] Jean-Joseph-Thérèse Pinaud, "Eloge historique de Louis XVI et de Louis XVII, prononcé en séance publique de l'Académie . . . le 19 janvier 1815," *Recueil de l'Académie des Jeux Floraux 1814–1816*, second pagination, p. 51.
[15] *Ibid.*, p. 54.
[16] *EM*, May 10, 1822.
[17] *Ibid.*

practice of all those virtues which she teaches. . . . no interests attached the life of the citizens to political concerns, and their fidelity, that pious obligation which united them to their prince by a bond as durable and no less sweet than that of conjugal tenderness, rendered them capable of the greatest sacrifices.[18]

They denied that the Old Regime had been a restriction to liberty, since they defined liberty in terms other than those of liberalism. Liberty was the right to exist peacefully within the structure of duties laid down by divine wisdom. Toulouse before the Revolution enjoyed a system of administration admired by all France, sanctioned by the "espèce de pacte" between the King and his people that permitted the gradual removal of admitted but minor abuses which existed.[19] The advocate Pinaud granted that Bourbon tolerance of the Parlement's political activity was mistaken since the opposition to the royal power had caused their mutual destruction.[20] Yet, in their social action, the Parlements were admirable. The venality of office set up a line of families devoted to study of the laws, thereby demonstrating that if a body of men is well constituted, even that which is apparently most harmful can have good results.[21]

The ultras placed the major blame for the undermining of the throne (the symbol of national stability) on incessant carping criticism by the *philosophes*, which stimulated popular violence during the Terror.[22] Pinaud thought this especially serious in a nation characterized by violent passions, impetuosity, and "her swift tendency to excess."[23] Diderot's *Encyclopedia*, the masterwork of the "têtes fortes," was a *summa* of anti-social doctrines.[24] In turn, these destroyed the many institutions with overlapping authority that so annoyed the legislators of 1789 who were obsessed with a desire for uniformity and regularity. When these institutions were stripped from her, France became a nation of individuals lacking unity and no longer able to fight off tyranny.[25] Burke was invoked in this

---

[18] *AR*, March 31, 1818.
[19] Pinaud, "Eloge historique," p. 5.
[20] *Ibid.*, pp. 6–8.
[21] *EM*, January 7, 1822.
[22] *AR*, August 27, 1818.
[23] Pinaud, "Eloge historique."
[24] *AR*, October 2, 1815, *extrait Journal du Gard*.
[25] Aubuisson de Voisins, *Considérations sur l'autorité*, p. 190.

criticism of the failure of reformers to provide stable institutions for the protection of property, persons, and civil and political rights, while true independence rested in the conscience of man that forbade committing evil acts even when ordered to do so, and did not revel in destroying the past.[26] Pinaud considered *philosophe* criticism of the origins of the state and its constitution exemplified by disgust for the condition into which one was born, indifference on religious matters, and a doctrinaire belief in progress and human perfectibility, all of which coalesced to break down the structure of political administration.[27] The Revolution split the chain of the past and the present; the execution of Louis XVI was the "murder" of a society.[28] Was he not the father of his people? This, it was said, was the result of the "pernicieuses maximes" of the *philosophes*.[29]

The Revolution caused many faithful royalists to leave France. The ultras wished to justify and glorify the emigration in the eyes of those who saw it as treasonable. The question of the moral or territorial nature of the native land exercised the *Echo du Midi*: "For every true Frenchman, the fatherland is always where the King is."[30] Far from being traitors, the émigrés were "virtuous chevaliers, nobles, and plebeians" who sacrificed their material well-being to uphold the Bourbon dynasty's sacred rights.[31] The Revolution had taken their property in an attempt to destroy them; if law, commerce, and property were to be maintained in the future, power should be given only to those with much to lose in civil disturbances. The poor were encouraged to realize that the Revolution was not to their real economic advantage, for the revolutionaries were selfish and gave neither the charity nor the work that had been provided by the wealthy landowners of the Old Regime.[32]

The holocaust of the Revolution, with its systematic persecution of the royalists during the Terror, the massing of priests and nobles in jails, confiscations and frequent executions, was clearly divine punishment visited on an irreligious century. Napoleon fitted into this scheme of things and represented Order, but it was Order imposed by the cumulative exhaustion from evil-doing. The *philosophes*

[26] *AR*, June 16, 1818; July 2, 1818.
[27] Pinaud, "Eloge historique," pp. 8, 14.
[28] *AR*, January 21, 1819.
[29] Pierre-Catherine Amilhau, *Eloge de Louis XVI* (Toulouse, 1817), p. 8.
[30] *EM*, April 26, 1822.
[31] *Annuaire de la Haute-Garonne* (Toulouse, 1825), p. 96.
[32] *AR*, April 9, 1817.

destroyed the Old Regime; Jacobin excesses turned the violence of the Revolution against itself: and the ultras were convinced that the liberals were now plotting to destroy the Restoration. The Hundred Days confirmed them in their paranoid suspicion of all who disagreed with them in any particular.

The Restoration meant peace for France. The ultras contrasted wars, executions, imprisonments, and violent disturbances in Europe which resulted from the Revolution with the benefits of legitimacy which would cause the economy to flourish and the good old ways to reappear. As one local poet put it in doggerel verse:

Tout germe et tout se revifie
Rien des beaux arts ne suspend plus le cours,
Le commerce reprend la vie,
De la toute-puissance expliquant les décrets,
Les Ministres du culte enfin exempts d'alarmes,
N'auront plus à sécher nos larmes,
Et de Louis nous traçant les bienfaits,
Loin de nous inviter à recourir aux armes,
Nous prêcherons des paroles de paix.
Ce ne sont là que de faibles images
Du bien que l'on doit pressentir,
Et dont depuis trois ans, comme dans les villages,
Nos coeurs commencent à jouir
Dans la ville des Tectosages.[33]

The Restoration was also the return of paternal kindness and authority which would regenerate the essential sweetness of France.

As a result of their interpretation of the Revolution, the ultras were obsessed with the danger of any further spread of Jacobinism in Europe, and indeed, throughout the world. Joseph de Villèle noted in 1817 that Toulouse was calm, but he visualized a vast European conspiracy secretly planning a revolution.[34] These views

[33] Everything germinates and revivifies/ Fine arts are no longer blocked in their course/ Commerce becomes active again./ Explaining the decrees of the Almighty/The ministers of religion are finally free from fears/And shall no longer have to dry our tears – /Telling us of Louis's goodness/Far from calling on us to take up arms/They shall preach peace./These are my feeble pictures/ Of the good that can be hoped for/And which we enjoy as in the villages/ In our hearts in the city of the Tectosages [Toulouse]. *Sur la fête de Saint Louis.* Toulouse, August 25, 1817.
[34] AV, Joseph de Villèle to Desbassyns, April 22, 1817; June 21, 1817.

also had popular currency, and are illustrated in an anonymous letter sent to the mayor by a scarcely literate individual who denounced subversion in 1817:[35]

Monsieur/il Est etonan que vous ne/Connessa pas linnorme conspira/ tacion qui ce prepare en France/ tous va eclater à la foi la/Sassin du roy toute la/famille royalle toute la/noblesse le clergé dois y/perire ce en ne fait ci tous/les ministre ne son pas/arrêté de suite est pendu/de suite je vous avertis/avertisse vite le roy/est la famille royal. Meffié vous de demi so/est des fédéré est des aquereurs des biens/je sui français nasionneau/le ler 7bre 1817.

The evil represented by the Revolution was widely present in Europe. The *Echo du Midi* always showed a close interest in the politics of the Iberian Peninsula, and reported carefully on the struggles between the partisans of the Revolution of 1820 and the *serviles* in Spain, as well as the contest between royalists and liberals in Portugal. In the later 1820's, there was a regular column in the newspaper entitled "Nouvelles d'Espagne et des frontières." On January 2, 1827, the *Echo* reported increasing support for the royalists in Portugal, and compared this to the heroic Spanish attitude at the time of the War of Independence, an analogy which placed English troops in the same unfavorable light as the armies of Napoleon. The criticism of foreign and domestic liberals who encouraged Spanish and Portuguese liberalism and of the English who profitted from their ascendancy over the Portuguese court were part of a generalized critique of subversion.

Anglophobia had already emerged as a characteristic right-wing attitude; the ally of the revolutionary and Napoleonic period was now showing her true face. In the course of 1827, there was a series of reports on the situation in Portugal, many of them supplied to the *Echo* by a Portuguese reactionary, Ponte Negrão, who was living in the city. "Unfortunate Portugal owes then to the English the frightful state of exhaustion, misery and anarchy in

[35] "Monsieur, It is astonishing that you do not know of the enormous plot which is preparing in France. Everything is going to explode simultaneously: the King, the royal family, the nobility and clergy must all be assassinated if this is not done—if the ministers are not immediately arrested and hanged. I warn you: warn quickly the king and the royal family. Beware of the demi-soldes and of the *fédérés*, and of the owners of *biens nationaux*. I am a national Frenchman. 1 September 1817." AV, Anonymous letter to Villèle, postmarked Toulouse.

which she is plunged today."[36] Earlier in the year, the Ancient Alliance had been characterized by an excuse for the British to plunder Portuguese commerce. London was seen as a center of crime and political exiles, men whose names recalled the most horrible of crimes and who lived in a city where thieves and prostitutes abounded. In their seditious pamphlets, they appealed to the worst popular violence. Clearly they were in favor of the triumph of the "system" of Robespierre, Marat, and Danton. The Protestant English, with their crime and political freedom, essentially different in character from the Europeans as a result of their history, climate, and temperament, encouraged the liberals of Paris, Madrid, and Lisbon in their sinister conspiracy against society.

Happily, the Catholic peasantry of Spain and Portugal were motivated by more moral ambitions than those of the educated and free-thinking. The *Echo* constantly attacked the *Journal de Toulouse* for its maligning of the Spanish church. Only with a divine *misericorde* would Spain return to the principles of order and of morality.[37] Many Toulouse ultras put their approval of Spanish royalism and Catholic practice into a tangible form by giving assistance to the Marquis of Mataflorida and the Spanish ultras of the Urgel Regency, some of whom passed through the city.[38] The contrast between lands of good principles and those of bad ones were drawn widely. The Philippine islands were given a glowing description:

Amid the troubles and revolutions of Europe, this land keeps its peace, its institutions and its good thinking. Religion flourishes there . . . three million Indians [sic] are tranquil and submissive. The inhabitants of the Philippines have not been led astray by the bad books which are so widespread in Europe in recent years: they have no doctrinaire systems in religion and politics: they walk in the same paths as their fathers. Happy land where nobody thinks at all of revolutions![39]

The ultra deputy, Chalvet de Rochemonteix, kept notebooks in which he recorded interesting current events, especially insurrections and revolutions, as part of an amateur concern with the way

[36] *EM*, March 27, 1827.
[37] *EM*, April 11, 1823.
[38] *EM*, June 16, 1823. J. L. C. Garcia-Llera, *Los realistas en el trienio constitucional, 1820–1823* (Pamplona, 1958), *passim*.
[39] *EM*, January 11, 1827.

in which these disturbances developed. He filled several pages with details of unrest in Brazil.[40]

These studies strengthened the ultras' conviction that administrative purges and censorship were needed to end subversion. "The King and the country are exposed to evils from which we have hardly been delivered by the maintenance in their positions of men, almost always servants of every party and instruments of evil."[41] The sentiments of provincial royalism were purifying, and were carried to Paris by the deputies of the Chambre Introuvable. In contrast, Paris—"this immense Babylon" full of bandits and unemployed ruffians—was essentially corrupt, "a capital which will finish like London by becoming the monstrous head of a degraded body."[42] While a significant shake-up in the personnel of the ministries and prefectures took place after 1815, it was never sufficient to satisfy men like Chalvet-Gaujouse who lamented to a friend: "one must not deceive oneself: we are in a Republic which has the false appearance of Monarchy."[43] Disappointment because of the indulgence of the government of Louis XVIII was often intense. A manuscript poem sent to Villèle describes "a troubador grown old far from Occitania/ arrived with joy from American shores" who enters the city on January 21, 1816 (anniversary of the execution of Louis XVI), and finds it in mourning because of the King's misguided pardon of obvious subversives.[44] After 1815–16, as a result of the evident economy of the government in appointing men to various governmental offices, ultra concern focused more on the need for effective censorship than the need for purges.

What century is more fertile than ours in bad books of all kinds, and in what era would there be stranger abuse of the press? The apostles of incredulity, known under the name of brilliant wits [esprits forts], and who should be called brilliant fools, do not content themselves with sharpening their pens against religion and good morals, but in order to hasten the sublime work of corrupting humanity they do not cease to reproduce the writings of their predecessors whom public indignation had willed to eternal forgetfulness.[45]

[40] AB.
[41] ADHG, 4 M 35, Savy-Gardeilh report, July 20, 1815.
[42] AR, May 21, 1816; Où en sommes-nous? pp. 14–15.
[43] Jean Barada, "Toulouse et la vie toulousaine . . .," Annales du Midi, XLV (1932), 450.
[44] AV.
[45] AR, August 1, 1818.

Liberal journalists were accused of stirring up religious strife and of attacking southern loyalists.[46] Chalvet de Rochemonteix deplored what he called "variations in opinions and principles" as much as he did the policies followed by the bureaucracy. Discussion of public and intellectual issues, the restatement of differing positions, seemed bound to produce discontent to the ultras.[47] The *Echo* even found itself praising the Empire:

> Under the peaceful reign of our legitimate Kings has been seen what was never seen under the usurpation: impiety, anarchy and libertinage insolently setting up school in the shops and at the cross-roads.[48]

Liberty of the press encouraged that enquiry and discussion which made intelligence seem Jacobin, since it questioned ultraroyalist ideas. The *Echo* berated its local target in this connection, the innocuous *Journal de Toulouse*. In 1826, the *Courrier français* was attacked for its hostile commentary on what was described as a religious decision of the *Arrondissement* council of Toulouse.[49] In 1828, a blanket of venomous reproof fell over the opposition newspapers: "these scandalous publications daily undermine the bases of religion and weaken the Bourbon monarchy. Already the Revolution no longer takes the trouble to disguise its plans. . . ."[50] The *Echo* commentators frequently returned to the need for censorship. They denounced the attack on the Jesuits which had been stimulated by Montlosier's book, the *Mémoire à consulter* (1826). They objected to the obvious glee in the liberal press reporting of crimes committed by priests. In an attempt to counterbalance this press campaign, the *Echo* published in 1827 extracts from debates in both the Chambers which favored the Jesuits. They carried in full a speech by Clermont-Tonnerre, arguing that the Society of Jesus to which the parlementarians had been so opposed during the eighteenth century and which had been condemned by the Parlements in 1761–62 no longer existed in the same form. This was to remind the ultras of parlementary antecedents that they should abandon the familial tradition of hostility to the Jesuits.

[46] *AR*, October 15, 1818.
[47] *AB*, Chalvet de Rochemonteix, May 25, 1820.
[48] *EM*, November 1, 1824.
[49] *EM*, August 17, 1826.
[50] *EM*, May 24, 1826.

Somewhat inconsistently, the Archbishop continued that permission for Jesuit organizations to exist was not necessary at a time when "so many groups form freely for selfish motives, for petitions, for Free-masonry, for industry and commerce: is a particular permission required so that priests can meet together and meditate in silence?"[51] The *Echo* printed extracts from other papers which returned to the timeworn argument that the liberals favored freedom of the press in order to hasten a new Revolution. A subscriber's letter was printed on March 3, 1827, criticizing Chateaubriand for his shift of views on the subject of censorship, and contrasting them with those he held in 1820, at the time the Duke of Berry was assassinated: then Chateaubriand declaimed against the spread of sedition; now he was mistakenly fighting against government measures on censorship. Ricard, the pious deputy, described the Press Law of 1827, painting vividly the ravages of unbelief and disorder caused among the country laborers and those royalists, concerned only with agriculture and the welfare of their large families, when they were exposed to "ces résumés pestilentiels" hawked by the liberals through France. The country people and the artisans were to be protected from these perverse publications; what father, asked Ricard, does not keep a dangerous weapon out of the hands of the child he loves?[52]

The appointments of Decampe, an inspector at the Toulouse *Académie*, and of Pujol, a Faculty of Letters professor, as censors in the Haute-Garonne was approved by the *Echo*. The editor noted the widespread concern throughout France about the mockery of religion and the vilification of royalism, for the control of which so many *conseils généraux* had asked the government in 1826. The Haute-Garonne council described Paris as the center of corruption whose agents took a vicious pleasure in working for the "downfall" of the young, and in placing in the poorest individual's grasp the subversive books which were sold from one end of France to the other.[53] The ultra newspaper *La Quotidienne*, published in Paris, was under the control of those members of the group in the capital who had been hostile to Villèle since the *amortissement* affair. The *Echo* replied tartly to a reproach from that paper for having praised Villèle when he left office by observing that royalism had

51 *EM*, February 13, 1827.
52 *EM*, March 22, 1827.
53 *EM*, July 5, 1827.

deep roots in the provinces. The *système de haine* which the *Quoti-dienne* stimulated among the ultra ranks in Paris was deplorable, since it could only benefit the opposition.[54] Just as liberal papers were regularly castigated for also opposing the work of the minis-try, the best ultra newspapers were quoted and praised. The *Echo* often quoted from the *Gazette de Lyon*, "of which the highest praise is to merit the sarcasm and insults of the organs of revolu-tion,"[55] and from the Bordeaux paper, the *Ruche d'Acquitaine*.

Subversion resulted from freedom of the press. The hand of God was necessary to protect society from this destructive force. In August, 1815, at the height of the White Terror, the *Ami* cited the maxim of Bonnald [sic]: "The Revolution began with the declara-tion of the rights of man; it can only end by the declaration of the rights of God." Religion, law, and education are the triple brakes on human passions, the editorialist continued, and the same limita-tions should be applied to the nation at large.[56] Only hypocritical unbelievers argued that the Church should stand aside from na-tional life. Was not morality in politics of vital public concern? Both law and education should carry the mark of religious concerns. These ideas were to recur frequently when ultras saw the effect of divine providence in politics. Archbishop Clermont-Tonnerre not only instructed his clergy to influence elections, but saw royalist successes in the 1824 campaign as a sign of divine purpose. "The designs of God are no longer mysterious: the genius of evil is con-founded and keeps silent."[57] Military success in the Spanish interven-tion by the forces commanded by the Duc d'Angoulême was a sign of divine favor for the Bourbons. The *Echo*, during the Greek War of Independence, was sarcastic in its appreciations of liberal sym-pathies for Christians fighting against the Turks, and contrasted this with their hostility to religion in France.[58] It was important to keep a consistent concern with God's purpose: Montlosier was de-nounced for his "horrid doctrines" which weakened the influence of religion in education and politics.[59] The same principle was invoked even in more mundane spheres: mayor Montbel was praised for his

[54] *EM*, January 26, 1828; Irene Collines, *The Government and the News-paper Press in France 1814–1881* (London, 1959), pp. 42–46.
[55] *EM*, February 7, 1828.
[56] *AR*, August 21, 1815.
[57] *EM*, March 22, 1824.
[58] *EM*, May 25, 1826.
[59] *EM*, June 27, 1826.

ordinance against gambling houses, which was "a great act of religious morality."[60]

The missions which tried to reconvert France to the level of religious observance which had existed before the Revolution were particularly esteemed because of the unity of outlook they postulated between Catholicism and royalism.

It is well known that wherever the missionaries have been, God and the King have more faithful servants, that there is less disposition to opposition, to discontent, to complaints; that there people are more given to order and submission. These happy effects disrupt the advance of the liberals, and that is why their newspapers have recently been struggling against the missions. That there are no priests in the countryside is not, in the eyes of those gentlemen, a major misfortune. The peasantry will be only more easy to mislead. Instead, they will be sent *père Michel* to endoctrinate them; as in 1789, pamphlets will be circulated against the nobles and the priests, and thus the seeds of Revolution will be sown.[61]

The prefect in May, 1819, noted the community of interests between those who were the most active supporters of the missions and the ultras: they were often one and the same person.[62] Certainly the missions did not conceal their propaganda functions. At the end of one religious ceremony, the presiding priest was greeted with cries of "Vive la croix! Vive le roi!"[63] At a cross-planting, one of those ceremonies which covered the squares and roads of nineteenth-century France with wayside crucifixes, the congregation intoned:

Venez français, le Dieu dont la puissance
Fait triompher et le trône et la foi,
Vient aujourd'hui qu'on chante dans la France
Gloire au Très-Haut, vive notre bon roi!
Vive la France! Vive le Roi!
Toujours en France,
Les Bourbons et la Foi![64]

The mission of 1826 showed its own direct form of reducing the numbers of seditious books in circulation by burning in a public

[60] *EM*, July 29, 1826.
[61] *AR*, August 29, 1818.
[62] *AN*, F⁷9659.
[63] *AR*, January 23, 1819.
[64] *AR*, May 17, 1819.

ceremony five hundred volumes of Rousseau and Voltaire, those apostles of disorder and unbelief, to the great satisfaction of the *Echo*.[65]

Atheism, the principal product of *philosophes* of the eighteenth century in the opinion of the ultras, was a cause of the Revolution and thus of liberalism. The *Ami du Roi* cited the cries against God and religion which were heard at Toulouse during the Hundred Days as an example of this.[66] Religion was the panacea which could cure the disease of atheism. The abbé Salvan looked to missions and the foundation of a community of Notre Dame de L'Espérance for the revivification of royalist sentiment, and the *Ami du Roi* thundered in amazement that the liberals should represent the Revolution as a time of regeneration. French youth should be protected against such wicked and irreligious ideas.[67] Indeed, it was clear that too much rationalism was bad; emotionalism was a basis of politics as faith was of religion.

Besides institutions, laws, and doctrines, sentiment is also necessary to a people. The politician calculates, judges, makes combinations: the people feels. It is necessary to teach it to feel strongly what is just, good, agreeable: it is as important to touch its heart as to persuade its reason.[68]

The *philosophes* had been excessively rationalistic while the progress they described was really disorder. The same could be said of those elements of the Old Regime which the liberals approved of, like Gallicanism: "The friends of liberty pushed the liberties of the gallican church so far that they wanted to separate it from the center of unity."[69] The religion of Charlemagne, Clovis, Saint Louis, and Henri IV should not be distorted by the attacks of "apprentice philosophers." Manavit, who was a bookseller specialising in religious and ultraroyalist tracts as well as the editor of the *Ami* and *Echo*, was enthusiastic about the new work of abbé Lammenais, *Essai sur l'indifférence* (1817). He published extracts from it in January, 1818, and subsequently was loud in appreciation of the

[65] *EM*, June 20, 1826.
[66] *AR*, January 23, 1819.
[67] Abbé Salvan, "Mon temps, 1814–1826," Mss. 1149, *BMT*; *AR*, July 21, 1818.
[68] *EM*, January 11, 1822.
[69] *AR*, January 8, 1819.

Paris newspaper, the *Mémorial* (1824–30), which was an exponent of the ideas of Lammenais.[70]

God would save a sinful world through the church, the missions, and on the local level through the confraternities which were re-established during the Empire. These pious associations with their secret meetings, signs, and ritual costumes had a persistent fascination for the people of southern France. In a sense, these confraternities and penitential associations were a blueprint for the royalist plots and groups active during the Revolution and Empire, the most famous of which was the *chevaliers de la foi*, whose strength was largely southern.

For the ultras, the Revolution was above all an attack on the family. Had not the Revolution executed Louis XVI, the father of his people? The family, the basic unit of society, produced and conditioned children or, as Bonald put it, conserved them. The mother was particularly responsible for initial education of children; enveloped in the folds of her skirts, children would learn the basic principles of Christianity and obedience. However, the teaching of children had to take place on a wider scale, beyond the family, and a system had to be devised to prepare children for their place in society. The ultras looked to the educational system to prepare children not only in culture and crafts, but also to train them to a world of ordered duty and repose.[71] They feared, and did not understand, the attraction of revolutionary violence to the young, although some could remember the excitement generated during the Terror. If children and the young renounced established ways, this was a consequence of laxness on the part of the parents (so ran the accepted wisdom of the ultras), and only by enforcing discipline more strictly could this social turbulence be brought under control. This was the duty of education: to indoctrinate and control the young.

The Toulouse ultras, as elsewhere, suspected the liberals of trying to perpetuate social agitation by education. The *Ami du Roi* attacked the liberal journal, *La Minerve*, for an article on new educational methods. These innovations produced dissatisfaction with the social position into which the individual was born, thus causing an upset in the hierarchy of professions. Continuous strife resulted;

[70] *AR*, January 29, 1818.
[71] Raymond Deniel, *Une image de la famille et de la société sous la Restauration, 1815–1830* (Paris, 1965), pp. 147–99.

and since all individuals could think themselves suitable to command, none wanted to obey.[72] This education in the manner of Rousseau and Voltaire did worse than to make the common people disdain useful trades: it spoiled them. Naive and ignorant servants were preferable to those with education; it was the "good, ignorant peasants" who saved the landowners during the Revolution, while the educated—the doctors and school teachers—denounced them to the Revolutionary authorities.[73] But education, by which was meant religious instruction, was needed to end the rapidly rising crime rate.[74] The ultras held firm to the commonplace of the eighteenth century that religious education was necessary to keep the people obediently in their place. The *Echo du Midi* cited approvingly the letter of Mgr. Frayssinous, Grand Master of the University, circulated soon after his appointment on June 1, 1822, which proclaimed that morality and religion were more important to education than literary and scientific pursuits, and that in consequence the clergy should be closely involved with teaching establishments.[75] Certainly the landowners saw little need for educated, overly-forward commoners. Half a century later, Pariset cited local landowners who argued that education would only take people from the land and, therefore, that peasants should be discouraged from studying. In both town and country it was hoped that the lower classes would remain docile; all they needed was a smattering of religious instruction and the rudiments of literacy.

Not everybody in the city subscribed to this view about education. In a speech of 1824, the moderate liberal Malaret, a former mayor of the city during the Empire and president of the Academy of Sciences of Toulouse, attacked the idea that education could corrupt or cause discontent among the lower classes. While he believed universal education could only have beneficial effects, instruction should be grounded in monarchical and religious principles. A year later he was again defending religion for its social utility: it was the most powerful of civilizing forces which produced "respect on earth for these indispensable inequalities which will later disappear before the majesty of the Eternal One."

The Brothers of the Christian Doctrine, better known as *igno-*

[72] *AR*, November 14, 1818.
[73] *AR*, October 13, 1818.
[74] *AR*, August 1, 1818.
[75] *EM*, July 22, 1822.

rantins, were especially involved in primary education in the city. They first established their schools there, with the help of rich patrons, in 1784. The Ursulines had a school for girls. In the villages, the *régent* or *régentes* provided instruction. These schools were broken up by the revolutionary disruption of the educational system. With the return of order, the *ignorantins* returned to primary education in March, 1803, with 360 children in their classes. Portalis, the *conseil général*, and the municipality of Toulouse all called for religious and submissive primary education, and the *ignorantins* soon expanded the numbers admitted to their lessons. The municipality of 1808 was pleased that a free school for girls, located in the *maisons de charité*, had been very successful, and requested the brothers to provide a similar service for boys, such moral instruction being especially useful to the indigent after a Revolution which had destroyed all social bonds. As a result, each of the eleven brothers who taught in the four *arrondissements* was voted a lump sum of 600 francs.[76] The number of *ignorantins* increased in the department after the establishment of a noviciate, and it was hoped that schools could be started in each *chef-lieu d'arrondissement*, and eventually in each *chef-lieu* of the cantons.[77] During the Restoration, there was no change in outlook. The prefect called for an increase in the number of *ignorantins* in the city from eleven to fifteen, which soon ensued, and the brothers were praised for their excellent work in ensuring that public institutions of learning were run on religious, monarchical, and moral lines.[78] In 1823, the *conseil général* offered an incentive of 6,000 francs to the first commune which provided lodgings and an operating budget of 2,000 francs to run an *ignorantin* school, in order that the benefits which Toulouse enjoyed could be appreciated elsewhere. Since the order of the Christian Doctrine had so prominent a place in local primary education, the granting of the power to bishops in March, 1824, to license primary teachers was not of particular significance to the city. In the autumn of that year, the Toulouse schools contained some 800 pupils, and 400 in the "petites classes." The chevalier Dumège estimated in 1829 *ignorantin* enrolment at 1,300 chil-

[76] Register, *AMT*, July 11, 1807.
[77] *AN*, F^{1c}V, (Garonne, Haute-) 2.
[78] *AN*, BB^{3}238 (dossier 4).

dren.[79] What this system lacked in speeding up the acquisition of literacy in the department was compensated for by its good propaganda work. Among the army recruits of 1828, only half could read or write, but those who could do so showed excellent sentiments: "Vive Charles X! Vive le Roi quand même! Vive le Roi et les Bourbons!" These recruits, noted the *Echo du Midi*, had been isolated from irreligion and revolutionary doctrines: "The majority of the young people about whom we are speaking belong to the poorer classes of society, where the spirit of Revolution has perhaps made the least progress."[80]

The *ignorantins* and their supporters were hostile to rival methods of education. The system of mutual instruction, where older pupils taught younger ones, called the Lancastrian system, was particularly suspect, because it did not sufficiently emphasize the authoritarian aspects of the submissive child obeying the teacher. Such a school was founded on All Saint Day, 1819, under the direction of Mme Blanc and under the patronage of the poet Alexandre Soumet; MM. Echaux and Charrière were in the official protection of the prefect, mayor, and rector of the Academy. The children were to learn French and Latin grammar, some arithmetic, geometry and other branches of mathematics, drawing and architecture, geography, and ancient and modern history. Religious instruction was to be given by the parish curés.[81] It soon became apparent that the last named were very hostile to the new schools, which had little success. In 1829, the system was revivified with the establishment of free schools of mutual instruction, but this time it was much more clear that the most noted liberal personalities of Toulouse were involved, like Romiguières, lieutenant-general Cassagne, de Tauriac, Pagès, and Malpel. The list of patrons was enough to damn this "Protestant" experiment in the eyes of the ultras.[82]

The secondary system was more complex, for only the children of the rich and well-born attended these schools, together with a number of scholarship boys. Their primary education was provided at home by tutors or by a local curé. Before the Revolution, the children of such families were in the care of teaching orders like

[79] *EM*, September 15, 1824; A.L.C.A. Dumège, *Statistique générale des départements pyrénéens* (Paris, 1828–29), II, 531.
[80] *EM*, July 29, 1828.
[81] *JPLT*, January 19, 1820.
[82] *Le Moniteur*, February 18, 1829.

the Oratorians or the Benedictine fathers at Sorèze. The Revolution smashed this clerical system, and when Napoleon re-established the secondary system, it seemed to the ultras that the new *lycées* were more like barracks than peaceful places of spiritual and cultural development. Moreover, the clergy was decimated by age and by the effects of the Revolution; few new priests could be consecrated, or were suitable to provide teaching. After the fall of Napoleon, it was clear that it was important to reconstitute the *lycée* as the *collège royal*, to re-establish a second college as a *petit séminaire*, the *Esquile*, and to enlarge the seminaries, if the ultra aims in education were to be put into practice.[83] Many of the most prominent ultras in the city (such as Villèle and the advocate Pinaud) had attended the *collège royal* before 1789, and this heightened their awareness of the need for reforms. The staff seemed more than amenable to this royalist outlook; during the Hundred Days, a number of teachers had refused the oath of submission to the Emperor and had been dismissed.[84] The staff in charge of the seminaries had even stronger ultra enthusiasms, and they instructed both future priests and youths who did not intend to take orders. In June, 1814, ecclesiastical schools had been separated from the surveillance of the *Université*, and in February, 1821, privileges accorded to the *collèges royaux* were granted to private schools. All this permitted ultra influence on education to increase rapidly.

This was shown in the very selection of pupils, especially in those places not subject to the nomination by the Minister of Public Instruction. There was a continuous dispute over the number of places to be made available and over the amount of scholarships to be paid; since the scholarships were given out in part by the municipal council, this was an obvious form of patronage and encouragement to deserving ultra families.[85] However, there were signs that the youth of Toulouse did not live up to the pious expectations of their ultra sponsors. Apart from the usual boarding school scandals over mores and general discipline, the *collège royal* was disturbed by political controversy. The *surveillant* Laserre arrived in the dormitory one night to find two pupils in their nightshirts fighting and pulling hair, and as he tried to separate the belligerents, he heard the awful words: "The King is a Pig! Yes! Yes! He

[83] *AN*, F1cV, (Garonne, Haute-) 2.
[84] *AN*, F79055.
[85] *ADHG*, 2 T 19.

is so!" Two other boys were also suspected of subversive opinions
and all three were expelled.[86] The mother of one of the pupils reported that, among the adolescents at the *lycée*, were *monstres* who
rejoiced at the news of the assassination of the duc de Berry by
Louvel.[87] Later in 1820, abbé Ferrouil de Montgaillard, the new
proviseur at the college, called on the boys to emulate a former
student in their institution, Villèle. Prize-giving ceremonies, church
sermons, and lessons in French history, were all used to drive home
the need for loyalty to the Restoration and the Bourbons. One historian of the school suggested that this conspicuous loyalty and
religiosity were partially a defense against clerical interference in
the running of the establishment. But it is hardly surprising that
the boys took revenge in playing tricks on one teacher, the indefatigable M. Viguier, who was particularly assiduous in searching
for subversion under every dormitory bed and who corresponded
with Villèle on the subject of the necessary reforms.

The University of Toulouse, founded in 1229, was a source of
pride to the city, although it had fallen away from its earlier academic distinction by the end of the Old Regime and had become
essentially a technical school with faculties of Law, Theology,
Medicine, and Arts. There was more intellectual innovation and
enquiry in the *Académie des Jeux Floraux*, the *Lanternistes*, and the
Academy of Science than in the lecture halls of the university.
On the other hand, although not endowed with funds, the university gave a stimulus to the town economy through the expenditures
of the student body. Like the Parlement, it was suppressed during
the Revolution, although some higher education continued in a
truncated form in the *Institut Paganel* from 1794 to 1796, and subsequently in the *Ecole Centrale* from 1796 to 1804. A number of
university professors taught in the new establishments, and some
students remained in the city, like the young Ingres who studied
art and made money on the side by playing in the orchestra of the
municipal theatre located in the *Capitole*. There was a marked
decrease in the contribution of the higher learning to the purses of
the inhabitants of Toulouse.

The University was re-established under the Empire in the form
of separate faculties. The Law School was established with five

[86] Gaston Martin, *Le lycée de Toulouse de 1763 à 1881* (Toulouse, 1930),
pp. 39–40.
[87] AV, Mme de Villèle to Joseph de Villèle, February 21, 1820.

chairs in 1804 and became a faculty in 1808; the Imperial School of Surgery and Medicine dated from 1806 (and became a secondary school in 1820); the Faculty of Letters, the Faculty of Sciences, the Faculty of Catholic Theology, and the Faculty of Protestant Theology completed the organisation which took form between 1808 and 1810. This whole structure was under the care of the Rector of the Academy, who was responsible for primary, secondary, and higher education. The language of instruction was French; the area served by the Academy was four departments.

The structure remained essentially unchanged during the Restoration, although the innovations which affected the universities in general, like the appointment of Frayssinous and the increase in clerical influence, had their impact on the situation in Toulouse. The staff of the faculties was close to the noble and royalist circles in the city, especially in the Law Faculty, heavily influenced by the robe traditions of the city. Professor at the law faculty Jamme and the rectors of the academy between 1809 and 1830, de Ferrand-Puginier and Larrouy, were all ultras. (A priest, Maurice Ranc, served during the Hundred Days.) The secretary-general Batbèze and dean of the Faculty of Law Bastoulh held the same outlook.[88] Jean Ruffat, an advocate and doctor of law at the Parlement, was appointed professor of Law in May, 1816, and a municipal councillor in the same month. His father Barthelémy had also been a university professor, and his mother was imprisoned during the Terror. He taught Montbel, the future minister of Charles X. He was appointed *econome* of the *collège royal* because of the purity of his ultra principles.[89] In 1824, he delivered a eulogy of Clemence Isaure at the *Jeux Floraux*, in which he praised the Duchesse d'Angoulême for upholding "the precepts of a charitable and consoling religion too long put in question by the ravages of skepticism" and throughout the Restoration he was an exponent of ultra ideas. In 1830, he was dismissed from his chair and remained an important Carlist until his death in 1842.[90]

One of the inspectors of the Toulouse Academy, the advocate L.-A. Decampe, was very critical of university students. In 1816, he became a member of the *Jeux Floraux*, and described the Midi as

[88] *L'Université de Toulouse 1229–1929* (Toulouse, 1929), passim.
[89] *AN*, F1b, (Garonne, Haute-) 26; A. Brémond, *Annales du XIXe siècle de la ville de Toulouse de 1800 à 1850* (Toulouse, 1865), p. 90.
[90] *EM*, May 7, 1824; *ADHG*, 4 M 48.

"keeping the sentiments of the past for the blood of its masters."[91] In 1820, he was appointed a member of the Toulouse censorship commission.[92] The best summary of his views was a pamphlet under the title: *Considérations sur l'état actuel des moeurs de la jeunesse française et sur les moyens d'améliorer l'esprit de celle qui doit lui succéder* (1822). He argued that the irreligious and immoral influences of the Napoleonic era were still present in the French university in the form of Napoleonic appointments, and that this spirit infected the university students. The prefect in 1816 also thought the half-pay officers had an ascendancy on some members of that faculty who had showed themselves hostile to the extremism of the *verdets*.[93] On the other hand, the eight to nine hundred students in the law school spent more time in the theatre than in the lecture hall and enjoyed cheering whatever they construed as political allusions in plays. The rest of the time, they tended to be occupied with the excursions, love-affairs, and duels which Etienne de Jouy thought to be their habitual concerns.[94] Decampe and others were very suspicious of student radicalism, and constantly stressed the need for good political principles, as in Decampe's *Eloge historique de Louis XVIII* (1826). He was appointed rector of the *Académie de Lyon* towards the end of the Restoration, but during the July Monarchy he returned to Toulouse where he was suspected as an influential Carlist, closely associated with the abbé Berger who had been a founder of the *Société des Bonnes Etudes*.[95] These staff members hoped for the re-establishment of a decentralized system of universities, with at least a degree of autonomy preserved from the Napoleonic system. They nostalgically described earlier times when the university was responsible for keeping order and was part of the structure of local independence. The Faculty organized competitions for the selection of its own staff, in collaboration with the presidents of the Royal Court, and suggested candidates for other Faculties of Law, for example, Poitiers. Three additional chairs in the Faculty of Law were created during the Restoration to increase the number of professors.[96] The five who

[91] *AR*, August 31, 1818.
[92] Ordonnance royale, April 1, 1820.
[93] *AG*, D³90, Liger-Belair to Minister of War, April 11, 1822.
[94] Etienne de Jouy, *L'Hermite en Province* (Paris, 1818–27).
[95] *ADHG*, 4 M 48; papers in J150.
[96] *AN*, F¹ᶜV (Garonne, Haute-) 2.

were initially appointed were overburdened with a very heavy load of teaching. In 1805, Toulouse had the second largest law faculty in France. The Law School in particular was hard hit by the Revolution of 1830; almost half of the teaching staff refused to take the oath of allegiance to the House of Orleans and subsequently were dismissed. Moreover, the university authorities suspected continuously the Law Faculty of Carlist sympathies during the Monarchy of July.[97]

The virtues of these ultra ideas and institutions were self-evident, at least to the *supériorités sociales,* and were passed on to the young by the educational system. Other vehicles of propaganda and discussion existed in Restoration Toulouse. The most important was the *Académie des Jeux Floraux,* claimed to be the oldest academy in Europe. The religious confraternities and penitential associations, the *Société des Bonnes Etudes,* and the more informal gatherings in particular cafés like that of the Place Rouaix made up the social context of Toulousain ultraroyalist propaganda in addition to the individual salons like that of Mme D'Hargicourt.

The *Jeux Floraux* flourished before the Revolution and was the main support of the claim of Toulouse to be "la cité palladienne." The academy grouped local poets and *savants,* many of whom were parlementarians. To this extent, it was typical of southern academies.[98] Advocates with literary ambitions were well represented. One of them was Barère de Vieuzac, later a member of the Committee of Public Safety. Pre-revolutionary *mainteneurs* included clerics and higher magistrates, but only two doctors, one painter, and one banker had held the office.[99] Suspended during the Revolution, the Academy reopened during the Empire, and in 1806 included a number of members from the Old Regime. From 1806 to 1814 the Academy celebrated Napoleon in verse and prose, but made a great show of royalist emotion at the first Restoration. Certainly the number of prominent ultras like Hocquart, Pinaud, Montbel, and Rességuier suggests that association with the academy was a positive recommendation to the Bourbons, although the succes-

[97] *L'Université de Toulouse 1229–1929,* pp. 127–28.
[98] D. Roche, "Milieux académiques provinciaux et société des lumières," in *Livre et Société au XVIII siècle* (Paris, 1966), 93–184.
[99] Axel Duboul, *Les deux siècles de l'Académie des Jeux Floraux* (Toulouse, 1901), I, 72–74.

sion of *sécrétaires perpetuels* showed some variation in political opinion.

Serres de Colombars, known as a cultivated and pious man and "an excellent royalist" before the Restoration, was dismissed during the Hundred Days. He called for legitimist writers to publicize the ultra view of society and politics.[100] Candidates for prizes in 1819 were encouraged to uphold the taste for study, work, and good principles.[101] The various eulogies, *remerciements*, and *résponse au remerciement* given at membership ceremonies provided frequent opportunities for public declarations of ultra principles. Much literature submitted to the Academy had legitimist themes, like the odes of the adolescent Victor Hugo on the re-establishment of the statue of Henri IV or the Virgins of Verdun.

The desire to spread ultraroyalist ideas was behind the foundation of a *Société des Bonnes Etudes* in 1823, in imitation of that of Paris. The opening ceremonies were attended by the prefect, the commander of the military division, the mayor of the city, the rector of the academy, and the archbishop of Toulouse, in an impressive display of 'official favor toward the new enterprise. The society intended to provide lectures on Roman and French law as related to public morality and institutions, literature, philosophy, physiology, and other subjects. Abbé Berger was the main organizer, helped by Pinaud, at this time the *sécrétaire perpetuel* of the *Jeux Floraux* and a councilor at the Royal Court; de Lartigue, who was vice-président of the *tribunal civil*; two university professors, Ruffat and Delpech; a philosophy teacher, Saurimont; and Decampe.[102]

Decampe, discussed above, delivered a speech on eighteenth-century philosophy, which he characterised under "three hideous heads"—atheism, materialism, and sovereignty of the people.[103] His speech attacking the consequences of such ideas was often interrupted by enthusiastic members of the audience leaping to their feet with shouts of "Vive le Roi!" Young Maxime de Roquette, writing to his friend, the son of Villèle, said that the meeting was "the most brilliant religious and monarchical ceremony which has

[100] J. A. L. A. Serres de Colombars, "Eloge de Clémence Isaure prononcé dans la séance du 3 mai 1816...," *Recueil des Jeux Floraux* (Toulouse, 1817), p. 8.

[101] *AR*, January 19, 1819.

[102] *Annuaire de la Haute-Garonne* (Toulouse, 1824), pp. 245–47. J. Fourcassié, *Une ville à l'époque romantique* (Paris, 1953), p. 239.

[103] *EM*, March 14, 1823; *AN*, F⁷6696; *JPLT*, April 24, 1823.

ever taken place in Toulouse." He went on to say in his obsequious style that the subject of the new society was on every lip in the conversation in the archepiscopal and prefectural salons.[104]

The society enjoyed substantial success for some time. It was divided into three sections: jurisprudence, medicine, and literature and philosophy, each with its own director and secretary as well as a *maître de conférences*. The council, its founders, and others associated with the society represented the epitomy of pious ultra society.[105] Such topics were discussed as Lammennais's doctrine of evidence, why sovereignty of the people inevitably leads to absolute despotism, and the need for intervention in Spain. While some ultraroyalist literary figures in Toulouse (for example, the Marquis d'Aguilar, member of the *Jeux Floraux*) argued against the innovative mania which was destroying the classic standards of French literature set in the century of Louis XIV, those involved in the *Société des Bonnes Etudes* were more sympathetic to romantic emotion. "Happy he who touches the heart-strings . . . and who impresses youth by the warmth of sentiment with the lessons of morality and fidelity."[106] Victor Hugo described the "excellent M. Pinaud." Olmade, an ultraroyalist *chef de division* at the city hall, was also a supporter of literary romanticism. The society published a *Journal de la religion et des bonnes etudes* which gave a prominent place to poetry, publishing the work of Jules de Rességuier and Alexandre Soumet. A committee was established in January, 1825, in cooperation with the *Jeux Floraux*, to encourage and assist deserving publications.[107]

Even the medical section of the society was able to acknowledge publicly its ultra outlook. It asked whether the study of medicine necessarily led to materialism, observing that if this was indeed the case the healing arts would have to be suppressed, since they were less vital to the social organization than true principles.[108]

A remarkable feature of the ultraroyalist newspapers and societies was the very slight attention paid to the commercial and industrial groups in France. De Maistre and others produced an eco-

[104] AV, Maxime de Roquette-Buisson to Henri de Villèle, April 22, 1823; May 31, 1823.
[105] EM, August 6, 8, 1823.
[106] EM, June 4, 1823.
[107] JPLT, January 26, 1825; Joseph Dédieux, "Le romantisme à Toulouse," *Les annales romantiques*, X, 1913, 1–26.
[108] EM, August 15, 1823.

167

nomic explanation of the origins of the Revolution in ascribing it to the machinations of financiers who sought immoral profits from the manipulation of state capital, aided by the *philosophes* and the irreligious. There was a potential distinction between the honest artisan and manufacturer on one hand and the capitalist who gained wealth through speculation on the other. The financiers had interests at variance with the former. The *Mémorial* described the pillage of wealthy merchants in Mexico City in 1829 as an object lesson of how revolutions could backfire:

In France also there exists in the so respectable class of bankers, merchants, and manufacturers of all kinds men who await, if they do not assist, a new revolution. May the appalling reports of the misfortunes of Mexico, of the disasters of the capitalists and businessmen of that unfortunate city, open their eyes finally, and prevent them from plunging into the revolutionary abyss and dragging us with them![109]

The ultras saw that the French Revolution had caused serious dislocation of credit and business.

This tacit criticism of business was tempered by two features of local ultraroyalism. One of these was a sense of regional interests best expressed by the Toulouse Agricultural Society. The other was the appreciation of the extent to which agricultural prosperity was related to industrial activity and strong consumer demand for its products.

The Agricultural Society (Société d'agriculture de la Haute-Garonne), met for the first time in its modern form on July 8, 1798, with twenty-three members. The Society attracted the most able and interested farmers of the region, and constantly increased the number of members. In 1817, there were 145 members and a further 69 corresponding members. The latter included the Duke of Wellington, the librarian of the Madrid botanical gardens, and other foreign agronomists. The Society regularly published a *Journal des Propriétaires ruraux des départements du Midi* which had a wide circulation. Even more than the *Jeux Floraux*, the Society was a forum for prominent local ultras: Marcassus-Puymaurin, d'Escouloubre, Louis de Villeneuve, Villèle the elder and his son, Reversat de Marsac, Chalvet de Rochemonteix, Bruno and Armand Dubourg, Limairac, Ricard, Hocquart, and Rességuier were all members. It

---

[109] *Mémorial de Toulouse, journal politique, littéraire, commercial . . . dédié à tous les amis de la réligion et de la monarchie*, March 5, 1829.

would be wrong to suggest that all model farmers were ultra— Baron Malaret and Picot de Lapeyrouse, excellent farmers, former mayors of Toulouse and both known as liberals, cooperated well with royalist colleagues on the neutral ground of agricultural interests. Malaret was president of the Society for some years and constantly hammered home the theme that Southern agriculture needed to be put on a commercial footing. At the session of June 24, 1827, attended by Hocquart, Baron de Raynaud, "the most distinguished people of the city, and especially many ladies," Malaret called for an end to the excessive reliance on wheat growing in the Toulousain and added: "Landowners must think of themselves as manufacturers and adopt those means of prosperity which are applicable to all industrial enterprises."[110] The ultras were open to a measure of self-criticism on matters of agricultural technique. The *Conseil Général* constantly regretted the backwardness of farming methods used in the Haute-Garonne, the poor course of crop rotations, the lack of pasture, the rare cultivation of rootcrops and poor quality livestock." Wine was bad in an area believed capable of an excellent product, the use of fertilizers was scarcely appreciated, deforestation was going on, and *métayage* inhibited tenants from making improvements in the farms.[111]

The ultras sometimes realized the significance of commercial developments. Villèle's kinsman Montbel took the initiative to encourage local commerce when he was mayor of Toulouse, and in 1827 he organized an exhibition of industrial products at the town hall. Such exhibitions in France dated from the series which took place in Paris between 1798 and 1806. In 1819, a royal ordinance called for an exhibition in the capital every four years. Various provincial cities imitated this project: the Toulouse exhibition followed the examples of Caën, Rennes, Nantes, and Lyon. A series of articles in the *Echo* emphasized the importance to Toulouse, "this metropolis of the Midi, so well placed for commerce and industry," to show awareness of technology that brought prosperity to the English. These views were placed in a political context, as when the editorialist asked if the partisans of old ideas in politics need necessarily find themselves at loggerheads with the supporters of innovation even on questions of machinery.[112] Toulouse had to show

110 *EM*, June 26, 1827.
111 Godoffre, *Conseil général . . . déliberations*, I, 511.
112 *EM*, May 31, 1827.

herself receptive to new industrial ideas if she was not to fall too far behind other parts of France.

Montbel put considerable support behind the campaign to state the need for more technical education. He praised the night-school course given by a young architect, Urbain Vitry. This course would help the city advance in "the great industrial movement of our era," and the future was bright for southern France and for Toulouse in particular:

Far from the riches brought to the capital by massive consumer demand, held back, perhaps, by the memory of some local institutions, our progress has been less rapid. But this is the period when, learning to utilize its immense resources, the Midi will be able to rival the North in industrial advantages.[113]

The nightschool course was attended by "heads of businesses, manufacturers, and ordinary workers" who appreciated that scientific knowledge would deliver them from the burdens of routine and prejudice. Apparently, Vitry's teaching did not fall on deaf ears; in December, 1827, a prospectus appeared, describing a publication which was to appear in the following year: *Le propagateur des procédés industriels dans le Midi de la France*. This newssheet of new techniques was to be produced by an association of "manufacturers, industrial artists and scientists of Toulouse" and subscriptions were solicited.[114] Once again, the persistent sluggishness of Toulouse in commercial and manufacturing initiatives seems to have manifested itself. There is no trace of the appearance of the newssheet in the city, presumably because no support was forthcoming. In the conversations and correspondence of the ultras, in the speeches by the Haute-Garonne deputies, and in the columns of the ultraroyalist newspapers of the city, it was the interests of the landowners which excited the greatest response.

[113] *EM*, December 31, 1827.
[114] *Ibid.*

VIII

THE JULY REVOLUTION
AND LEGITIMISM IN TOULOUSE

ONCE ESTABLISHED, the July Monarchy carried out a sweeping renewal of administrative personnel in Toulouse and the department. Only one of the senior officials of the prefecture remained, the *conseil général* and the *conseil d'arrondissement* were entirely renewed, 412 mayors and 358 *adjoints* were replaced, the justices of the peace were changed in large numbers, and so were the compositions of the various courts. Two of the three *receveurs particuliers*, the departmental *payeur*, two *receveurs principaux*, *the receveur* of the hospitals, the officer of weights-and-measures, major officials and subordinates in the customs, municipal departments of the *octroi* and the public works, and nine of the police *commissaires* were dismissed. The purge extended even to the municipal library and the observatory.[1] The web of patronage woven during the period of ultra dominance was torn apart. The new prefect was understandably indignant at an accusation brought up in the Chamber of Deputies that Toulouse was still largely under the control of legitimist officials: he retorted that there was probably no other city in France where so many dismissals had been made of those who might obstruct official business.

The victims of these dismissals, together with the majority of the local nobility, became supporters of legitimism. D'Encausse, a relative of Villèle and a *commissaire du roi à l'hôtel de monnaie*, dismissed in 1830, was among the "sommités légitimistes." Delpy, the *secrétaire général* at the prefecture throughout the Restoration

[1] *ADHG*, 4 M 49; Prefect to Minister of Interior, August 30, 1831.

whose initial appointment had been made by Angoulême in 1815, was another. Bastoulh, former *procureur du roi*, was a well-known legitimist. The advocates Dugabé and Bahuhaut were members of a legal-aid organization. Men protected by tenure in the courts, for example, Moly, also made no secret of their legitimist sympathies. The legitimists were reinforced by the retirement to Toulouse of men who had been army officers or officials elsewhere in France before July 1830 and who remained loyal to the former dynasty. Pinaud returned to Toulouse from Grenoble, where he had been *procureur du roi*. St. Félix Mauremont, a former prefect and deputy, and Puységur, an officer of the royal guard, arrived back in Toulouse. The leadership of the legitimists was drawn from the familiar parlementary families; names like Rességuier, d'Aguin, Rigaud, Cantalause, and Dubourg appear in police reports and in the columns of the *Gazette du Languedoc*, the legitimist newspaper published in the city. Naturally enough, Joseph de Villèle was considered the elder statesman of the partisans of Charles X, although he had disapproved of the maladroit policies of the Polignac ministry. Popular royalism had weakened during the Restoration, but there were legitimists among the artisans and former *verdets*.

Opinions were divided among those who wanted to see Louis-Philippe replaced on the throne. The older men and the émigrés— crusty veterans of the counterrevolution—could not bring themselves to abandon the brother of Louis XVI; to them, the chain of disasters which Charles X had brought on French royalism, from Quiberon to the July ordinances, seemed to have a pathetic grandeur. They hoped for his return to the throne. The majority looked to the young Henri V. Such a regime would maintain the achievements of the Restoration in parliamentary government without continuing the trend towards liberalism; above all, it would give a different tone to public life and reward the faithful servants of the Bourbons. The police thought this view was especially favored by commoner legitimists. Among the nobles, a third opinion prevailed, that of the "Henriquinquistes absolutistes." This was the conviction that the Restoration failed because of too much liberalism, and the belief that the regency would provide the opportunity for an increase in noble power.[2]

[2] *ADHG*, 4 M 49; police reports. Jeanne Lesparre, "Les partis politiques en Haute-Garonne sous la monarchie de juillet" in J. L. Godechot, ed., *La Révolution de 1848 à Toulouse* (Toulouse, 1848), pp. 31–40.

During the autumn following the proclamation of Louis-Philippe as king, the legitimists began to set up an organization to direct their opposition to the new regime. Like the *Institut Philanthropique* which had been in operation during the Directory and the *chevaliers de la foi* who conspired during the last years of the Napoleonic Empire, the *association légitimiste* used a charitable and religious motive as a pretexte for its existence. During the Restoration, the point was often made that the Bourbons and the Faith were at one. The emotion-packed meetings of the evangelizing missionaries and the pastoral letters of the Cardinal Archbishop Clermont-Tonnerre exalted the union of throne and altar. In a city noted for religiosity among the women and devout lower classes, this still had its political utility. However, the new archbishop of Toulouse under the July Monarchy, d'Astros, despite his personal sympathies to the former dynasty, made it clear to his clergy that they were to keep out of politics.[3]

The *association légitimiste* was established by April, 1831. The central coordinating committee was called the *Grand Prieuré*. Toulouse was the headquarters for an area extending over five departments: the Tarn, Gers, Ariège, Tarn-et-Garonne and the Haute-Garonne.[4] The other regional centers in southern France were at Bordeaux, Lyons, Marseilles, and Nîmes. In Toulouse, it was reported that 150 men had titles as civil and military officials, and the total number of adherents was said to be between one thousand and twelve hundred. These figures and details of organization were provided by the police. French historians have recently received a powerful warning from R. C. Cobb against taking the reports of time-serving professional police officers too literally. At any event, these reports provide a genuine insight into the world of "it is rumored that" which, in a tense political situation, has its own reality. There was doubtless some kind of organization. The supreme council of the organization was called the *Grand Prieuré*. It met intermittently either at the town house of Villèle on the Rue Vélane or at that of the Comte d'Hautpoul, the most active member, and implicated in the Ramel assassination of 1815. Delpy, the former *secrétaire général* of the prefecture, and Puylaroque, a

---

[3] P. Droulers, *Action pastorale et problèmes sociaux sous la monarchie de Juillet chez Mgr. d'Astros* (Paris, 1954).

[4] *ADHG*, 4 M 50. The detailed report of November 20, 1833, which came from an informer described the organization of the *Association Légitimiste*.

parlementary noble whose estates were in the area of Montauban but who lived mostly in Toulouse, were among the major figures. Below this high command were *Petits Prieurés* in the *chefs-lieux* of each *arrondissement*. They grouped former officials, nobles, retired soldiers and some merchants, and were responsible for the legitimist organization in their area and the transmission of funds to the *Grand Prieuré*. The police claimed that the *Prieurés* had decided to exclude merchants, but at the same time listed a number of men involved in commerce, like Servat, a merchant involved in supply, a "richissime boulanger," and a pharmacist, as enjoying positions of trust. Vignes, the former city *receveur*, was a member of the *Petit Prieuré*. At the cantonal level, a *commissionnaire de roulage* and a newspaper seller of the *Gazette du Languedoc* were listed as militant supporters of Henri V. Beneath the cantonal organization existed a network of *chefs de quartier*, men like the cabinet-maker Gerbousc, who was responsible for the area around the Jardin des Plantes. The *dizeniers* who collected contributions from individual members reported to them, handing over the contributions which were levied on a daily rate according to means. Indeed, some legitimists at this level received money given to support the legitimist counter-police, needy military men, and officials dismissed in 1830 for whom it had not been possible to find alternative employment with the *Gazette* or elsewhere. The counter-police were said to be a drawing master, a tailor from the Place du Salin, a wigmaker, and a former employee of the *Octroi*, and were led by an employee of a liberal merchant. Funds were also made available to provide a winter allowance of up to eight pounds of bread weekly to needy members of royalist companies. The rank and file of the seven companies of royalist volunteers was composed of "workers and day laborers from Toulouse itself, and from former *verdets*." Legitimism found most support in Toulouse; in the country, there was only a skeleton organization. The *arrondissement* of Muret was the most royalist and St. Gaudens the least royalist of the four in the department, but in general there was little sign of peasant support.

The memory of the bloody failure of the insurrection of the year VII was still alive, and the religious policy of the government was not one which inspired much resistance, except perhaps on the matter of the schools run by the *ignorantins*. The oppressive weight of the system of *métayage* directed by the legitimist landowners did not lend itself to much genuine sympathy on the part of the peasantry, despite their protestations of loyalty. At all events, legitimism in the Toulousain, as elsewhere in the Midi, was mostly urban in nature.

The *Association Légitimiste* was not the only focus of legitimism; indeed, the secrecy with which its acts were shrouded tended to lessen its effects. The masonic lodge *La Sagesse*, on the other hand, was notoriously *Henriquinquiste*. The members were able to cover royalist allusions and wishes with the ceremonial of masonry. Another, more public, forum was the *Société de Défense Mutuelle* which borrowed the ideas which had appeared among liberals during the Restoration. The society was dedicated to the fight against "a centralisation made daily more despotic, which crushes France, chains the provinces, torments the citizens who are ceaselessly delivered to the arbitrariness of a gendarme or a prefect."[5] Legal and practical advice was offered to those who found themselves at odds with the bureaucracy. There were societies in the Tarn-et-Garonne, Tarn, Ariège, Gers, and Haute-Garonne: the area controlled by the *Grand Prieuré* of Toulouse. The secretary Soulé was a neighbor of Villèle on the Rue Vélane. The membership included a rich tailor, a vintner, a clockmaker, several *avocats*, a hatmaker, a former subprefect, and other ex-officials. A legitimist association existed among the students of the University of Toulouse.

Legitimism was strong in the religious confraternities which were typical of the city. The convent school of St. Antoine du Salin was considered the best *Henriquinquiste* education for upper-class girls. The convents of the Compassion, St. Vincent de Paul, and the Feuillantines, if less fashionable, were no less fervent in their attachment to the cause of the exiled Bourbons. The *sociétés de secours* provided jobs for those who were right-thinking. The Confraternity of St. Louis at the St. Exupère church was full of men who had been *verdets* in 1815; the Black Penitents at the Nazareth Church were presided over by Léopold de Rigaud who had been active during the White Terror. The confraternity of the Ste.-Epine boasted among its members Anglaret, a former lieutenant of the *verdets* implicated in the assassination of General Ramel. These confraternities joined the nobility and other legitimists in observing the anniversary of the execution of Louis XVI

---

[5] *Gazette du Languedoc*, January 20, 1832.

on January 21, and of the assassination of the Duc de Berry on February 13. Only rarely did these events cause any political disturbance. The very nature of these lugubrious ceremonies discouraged any active opposition. The police appreciated this and showed little concern about them, although the congregation was often quite large, as on February 13, 1834.[6]

Legitimism was at the root of some scandals within local institutions. The Royal Court was shaken when in August, 1832, Baron Corbière, the former *procureur général* of the court during the Empire (recalled to office by the July Monarchy), took advantage of the law dealing with the presence of witnesses at the time of court hearings and placed Samuel de Panat, a legitimist nobleman from Saint Gaudens, under confinement in Toulouse. Hocquart, the former ultraroyalist deputy who remained First President of the court under Louis-Philippe, was aggrieved at this officious behavior toward his son-in-law de Panat, who had in fact promised to attend the court when called to do so. This affair was aggravated by the publication of a pamphlet by Corbière, entitled *Ma réponse aux cris de M. le Vicomte de Panat.* Hocquart deplored this publication even more than the original affront. In the *Gazette du Languedoc* he described the behavior of the *procureur général* as "a hitherto unheard of way to clarify points at issue between two magistrates, and especially between the chiefs of a high court."[7] The whole incident arose from Corbière's desire to humiliate the legitimist group in the court which excluded him from public office for fifteen years. Tongues wagged furiously in the legitimist salons over this squabble, just as they did later in the same year over a dispute at the *Académie des Jeux Floraux.* A replacement for the seat vacated by Archbishop Clermont-Tonnerre was pushed through early in the meeting and a physics professor was elected. When the legitimist members of the *Académie* arrived and discovered the election had already taken place, there was a heated shouting match and the session was suspended.[8]

This kind of trivial incident did not affect public order. To the legitimists, they seemed to typify the animosity of the Orleanist regime, but they were hardly substantial issues which affected the decisions of the new administration. The *Gazette du Languedoc,*

[6] *ADHG,* 4 M 51, rapport, February 14, 1834.
[7] *ADHG,* 4 M 35; *Gazette du Languedoc, supplément,* December 4, 1832.
[8] *ADHG,* 4 M 49, report to prefect, September 3, 1832.

subtitled the *Journal des intérêts régionaux*, criticized relaxation of the protectionist legislation on grain imports, but this was an issue which only excited the landowners. The attempt to keep the sympathy of the poor by charity continued, but there were new rivals who offered other alternatives to the selfish social policy of the *juste milieu*. The Saint-Simoniens had appeared in the city, and there was now a significant Republican movement such as had not existed under the Restoration. The legitimists of Toulouse made little effort to win new members into their ranks which were dominated in their upper levels by the prejudices of the nobility. The *Gazette du Languedoc* often published sarcastic literary "vignettes" on the vulgarity of "un bal bourgeois," the lack of refinement of the Orléans family, and the gross manners of the *juste milieu*. While this provided self-satisfaction to noble legitimists, it was ill-calculated to win new sympathies.

The legitimists were a classic example of a group so deeply imbued with a set of religious, political, and cultural prejudices as to be unable to adjust to a changing situation. They were frustrated by change and wished it would stop; they were worried by new ideas and political debate. These social fossils tried to ward off the disruption of the society they had dominated by invoking a conspiratorial explanation of French history. They were an opposition which it was not crucial to placate as they progressively isolated themselves from new skills and attitudes. The noble landowners of the Toulousain began to loose their landed wealth as well as their political influence when the great estates began to splinter as a result of rural depopulation from the mid-1840's on. While they had always kept precise records of the process of rack-renting the *métayers* and *maître-valets*, the poor yield of the area showed how little genuine innovation of new methods took place in the first half of the nineteenth century. The English translator of the exceptional farmer Picot de Lapeyrouse, a man with a specialized knowledge of current agricultural techniques, noted that the agriculture of the Garonne Valley was far behind that of other parts of France.[9]

During the Restoration, commerce and industry in Toulouse was too weak to produce a group of wealthy commoners able to fight against the ultra ascendancy. Certainly men like Chaptive, Viguerie,

[9] P. Picot de Lapeyrouse, *The Agriculture of a District in the South of France* (London, 1819), 92; R. Brunet, *Les campagnes toulousaines*, Toulouse, 1965.

177

Barre, and Cassaing were liberal merchants who made plain their hostility to all that was proclaimed by Villèle and his colleagues at the town hall, at the *conseil général*, and among the deputies. They had less access to power than the conservative faction in city business circles—men like Félix Gounon, Duchan, Saint-Raymond, and Ville-Teynier—who sympathized with the Old Regime organization of trade and city government from which their families derived their social position. The presence of a very conservative political opinion among merchant groups was characteristic of many southern cities. In the Eure, one of the most economically advanced parts of France, the rule of local landowners during this period was increasingly opposed by merchants and manufacturers who found an electoral following. The same could be said of Alsace. However, in Toulouse, and to some extent in other southern cities like Montauban and Nîmes where religious frictions played a part, or in Bordeaux, Marseille, and Montpellier where Old Regime families still kept an important place, there was a strong body of conservative opinion in the business elite.

The ultraroyalist views on the nature of society, which had emerged during the Restoration, were crystallized in local legitimism. The animosity against the rejecters of traditional values intensified. The Revolution of 1830 seemed yet another confirmation of ultraroyalists' suspicions of the big cities, bureaucrats, and speculators. They despised "this Parisian bourgeoisie, composed of shopkeepers and jackals [*loup-cerviers*] on whom the salvation of the *juste-milieu* has so often depended."[10] In a long article praising Villèle, the *Gazette* wrote in the same vein:

There will be neither rest, prosperity, nor order in this land for as long as society is led by men of letters and advocates. Men of letters govern their little republic very ill . . . as for the advocates, vain chatterers, they bristle with difficulties and are full of disputes and chicanery. Nothing can succeed with them. The restored France will wish to be led by its natural leaders [*les grandes influences*]: men of the soil, of war, of the magistrature, of the priesthood, and by large-scale industry, the only realities of a well-organised social order.[11]

The suspicion of the advocates which the parlementarians had voiced in 1789, the blame attached to the *philosophes* for causing

[10] *Gazette du Languedoc*, January 5, 1836.
[11] *Gazette du Languedoc*, January 25, 1836.

social disturbance, the hostility to centralization, the conviction that it was Protestants, Jacobins, and Napoleonic bureaucrats who had destroyed public "morality" were heard again in the legitimist press. These ideas, now stylized into prejudices, made them grotesque to less dogmatic contemporaries.[12] In almost petulant defiance of their critics, the legitimists of Toulouse long continued to repeat these ideas which affected southern France until the present century.

[12] E. de la Bédollière, "Le Languedocien" in *Les français peints par eux-mêmes, encyclopédie morale du dix-neuvième siècle* (Paris, 1841), II, 57.

APPENDIX I

ADMINISTRATIVE ORGANIZATION OF HAUTE-GARONNE

(Source: Almanach Royal, 1820)

HAUTE-GARONNE

Administrative Arrondissements:

1. TOULOUSE
   Prefect: Baron de St. Chamans
   Population: 125,854
   Electoral Representation: 1 elector to 147 population

   CANTONS *and chefs-lieux de justices* [sic] *de paix*

Cadours	Léguevin
Castanet	Montastruc
Fronton	Toulouse (4 jp) Verfeil
Grenade	Villemur

2. MURET
   Sous prefet: Bellefonds
   Population: 77,032

   CANTONS *and chefs-lieux de justices* [sic] *de paix*

Auterive	Montesquieu-Volvestre
Carbonne	Muret
Cazères	Rieumes
Cintegabelle	Rieux
Fousseret	St. Lys

   Electoral Representation: 1 elector to 387 population

3. St. Gaudens
    Sous prefet: Escherolles
    Population: 117,990

    Cantons *and chefs-lieux de justices* [sic] *de paix*

Aspet	Saint-Béat
Aurignac	Saint-Bertrand-de-Comminges
Bagnères de Luchon	Saint Gaudens
Boulogne-sur-Gesse	Saint-Malory
Isle en Dodon	Salies-du-Salat
Montréjeau	

    Electoral Representation: 1 elector to 1,053 population

4. Villefranche
    Sous prefet: Lacoste
    Population: 57,963

    Cantons *and chefs-lieux de justices* [sic] *de paix*

Caraman	Nailloux
Lanta	Revel
Montgiscard	Villefranche

    Electoral Representation: 1 elector to 204 population

Electoral Arrondissements:

1. Cadours, Fronton, Toulouse ouest, Toulouse nord, Toulouse sud, Verfeil
2. Castanet, Grenade, Léguevin, Montastruc, Toulouse centre, Villemur
3. As Villefranche Administrative
4. Muret and St. Gaudens combined

APPENDIX II

Distribution of Tax Payments by Profession of 773 Electors in the Electoral Cantons of Toulouse-Centre, -Sud, -Nord, -Ouest, from 1820 Electoral Rolls

Professions	Tax paid with approximate equivalent in revenue indicated in italics (in hundreds of francs)						LINE TOTAL	Percent, by main heading, of the 773 electors
	3–4 *20–25*	4–5 *26–31*	5–8 *32–51*	8–10 *52–65*	10–15 *66–99*	15– *100–*		
AGRICULTURE								
Landowners	48	31	68	25	65	81	317	40.5
PATRONAT								
Negociants	14	8	29	8	27	13	99	
Innkeepers, hoteliers	5	1	1	2	0	1	10	
Perfume, pottery, wax, clock, mirrors, blankets, harness-makers	7	3	4	1	0	1	16	
Linen merchants, retail and wholesale	8	6	5	1	2	0	22	
Lace, haberdashery, cotton merchants	2	2	2	0	0	2	8	
Blacksmith, tinmen, metallurgical trades	7	3	2	1	1	0	14	
Gold and silversmiths	3	3	2	1	0	0	9	
Food merchants and vintners	15	4	3	1	0	0	23	
Nurserymen and arborists	1	1	0	1	2	0	5	
Miscellaneous merchants: tobacco, furniture, etc.	4	3	0	0	0	0	7	

Wood merchants	3	1	1	0	0	0	5	
Leather merchants	3	1	0	0	0	0	4	
Grain and flour merchants; millers	5	2	2	0	0	0	9	
Drapers, wholesale and retail	2	3	2	2	2	1	12	31.4
SERVICE DU ROI								
Mayors and adjoints of communes	6	2	5	2	6	6	27	
Mayors and adjoints of Toulouse municipality	0	0	0	0	2	6	8	
Officials: tax collectors, the enregistrement	4	1	5	0	5	2	17	
Officials at prefecture	0	0	1	2	2	0	5	
Cour Royale	2	4	0	1	2	8	17	
Première instance	0	1	3	1	1	0	6	
Juge de Paix	1	1	1	0	0	0	3	
Avocats	3	1	6	4	1	2	17	
Notaires	2	2	1	0	0	2	7	
Avoués	4	1	2	0	2	1	10	
Miscellaneous legal (huissier, etc.)	1	0	0	0	1	1	3	
Soldiers and police	3	4	4	4	3	3	21	18.0
CLERGY								
Priests	5	2	2	2	1	1	13	1.7
PROFESSIONS								
Agents de Change	1	2	0	0	1	2	6	
Doctors and surgeons	4	4	5	0	1	0	14	
Pharmacists and druggists	3	5	3	3	1	0	15	
Teachers at Faculté and Collège Royal	1	2	2	2	2	2	11	
Miscellaneous: architect, printer, etc.	3	4	1	3	2	2	15	
Total								7.9
								99.5%

(Source: *ADHG*, 2 M 23)

DISTRIBUTION OF OCCUPATIONS ACCORDING TO TAXES PAID

Occupation	Taxes Paid (in Hundreds of Francs)						
	3–4	4–5	5–8	8–10	10–15	15–	
	%	%	%	%	%	%	
Agriculture	5.9	3.6	7.7	2.8	7.5	9.3	Percent of electorate
Patronat	10.5	5.4	7.0	2.4	4.5	2.4	according to main
Service du Roi	4.0	2.4	4.4	2.3	4.4	3.9	headings of the elec-
Clergy	0.7	0.3	0.3	0.3	0.1	0.1	tors of Toulouse Nord,
Professions	1.6	2.3	1.5	1.1	0.9	0.8	Sud, Ouest and Centre

Opinion	Agriculture %	Service du Roi %	Patronat %	Professions %	Clergy %	Note
Royalist	23.8	11.7	14.1	11.0	1.8	Percent of 453 electorate of 1st arrondissement, Haute-Garonne, 1820, by opinion, according to main headings
Liberal	8.1	0.2	7.7	6.6	—	
Doubtful R.*	0.7	1.8	0.9	0.2	—	
Doubtful L.**	5.5	0.2	3.1	0.4	—	
Royalist	18.8	9.4	7.4	5.9	1.0	Percent of 404 electorate of 2nd arrondissement, Haute-Garonne, 1820, by opinion, according to main headings
Liberal	15.3	2.2	17.6	5.2	—	
Doubtful R.*	2.5	0.4	4.5	0.7	—	
Doubtful L.**	3.5	—	4.7	0.7	—	
Royalist	23.4	22.9	3.5	6.3	0.6	Percent of 286 voters of 3rd arrondissement (Villefranche), Haute-Garonne, 1820, by opinion, main headings
Liberal	21.7	5.6	6.3	4.2	—	
Doubtful R.*	—	—	0.4	0.7	—	
Doubtful L.**	1.7	2.7	—	—	—	
Royalist	22.1	11.4	0.8	4.1	—	Percent of 122 voters, St. Gauden's section of 4th electoral arrondissement, Haute-Garonne, 1820, by opinion, main headings
Liberal	17.2	4.1	4.9	—	—	
Doubtful R.*	8.2	1.6	0.8	4.9	—	
Doubtful L.**	7.4	4.1	1.6	6.6	—	
Royalist	17.3	18.4	—	5.6	—	Percent of 196 voters, Muret section of 4th electoral arrondissement, Haute-Garonne, 1820, by opinion, main headings
Liberal	22.0	3.1	7.7	1.0	—	
Doubtful R.*	5.1	5.1	—	1.0	—	
Doubtful L.**	8.7	3.6	1.5	—	—	

*Doubtful royalist
**Doubtful liberal
SOURCE: *AN*, F¹ᶜ III (Garonne, Haute-) 6.

APPENDIX

III

THE MUNICIPALITY OF TOULOUSE[1]

Mayors: 1800–1830	Dates in Office	Origins of family nobility
°P. Picot de Lapeyrouse	1800–06	recent municipal
°G. de Bellegarde	1806–11	Empire ennobled
°J.F.M. de Malaret	1811–14	parlementary
°L.G.F. de Monstron d'Escouloubre	–14	military
°J.F.M. de Malaret	1814–15	parlementary
°J. de Villèle	1815–18	seigneurial
°G. de Bellegarde	1818–23	Empire ennobled
°T. d'Hargenvilliers	1823–26	military
°G. I. Baron de Montbel	1826–29	parlementary
°A. de Rességuier	1829–30	parlementary
J. Viguerie	1830–33	

Members of Toulouse Municipal Council

1. Bourbon nominated, 1814–1816

Name	Occupation	Years in Office
°T.J.H. Aldéguier	President at the court	1814–15
°J.L.C. d'Aubuisson de Voisins	landowner	1816–18
F. Baudens	négociant	1814–15
P.A.J. de Baudon	receveur général	1814–17
Bériolle	landowner	1816–30
°J.L. Castellane	maréchal de camp	1816–30
J.G. Cayre	juge d'instruction	1814–19
°P.G. Célès de Marsac	former advocate at the Parlement; landowner	1814–15

[1] Noble status indicated by an asterisk.

APPENDICES

Name	Occupation	Years in Office
Courtois elder	banker	1816–19
A. Chaptive	négociant	1814–15
G. des Essarts	receveur de l'enregistrement	1816–30
J.M. Dupau	négociant	–14
J.P.M. Espigat-Sieurat	landowner	1814–15
M. Espinasse	lawyer	1816–26
P.M.A. Fraissines	former procureur du roi at Parlement; landowner, tax inspector	1814–30
°A.G. Gary	procureur général	1816–25
Gaugiran	doctor	1816–22
J. L. F. Gounon	merchant	1814–18
°M.L. Hocquart	First President at the court; deputy	1816–30
G.J.A. de Joulia	wool merchant	1816–18
°G.M. Leblanc	landowner	1814–30
A.A. Marie	merchant	1814–15
°R. de Marsac	landowner	1816–30
°F. Martin d'Aiguesvives	councilor at the court	1814–15
°J. L. F. Palarin	landowner	1814–30
S. Pugens	notary	1814–15
°M. de Puymaurin	landowner, deputy	1816–30
°A. de Rességuier	landowner	1816–29
J.D.F.M. Ruffat	law professor	1816–30
M.P.C. Saget	landowner	1814–19

2. Municipal councillors appointed and reappointed in 1816

Name	Occupation	Years in Office
Amilhau, Jean-Pierre	notary	1814–30
°Bastoulh, Jean-Raymond-Marc	jurisconsult	1804–27
°Bellegarde, Guillaume	landowner	1806–11
		1814–23
		1830–37
Boyer de Tauriac	landowner	1804–19
Cassand, Marie-Guillaume-Rene	landowner	1804–30
°Escouloubre, Louis-Gaston-Monstron de, Marquis	landowner	1804–18
°Lavédan, Jean-Baptiste, Comte	landowner	1804–25

3. Municipal councillors appointed during the course of the Restoration, after 1816

Name	Occupation	Years in Office
Astre, Gilles-Francois	advocate	1824–30
°Bastoulh, Raymond-Marie-Hyacinthe	councilor	1827–30
Bosc, Jean-Baptiste	président du tribunal de commerce	1826–30

Name	Occupation	Years in Office
Flottes, Louis-Antoine	professor at law faculty	1830– ?
*Cambon, Alexandre	President at the court	1826–29
Cassaigne, Jean-Baptiste	juge de paix	1821–30
Courtois, fils	banker	1820–37
Dubor, Bernard	doctor	1818–30
Garrigou, Marie-Joseph	iron-merchant	1829–31
*Miegeville, Jean-Antoine	councilor at the court	1822–30
		1831–34
*Montbel, Guillaume-Isidore	landowner	1824–30
*Ricard, François-Louis-Charles	landowner	1809–16
		1825–30
Roucoule, Honoré, *père*	lawyer	1804–05
		1809–16
		1819–29
Roucoule, Honoré, *fils*	councilor at the court	1829–30
		1831–45
Tricou, Félix	directeur des domaines et forets	1818–30
*Villèle, Joseph	landowner	1820–30
*Villèle-Laprade, Guillaume	ex-colonel, payeur du départment	1826–30

SOURCES: Brémond, *Annales*; AN, F1bII, (HG) 8; ADHG, IM-74, IM-75.

188

APPENDIX IV

Table 1

Membership of the *Conseil Général* of the Haute-Garonne, 1815–16

Name[1]	Occupation	Annual Revenue (Approximate), Francs
Lafont-Cazeing	Landowner	200,000
Lassus-Camon	Landowner	60,000
°Escouloubre	Landowner	36,000
°Rességuier	Landowner	25,000
°Marsac	Landowner	20,000
°Villèle	Landowner	15,000
°Cambon	*Premier Président*	12,000
°Pérignon	Director of Mint	12,000
°Caffarelli	Landowner	10,000
°Davessens	Landowner	10,000
Thoron	Retired Merchant	10,000
°Palarin	Landowner	9,000
Romiguières	Lawyer	9,000
°Ustou-Morlhon	Landowner	6,000
Lasplanes	Landowner	6,000
Amilhau	*Avocat*	5,000
Goudin	Landowner	5,000
Marin	Landowner	5,000
Hémet	Merchant	3,000
Tatareau	Judge	3,000
Niel-Brioude	Landowner	2,500
Gonin	—	—
Lacombe-Bermond	—	—

SOURCE: *ADHG*, 2 M bis 2, 2 M bis 3, 2 M 19; *AN*, F1bII (Garonne, Hte) 7, F1bII (Garonne, Hte) 8.

[1] Noble status indicated by an asterisk.

189

Table 2

Restoration appointments to the *Conseil Général*, 1817–30

Name[1]	Occupation	Annual Revenue (Approximate), Francs
°Montbel	Mayor; deputy; Landowner	20,000
Prévost-Junior	Landowner; former *négociant*	20,000
Brettes-Thurin	Landowner, mayor	10,000
°Dubourg	Landowner, deputy	10,000
°Durand	Landowner, sous-prefet	10,000
°Hocquart	*Premier Président*	10,000
°Morier de Mourvilles	Landowner	10,000
°Roquette de Buisson	Landowner; deputy	10,000
°Saintegême	*Conseiller de prefecture*	10,000
°Villèle-Laprade	Landowner; *Payeur* of the department	17,200

SOURCE: *ADHG*, 2 M bis 2, 2 M bis 3, 2 M 19; *AN*, F[1b]II (Garonne, Hte) 7, F[1b]II (Garonne, Hte) 8.

[1] Noble status indicated by an asterisk.

BIBLIOGRAPHY

I. MANUSCRIPT

A. *Archives Nationales*, Paris [*AN*]

The most important documents used for this study are:
i) Personnel dossiers in the justice series from the *cour royale* at Toulouse:

BB¹15–17
BB⁵66–69
BB⁶61, 65, 81, 87, 96, 523, 532⁹
BB⁹325, 348, 374, 400, 427, 479, 498

ii) Reports from the *procureur général* containing information about political life in the city:

BB³⁰192, 236, 238 dossier 4, 245

iii) Reports on elections and deputies:

C24 (159); C281 (773); C130 (449) C1215
C*II 382, 732–742

iv) *Administration générale*

F¹ᵃ412
F¹ᵇI 244–248
F¹ᵇI*234, 240–241
F¹ᵇII (Garonne, Haute-) 1–8, 26
F¹ᶜIII (Garonne, Haute-) 1–6, 8–9
F¹ᶜV (Garonne, Haute-) 1–4
F³II (Garonne, Haute-) 24–27
F⁷4006–4008; 4349, 4444, 5107, 5116, 5117, 6258–6260, 6769, 6966, 7028, 7285, 7418, 7487, 7602, 9055–9059, 9234, 9235, 9659

F^{15}708–14, 20–22
F^{16}1003^A, 1086
F^{19}427, 603, 1009
v) *Secrétariat d'Etat*
AF^{iii} 1004–1005, 230
AF^{iv} 1944
vi) *Comité des recherches*
Dxxix bis 5, nos. 78
11, nos. 117
21, nos. 224, 228, 229
25, nos. 249, 250

B. *Archives du Ministère de la Guerre* [AG]

Correspondence of general commanding the tenth military division
D^3 1–7, 9, 20, 36, 40, 52, 65, 76, 90, 120

C. The majority of documents consulted for this study are kept at the *Archives départementales de la Haute-Garonne* [ADHG], Toulouse

i) Counter-revolution
L 262, 268, 270, 273–6, 285–333, 2292–94,
2264–2277, 2307–2309, 2281–90
J 690, 813
6J 90–95, 100

ii) The major collection of official documents concerning Toulouse during the period of the Restoration is kept at the departmental archives of the Haute-Garonne. The material consulted there can be classified as follows:

a) Financial information is sparse for the history of Toulouse in the first half of the nineteenth century, and the electoral lists of the constitutional monarchies provide invaluable knowledge of this subject:
2M 19–24
The *commune* totals of tax returns are also preserved:
P 244, 245
2P, 38–40
Details on the wealth of individuals can be found in the registers of the *enregistrement*, especially the *mutations par décès*:
WQ 5577–5601 (*mutations par décès*)
WQ 5572–5574 (*testaments et donations*)
b) The social positions of the Toulouse ultras were meas-

ured by indications scattered in a great variety of documents, but the registers of the *Etat civil* of marriages were especially helpful, as were the lists of the *six cents plus imposés*.

    4E 2774–2782, 4E 3034–3041

    2 M 7

Some registers from the *étude* of Me. Amilhau were consulted.

iii) Deliberations of the *conseil d'arrondissement de Toulouse*, the departmental *conseil général*, and nominations to these bodies:

    2M bis 2, 3

    1 N 8–15

    2 N 34–38

    (provisional numbering: X 1 M 57, 64, 72–75, 80, 83)

iv) *Administration Générale*

    M 106, 1017

    1M 65

    2M 19–24

    4M5, 35–50

    6M 13–26, 40, 49

    10M 21

    13M 76

    2T 13, 14, 19–21

    6T 1–2

    2V 29

    4V 5

    41Y1, 44Y1

D. *Archives Municipales de Toulouse* [AMT]

i) Registers of the deliberations of the Toulouse municipal council, VIII–1830

    2F 1–3

    HH36, 37, 41, 42, 47

    2H 39

    3H 1–5

    4S 20, 25–29, 32, 40, 42

    5S 94, 97, 101

    1S 4, 7, 8, 11, 36, 47, 55, 56

    GG 1012

E. *Bibliothèque Municipale de Toulouse* [BMT]

i) Adrien Salvan, "Mon temps, souvenirs toulousains, 1814–1826," mss. 1149

ii) "Notes politiques d'un prefet: l'Affaire Ramel," mss. 1158

F. *Archives of the Beaumont Family*, Château de Merville, Haute-Garonne [AB] (consulted by the kind permission of the Marquis de Beaumont)

  i) The correspondence of Chalvet de Rochemonteix

G. *Archives of the Castelbajac family*, Lauret, Gers (consulted by the kind permission of the Vicomte de Castelbajac)

  i) Correspondence of B. de Castelbajac, notably letters from Villèle, and the abbé Ducasse (1817–22)
  ii) "Réflexions et jugements d'ordre politique; la Chambre de 1815," unpublished mss. of B. de Castelbajac

H. *Archives of the Villèle family*, Mourvelles-Basses, Haute-Garonne [AV] (consulted by kind permission of the Comte de Villèle)

  i) Correspondence of Joseph de Villèle with local personalities
  ii) Diaries of J. de Villèle
  iii) Miscellaneous family correspondence
  iv) Electoral lists of the Villefranche arrondissement, 1827

II. PRINTED SOURCES AND BOOKS

A. Collections of Documents, Correspondence, and Publications of Toulouse Learned Societies

Adher, J. "Lettres inédites de A.-P.-H. Sermet, évêque constitutionnel de la Haute-Garonne, publiées par J. Adher." *Revue des Pyrénées*, X (1898), 101–3.
———. *Recueil de documents sur l'assistance publique dans le district de Toulouse de 1789 à 1800*. Toulouse, 1918.
Arrêté et supplications du parlement de Toulouse concernant les Etats du Languedoc. Du 21 Janvier 1789. Toulouse, 1789 (2 fascs.).
Arrêtés du parlement de Toulouse séant en vacations, 25 et 27 septembre 1790. . . . Toulouse, 1790.
Barada, J. "Toulouse et la vie toulousaine de 1786 à 1828 d'après la correspondance de Clément Daignan d'Empaillan." *Annales du Midi*, XLV (1932), 41–78, 163–203, 443–72; XLVI (1933), 66–87, 174–205.
Barthès, Pierre. *Toulouse au xviiie siècle, d'après les "Heures Perdues" . . . par E. Lamouzèle*. Toulouse, 1914.

Bénaerts, Louis. *Les commissaires extraordinaires de Napoléon 1er en 1814 d'après leur correspondance inédite.* Bibliothèque d'histoire moderne, 15. Paris, 1915.

Bouglon, J.-A.-R. de. *Les reclus de Toulouse sous la Terreur, registres officiels concernant les citoyens emprisonnés comme suspects.* Toulouse, 1893–1912 (3 fascs.).

Clermont-Tonnerre, Anne-Antoine. *Lettera pastorale dell'eminentissimo . . . arcivescovo di Tolosa . . . al clero e ai fedeli della sua diocesi.* Roma, 1823.

Cobbin, Ingram. *Statements of the Persecution of the Protestants in the South of France.* London, 1815.

Connac, E. "La réaction royaliste à Toulouse (1918–1816), trois lettres inédites de Picot de Lapeyrouse à l'avocat Romiguières." *Revue des Pyrénées,* X (1898), 431–51.

Douais, C. *Documents sur l'ancienne province de Languedoc.* 2 vols. Paris, 1901–4.

Fauré, Louis-Joseph. *Notes et réflexions d'un bourgeois de Toulouse au début de la Revolution d'après des lettres intimes.* Toulouse, 1917.

France. *Laws, ordinances, etc., Recueil des édits, déclarations et ordinances du Roi, arrêts du Conseil, du parlement de Toulouse et autres cours.* 8 vols. Toulouse, 1782–86.

Garonne, Comité de la Haute-. *Cahiers paroissiaux des sénéchaussées de Toulouse et de Comminges en 1789,* publiée par F. Pasquier et F. Galabert. Toulouse, 1928.

Godoffre, Ambroise, ed. *Conseil général du département de la Haute-Garonne, déliberations de l'an VIII à 1838 . . . Analyse des procès-verbaux.* 2 vols. Toulouse, 1869.

Martin, Henri, ed. *Département de la Haute-Garonne. Documents relatifs à la vente des biens nationaux . . . District de Saint Gaudens.* Rieumes, 1924.

————. *Département de la Haute-Garonne. Documents relatifs à la vente des biens nationaux . . . District de Toulouse.* Toulouse, 1916.

Procès-verbal et adresse des citoyens actifs et catholiques de la ville de Toulouse. . . . Toulouse, 1790.

Rémusat, Charles François Marie. *Correspondance de M. de Rémusat pendant les premières années de la Restauration publiée par son fils Paul de Rémusat.* 3 vols. Paris, 1883–84.

Rémusat, Claire-Elizabeth. "Letters de province, 1815–1817." *Revue de Paris,* IV–V (July–September, 1902).

Santi, L. de. *Notes et documents sur les intrigues royalistes dans le sud-ouest de 1792 à 1815. Extrait* Toulouse, Académie des sciences, inscriptions et belles lettres, *Mémoires*, 12 sér., IV (1916), 37–115. Toulouse, 1916.

Toulouse. Académie des Jeux Floraux. *Recueil de l'académie des jeux floraux.* Toulouse, 1814–50.

Toulouse. Académie des sciences, inscriptions et belles lettres. *Histoire et mémoires de l'académie royale des sciences, Années 1807–1841.* 6 vols. Toulouse, 1827–43.

Toulouse. *Comité des subsistances, (1793–1795).* Département de la Haute-Garonne, *Le comité des subsistances de Toulouse, 12 août, 1793–3 mars, 1795.* Toulouse, 1912.

Toulouse. *Cour royale: Extrait des Registres, trente août mil huit cent quinze.* Toulouse, 1815.

Toulouse. Curés: *Très-humbles supplication de MM. les curés de Toulouse à M. le comte de Périgord.* Toulouse, 1788.

Toulouse. *Noblesse: Procès-verbal, mandat, et cahier des doléances de la noblesse de la sénéchaussée de Toulouse.* N.p., 1788.

Villèle, Joseph-Séraphin de. "Toulouse en 1816, lettre de M. de Villèle à M. Laîné, ministre de l'intérieur, Toulouse 1 mai, 1816." *Nouvelle Revue Restrospective,* VII (1897), 311–20.

B. Biographical Dictionaries, Genealogies, and Works of Reference

Abel, Froidefont. *Tableau chronologique des noms de messieurs les capitouls de la ville de Toulouse.* Toulouse, 1786.

Annuaire de la Haute-Garonne. Toulouse, 1824, 1825.

Arnault, Antoine. *Biographie nouvelle des contemporains.* 21 vols. Paris, 1820–26.

Baour, Jean-Florent, *Almanach historique....* Toulouse, 1789.

Beaunier: *Liste des Bénéfices ... abbayes et prieurés de l'ancienne France ... provincia Tolosana.* New ed., Paris, 1905–41.

Biographie des députés de la chambre septennale de 1824 à 1830. Paris, 1826.

Biographie des faux prophètes vivans. 2 vols. Paris, 1821.

Biographie des ministres français depuis juillet 1789 jusqu'à ce jour. Bruxelles, 1826.

Biographie impartiale de 221 députés, précédée et suivie de quelques documents curieux. Paris, 1830.

Biographie nouvelle et complète de la Chambre des députés, contenant les députés nouvellement élus. Paris, 1829.

Biographie toulousaine, ou dictionnaire historique des person-

nages qui par des vertus, des talens, des écrits, de grandes actions, des fondations utiles, des opinions singulières, des erreurs, etc., se sont rendus célèbres dans la ville de Toulouse. 2 vols. Paris, 1823.

Boutaric, J.-F. de. *Traîté des droits seigneuriaux et des matières féodales.* Toulouse, 1775.

Braun, J.-B.-M. *Nouvelle biographie des députés ou statistique de la Chambre de 1814 à 1829.* Paris, 1830.

Brémond, Alphonse. *Etat actuel de la noblesse toulousaine pour toute l'étendue du ressort de la cour d'Appel de Toulouse.* Toulouse, 1871.

————. *Indicateur du nobiliaire toulousain,* Toulouse, 1868.

————. *Nobiliaire toulousain, inventaire général des titres probants.* Toulouse, 1863.

Caramel, A. *Bibliographie du Languedoc.* Montpellier, 1963.

Cauchois, Lemaire St. Ange. *Petit almanach législatif.* Paris, 1820.

Chambre [La] de mil huit cent vingt, ou la monarchie sauvée: galérie politique des quatre cent vingt-deux députés qui siègent dans la présente session. Paris, 1821.

Compte-rendu des impositions et des dépenses générales de la province de Languedoc, d'après les départements et les états de distribution. Montpellier, 1789.

Dantigny, P. F. *Annuaire administratif et statistique du département de la Haute-Garonne pour l'an 1811.* Toulouse, 1811.

[Delboy, publishers]. *Guide des étrangers dans Toulouse et les environs.* Toulouse, 1844.

Dictionnaire des girouettes, ou nos contemporains peints d'après eux-mêmes. 3rd ed. Paris, 1815.

Diocèse de Toulouse. *Rapport, ou comte-rendu des impositions de tout nature que ce diocèse supporte.* N.p., 1789.

Dumège, A.-L.-C. *Statistique générale des départements pyrénéens, ou des provinces de Guienne et de Languedoc.* Paris, 1828–29.

Faillon, L. *Annuaire du département de la Haute-Garonne.* Toulouse, 1807.

Fauré, Honoré. *Galerie administrative, ou biographie des prefets depuis l'organisation des préfectures jusqu'à ce jour.* Aurillac, 1839.

Frêche, Georges. *Les prix des grains, des vins et des légumes à Toulouse (1486–1868).* Paris, 1967.

La Bédollière, E. de. "Le Languedocien." *Les français peints par eux-memes, encyclopédie morale du dix-neuvièmè siècle,* II, 57. Paris, 1841.

La Roque, Louis de. *Armorial de la noblesse de Languedoc, généralité de Montpellier.* Montpellier, 1860.

Michaud, L.-F. *Biographie universelle.* 52 vols. Paris, 1811——.

Monnet, E. *Histoire de l'administration.* Paris, 1885.

Ramière de Fortanier, J. *Les droits seigneuriaux dans la sénéchaussée et comté de Lauragais 1553–1789.* Toulouse, 1932.

Robert, Adolphe. *Dictionnaire des parlementaires français.* 5 vols. Paris, 1889–91.

Saint André, J.-A.-D.: *Topographie médicale du département de la Haute-Garonne, . . . ouvrage basé sur les rapports qu'ont les diverses circonstances locales avec la santé des habitants de Toulouse.* Toulouse, 1813.

Toulouse. *Tableau de l'administration de la ville de Toulouse pour l'année 1785.*

Vilain, Jules. *La France moderne; grand dictionnaire généalogique, historique et biographique, Haute-Garonne et Ariège.* Montpellier, 1911–1913. Vol. 3, parts i, ii.

Woelmont, Henri de. *Notices généalogiques.* Paris, 1923.

C. Memoirs, Pamphlets, and Songs

Adresse aux gens de bien du languedoc, pour être communiquée à l'assemblée nationale, et aux bons français qui s'intéressent aux affaires présentes. N.p., n.d.

Amilhau, P.-C. *Eloge de Louis XVI.* Toulouse, 1817.

L'aristocratie enchaînée et surveillée par le roi et par le peuple . . . contenant un plan de constitution des provinces, suivi d'un mémoire de MM. les barons nés des Etats de Languedoc, et la réponse à leurs prétentions . . . 1er mars, 1789. 2nd ed. N.p., 1789.

[Belmontet, L.]. *La mission, épître à MM. les missionnaires.* Toulouse, 1819.

——. *Mon apologie.* [Toulouse, 1819].

Brassine, E. "Eloge de M. d'Aubuisson de Voisins." *Histoire et Mémoires de l'Académie de Législation de Toulouse,* ser. 3, I (1844).

Le Caméléon politique. Toulouse, [1819].

Cantique à MM. les pénitens d'Aurignac . . . en action de graces à l'heureux retour de Louis XVIII. N.p., n.d.

Castelbajac, L. de. *Mémoires de l'occitanienne, souvenirs de famille et de jeunesse.* 6th ed. Paris, 1927.

Caussade, A. *Dernier avis aux électeurs de 1824.* [Toulouse, 1824].

Cavaille, G. A. "Eloge historique de M. de Cardonnel ... 14 fevrier 1830." *Recueil de l'Académie Jeux Floraux.* Toulouse, 1830.

Chansons patriotiques dédiées à la garde nationale de Toulouse. N.d.

Chant nouveau pour le retour du prince et l'arrivée de la princesse à Toulouse. N.p., n.d.

Colombars, J. A. L. A. Serres de. "Eloge de Clémence Isaure prononcé dans la séance du 3 mai 1816." *Recueil de l'Académie Jeux Floraux.* Toulouse, 1817.

Correspondance de la municipalité de Toulouse avec celle de Bordeaux pour le pacte fédératif. Toulouse, 1790.

Couplets en l'honneur du P. Hyacinthe Sermet, nommé à l'évêché métropolitain du sud. N.p., n.d.

Couplets pour être chantés à l'éntrée de Monseigneur le duc d'Angoulême à Toulouse. N.p., n.d.

Decampe, M.-L.-A. *Considérations sur l'état actuel des moeurs de la jeunesse française et sur les moyens d'améliorer l'esprit de celle qui doit lui succéder.* Paris, 1822.

————. *Eloge historique de Louis XVIII.* Toulouse, 1826.

Délibération de la société des amis de la constitution, séante à Toulouse du 16 mai, 1792. Toulouse, 1792.

Délibération de la société républicaine de Toulouse proposée par elle à toutes les sociétés populaires de la République, 29 juillet, 1793. Toulouse, 1793.

Dénonciation d'un Languedocien à sa province. Toulouse, 1789.

Dumège, A.-L.-C. *Notice sur ... M. Pierre Magi-Duval.* Toulouse, 1825.

Garçons [Les] perruquiers de la ville de Toulouse ... a MM. le maire et officiers municipiaux, 8 avril 1790. Toulouse, 1790.

Gounon-Loubens, Joseph-François. *Discours prononcé par Mr. Gounon-Loubens, capitoul de Toulouse, aux Etats de Languedoc.* Toulouse, 1789.

Hauteville, R.-T. *Eloge du comte Joseph de Villèle.* Toulouse, 1863.

Lettre aux électeurs de la Haute-Garonne. Toulouse, 1827.

Lettre des avocats au parlement de Toulouse à Monseigneur le garde des Sceaux sur les nouveaux édits transcrits par les commissaires de S.M. dans les régistres du parlement le 8 mai (1788). Toulouse, 1788.

Lettre sur les pamphlets de Toulouse, ou bigarrures politi-

ques . . . *signé un membre de l'ancien Athenée.* N.p., n.d.

Livre sans titre, sans plan, sans sujet et sans fin: bavardage nouveau à l'instar de Paris par un auteur qui se cache par modestie, par amour propre, ou par prudence, comme on voudra. Toulouse, 1819.

Madrolle, A. *Défense de l'ordre social, attaqué dans ses fondements.* Paris, 1827.

Mailhe, J.-B. *Discours . . . sur la grandeur et l'importance de la Révolution qui vient de s'opérer dans l'Amérique septentrionale.* Toulouse, 1784.

———. *Requisitoire, fait par M. Mailhe, procureur-général-syndic du département de la Haute-Garonne, le 2 Octobre, 1790.* N.d., n.p.

Marcillac, P.-L.-A. *Souvenirs de l'émigration à l'usage de l'époque actuelle.* Paris, 1825.

Marrenx, François de. *Du principe fondamental de tous les partis révolutionnaires.* Toulouse, 1815.

———. *Lettre sur le gouvernement réprésentatif.* Auch, 1817.

———. *Lettre sur le pacte social.* Toulouse, 1815.

Mémoires de Tous. Collections de souvenirs contemporains tendant à établir la vérité dans l'histoire. Vol. 6, pp. 145–220, Rougé. Paris, 1837.

Montbel, G.-I. *Souvenirs du comte de Montbel.* Paris, 1913.

Observations sur la petition adressée aux Chambres par les propriétaires de vignes du département de la Haute-Garonne: par un officier d'artillerie, propriétaire de vignes et de forges. Toulouse, 1829.

Observations sur un point de la discussion relative au projet de loi concernant l'indemnité dû aux émigrés. Toulouse, 1825.

Ote-Toi de là que je m'y mette, ou quelques pages de vérité sur la députation toulousaine de 1830. Paris, 1830.

Où en sommes-nous? où allons-nous? ou courtes réflexions sur la situation de la France à l'approche des élections générales. Toulouse, 1827.

Palisse, J.-A. *Notice historique sur M.J.-A. Palisse (ancien commissaire de police de Toulouse) dont la nomination a été révoquée . . . par l'effet des événements du mois de mars dernier qui ont troublé un instant la tranquillité de cette ville.* Toulouse, 1822.

de Panat, D. S. J. P. "Eloge de M. d'Aubuisson de Voisins." *Receuil de l'Académie Jeux Floraux.* Toulouse, 1843.

Pescayre. *Tableau des prisons de Toulouse sous le règne de Robespierre et sous celui de ses satellites.* Toulouse, III.

Pétition des principaux propriétaires du département de la Haute-Garonne à la chambre de MM. les députés. N.p., n.d.

Pinaud, Joseph-Jean-Thérèse. "Eloge historique de Louis XVI et de Louis XVII, prononcé en séance publique de l'Académie . . . le 19 janvier 1818." *Recueil de l'Académie des Jeux Floraux 1814–1816,* 2nd pagination, p. 51.

Rapprochements historiques sur l'hospitalité des anciens; sur la formation de nos hopitaux, la nature de leurs revenus, et les divers systèmes qui se sont succédées dans leur administration; par un conseiller de préfecture [P. Dantigny?]. Toulouse, 1820.

Rémusat, C.-F. *Mémoires de ma vie . . . preséntés et annotés par Ch. Pouthas.* 5 vols. Paris, 1958–67.

Retraite ecclésiastique donnée à Toulouse par M. de MacCarthy de la société de Jésus, Octobre, 1829. N.p., n.d.

Ringaud. *Réponse d'un ami de la monarchie à un partisan du gouvernement républicain.* Toulouse, 1816.

Salvan, Abbé. "Mon temps, 1814–1826." Mss. 1149, *BMT.*

Savy, Abbé. *Oraison funèbre de Louis XVIII.* Toulouse, n.d.

Sur la fête de St. Louis, 25 août, 1817. Toulouse, 1817.

"Le 21 janvier, 1816, ou le troubadour à Toulouse. . . ." Mss, *AV.*

Villèle, Jean-Baptiste-Seraphin. *Mémoires et correspondance.* 5 vols. Paris, 1888–90.

Vitrolles, E.-F.-A. d'Arnaud. *Mémoires.* Paris, 1950–51.

D. Newspapers

Ami du Roi, Journal du Midi. Toulouse, Manavit, 1815–19. *ADHG, BN.*

Anti-Terroriste. Toulouse, February 1795–September 1797. *BMT.*

Echo du Midi, Journal politique, religieux et littéraire de la Haute-Garonne. Manavit, ed. Toulouse, 1821–28. *BN.*

Journal politique et littéraire de Toulouse et la Haute-Garonne. Vieusseux, ed. Toulouse, 1815–30. *BN, BMT.*

Gazette du Languedoc. Toulouse, 1831–36. *BMT.*

Journal de la religion et de la société des bonnes études. Vieusseux, ed. Toulouse, 1822. *BN.*

Mémorial de Toulouse. Toulouse, 1829–30. *BMT.*

Les quatre évangélistes, ou supplément aux actes des apôtres. Toulouse, [1790?]. Nos. 4–12. *BN.*

III. SECONDARY SOURCES

A. General Works

Artz, Frederick B. "Les débuts des partis modernes en France, (1815–1830)," *Revue d'histoire moderne et contemporaine,* VI (1931), 275–84.

———. "The Electoral System in France during the Bourbon Restoration, 1815–30," *Journal of Modern History,* 1 (1929), 205–18.

———. *France under the Bourbon Restoration 1814–1830.* Cambridge, Mass., 1931.

Aubuisson de Voisins, J.-F. de. *Considérations sur l'autorité royale en France depuis la restauration et sur les administrations locales.* Paris, 1825.

Bagge, Dominic. *Les idées politiques en France sous la Restauration.* Paris, 1952.

Baldensperger, Fernand. *Le mouvement des idées dans l'émigration française, 1789–1815.* 2 vols. Paris, 1925.

Beauvoir, A. Hiver de. *Histoire critique des institutions judiciaires de la France de 1789 à 1848.* Paris, 1848.

Bertier de Sauvigny, Guillaume. *La restauration.* 2nd ed. Paris, 1964.

———. *Un type d'ultra-royaliste: le comte Ferdinand de Bertier (1782–1864) et l'énigme de la Congrégation.* Paris, 1948.

Boas, George. *French Philosophies of the Romantic period.* Baltimore, 1925.

Bonnal, E. *Les royalistes contre l'armée, 1815–1820.* Paris, 1912.

Bourgin, Georges. *Les patrons, Les ouvriers et l'état. La régime de l'industrie en France de 1814 à 1830.* 3 vols. Paris, 1912–41.

Chaumié, J. *Le réseau d'Antraigues et la contre-révolution, 1791–1793.* Paris, 1965.

Cobban, A.B.C. *A History of Modern France.* London, 1968.

———. *Aspects of the French Revolution.* New York, 1968.

———. *The Social Interpretation of the French Revolution.* Cambridge, 1964.

Collins, Irene. *The Government and the Newspaper Press in France 1814–1881.* London, 1959.

Cremieux, A. *La censure en 1820 et 1821.* Paris, 1912.

Daumard, A. *La bourgeoisie parisienne de 1815 à 1848.* Paris, 1963.

Deniel, R. *Une image de la famille et de la société sous la Restauration.* Paris, 1965.

Doyle, W. "Le prix des charges anoblissantes à Bordeaux au dix-huitième siècle." *Annales du Midi,* 80 (1968), 65–77.

Egret, J. "L'aristocratie parlementaire." *Revue historique,* CCVIII (1952), 1–14.

Eyraud, —. *De l'administration de la justice.* Paris, 1825.

Foster, R. "The Survival of the Nobility during the French Revolution," *Past and Present,* 37 (1967), 71–86.

Fourcassié, Jean. *Villèle.* Paris, 1954.

France. Ministère de la justice. *Compte général de l'administration de la justice civile . . . 1820–1830.* Paris, 1831.

Garcia-Llera, J.L.C. *Los realistas en el trienio constitucional, 1820–1823.* Pamplona, 1958.

Gershoy, Leo. *Bertrand Barère.* Princeton, 1962.

Godechot, J. *La contre-révolution, doctrine et action, 1769–1804.* Paris, 1961.

Gruder, Vivian R. *The Royal Provincial Intendants.* Ithaca, 1968.

Hemardinquer, J. J. "Affaires et politique . . . un libéral: F. B. Boyer-Fonfrède (1767–1845)." *Annales du Midi,* LXXIII (1961), 175.

Higgs, D. C. "Politics and Landownership among the French Nobility after the Revolution." *European Studies,* 2 (1971), 105–21.

Hudson, Nora. *Ultra-royalism and the French Restoration.* Cambridge, 1936.

Hufton, Olwen. "Women in Revolution, 1789–1796." *Past and Present,* 53 (November, 1971), 90–108.

Jacomet, Pierre. *Le palais sous la Restauration, 1815–1830.* Paris, 1922.

Jouy, E. de. *L'hermite en province.* Paris, 1818–27.

Lépinois, Henri. *Histoire de la Restauration.* Paris, 1873.

Lepointe, Gabriel. *Histoire des institutions du droit public français au XIXe siècle, 1789–1914.* Paris, 1953.

McManners, J. *French ecclesiastical society under the ancien régime.* Manchester, 1960.

Marjolin, R.: "Troubles provoqués en France par la disette de 1816–1817." *Revue d'histoire moderne et contemporaine,* VIII (1933), 423–60.

Martin-Sarzeaud. *Recherches sur l'inamovabilité.* Paris, 1883.

Mellon, S. *The Political Uses of History.* Stanford, 1958.

Morris, R. N. *Urban Sociology.* London, 1968.

Muret, C. *French Royalist Doctrines since the Revolution*. New York, 1933.

Nisbet, R. A. "De Bonald and the Concept of Social Group." *Journal of the History of Ideas*, V (1944), 315–31.

Oeschslin, J.-J. *Le mouvement ultra-royaliste sous la Restauration*. Paris, 1960.

———. "Sociologie, organisation et stratégie de l'ultra-royalisme." *Politique*, III (1958), 231–59.

Perceval, E. de. *Un adversaire de Napoléon, le vicomte Laîné*. Paris, 1926.

Ponteil, F. *Les institutions de la France de 1814 à 1870*. Paris, 1966.

Pouthas, C. "La réorganisation du ministère de l'intérieur et la reconstitution de l'administration préfectorale par Guizot en 1830," *Revue d'histoire moderne et contemporaine*. IX, (1962), 241–63.

Pradalie, G. *Balzac historien: La société de la Restauration*. Paris, 1955.

Rémond, R. *La droite en France*. 2nd ed. Paris, 1963.

Resnick, D. P. *The White Terror and the Political Reaction after Waterloo*. Cambridge, Mass., 1966.

Richardson, N. *The French Prefectural Corps, 1814–1830*. Cambridge, 1966.

Roche, D. "Milieux académiques provinciaux et société des lumières." *Livre et Société au XVIII siècle*. Paris, 1966.

Rousseau, A. "L'idée décentralisatrice et les partis politiques sous la Restauration." *Revue de Bretagne*, XXIX–XXX (1903–4), 127–43, 329–41; 43–56, 231–37.

Rousselet, M. *Histoire de la magistrature*. Paris, 1957.

Sjoberg, G. *The Pre-industrial City, Past and Present*. New York, 1960.

Swart, K. W. *The Sense of Decadence in Nineteenth Century France*. The Hague, 1964.

Thureau-Dangin, P. *Royalistes et républicains*. Paris, 1874.

Tudesq, A. *Les grands notables en France 1840–1849*. Paris, 1964.

Viel-Castel, Louis. *Histoire de la Restauration*. Paris, 1860–78.

B. Toulouse and the Midi

Adher, J. "L'assistance publique au dix-huitième siècle; l'enquête de 1775 dans le diocèse civil de Toulouse." *La Révolution française*, LXX (1917), 132–66.

———. "La faculté de théologie de Toulouse au début de la

Révolution française." *La Révolution française*, LXI (1911), 134–40.

———. "La conspiration royaliste dans la Haute-Garonne en l'an IV et l'an V." *La Révolution française*, XLI (1901), 218–22.

Albert, A. *Eloge de Laviguerie*. Toulouse, 1844.

Albert, M. *Le Fédéralisme dans la Haute-Garonne*. Paris, 1931.

———. *La première Restauration dans la Haute-Garonne*. Paris, 1933.

Aldéguier, J. B. A. de. *Eloge du marquis de Castellane*. Toulouse, 1846.

———. *Histoire de Toulouse*. 4 vols. Toulouse, 1834–35.

Appolis, E. "La question de la vaine pâture en Languedoc au dix-huitième siècle." *Annales historiques de la révolution française*, XV (1938), 97–132.

Ariste, Louis. *Histoire populaire de Toulouse*. Toulouse, 1898.

Armengaud, André. "De quelques idées fausses concernant les pays de la Garonne vers 1840." *Revue d'histoire moderne et contemporaine*, VII (1960), 47–54.

———. "A propos des origines du sous-développement industriel dans le sud-ouest." *Annales du Midi*, LXXII (1960), 75–81.

———. *Les populations de l'est-aquitain, vers 1845 vers 1871*. Paris, 1961.

———. "Terre et societé en Toulousain au début de l'époque contemporaine." *Bulletin de la société d'histoire moderne*, ser. 12 (année 57), 8–9; (1959), 9–11.

Astre, Florentin. *De l'administration publique en Languedoc avant 1789*. Toulouse, 1874.

Bastard d'Estang, Henri Brune. *Les parlements de France; essai historique sur leurs usages, leur organisation et leur autorité; par le vicomte de Bastard d'Estang*. 2 vols. Paris, 1857.

Bégouen, H. "Les débuts des Cent-Jours à Toulouse." *Mémoires de l'académie des sciences de Toulouse*, ser. 12, III (1925), 483–531.

———. *Une société secrète émule de la compagnie du Saint-sacrement. L'Aa de Toulouse aux XVIIe et XVIIIe siècles d'après des documents inédits*. Paris, 1913.

Beyssi, Jean. "Le parti jacobin à Toulouse sous le Directoire." *Annales historiques de la Révolution française*, XXII (1950), 28–54.

Boddington, Mary. *Sketches in the Pyrenees with Some Remarks on Languedoc.* 2 vols. London, 1837.

Bourderon, H. "La lutte centre la vie chère dans la généralité de Languedoc au XVIIIe siècle." *Annales du Midi,* LXVI (1954), 155–70.

Bouyoux, Pierre. "Les six cents plus imposés du département de la Haute-Garonne, an X, étude sociale." Toulouse, typescript, 1957. *BUT.*

————. "Les six cents plus imposés du département de la Haute-Garonne en l'an X." *Annales du Midi,* LXX (1958), 317–27.

Brémond, Alphonse. *Annales du XIXe siècle de la ville de Toulouse de 1800 à 1850.* Toulouse, 1865.

Bressolles, Pierre. *Bernard-Antoine Tajan (1775–1845) et le barreau au lendemain de la Revolution, discours prononcé le 7 décembre, 1913, à la rentrée solennelle de la conférence des avocats stagiaires.* Toulouse, 1913.

Brunet, R. *Les campagnes toulousaines, étude géographique.* Toulouse, 1965.

Buchalet, François. *L'assistance publique à Toulouse au dix-huitième siècle. Extrait,* Bulletin de l'université de Toulouse, ser. B., no. 2. Toulouse, 1904.

Callon, G. "Le mouvement de la population dans le département de la Haute-Garonne au cours de la période 1821–1920 et depuis la fin de cette période." *Bulletin de la société de géographie de Toulouse,* 51 année (1932), 81–89; 52 année (1933), 57–64, 102–6, 113–20, 146–59.

Cappot, Jean Gabriel [pseudonym: Capo de Feuillide]. *Le Midi en 1815.* Paris, 1836.

Castéras, Paul de. *La société toulousaine à la fin du XVIIIe siècle (l'acien régime et la Révolution).* Toulouse, 1891.

Causse, Henri. "Un industrel toulousain au temps de la Revolution et de l'Empire, François-Bernard Boyer-Fonfrède." *Annales du Midi,* LXIX (1957), 121–33.

Cayla, Jean-Namert. *Histoire de la ville de Toulouse depuis sa fondation jusq'à nos jours, publiée sous la direction de J.M. Cayla et Perrin-Paviot.* Toulouse, 1839.

Cayre, G. *Histoire des évêques et archévêques de Toulouse depuis la fondation du siège jusqu'à nos jours.* Toulouse, 1873.

Cazals, Antoine Lucien. *Une page de l'histoire du Lauragais ou histoire de la ville et de la communauté de Montesquieu-sur-Canal.* Toulouse, 1883.

Chinault, Jules. *La chambre de commerce de Toulouse du XVIIIe siècle 1703–1791*. *Extrait*, Mémoires de l'académie de législation de Toulouse, fasc. 1. Toulouse, 1956.

Cobb, Richard. *Les armées révolutionnaires des departments du Midi, (automne et hiver de 1793, printemps de 1794), préface de Jacques Godechot*. Cahiers de l'Association Marc Bloch de Toulouse, études d'histoire méridionale, 1. Toulouse, 1955.

Connac, Emile. *Histoire de la Révolution à Toulouse et dans le département de la Haute-Garonne*. Toulouse, 1902.

Contrasty, Jean. "Les foyers toulousains d'enseignement et de bienfaisance détruits par la Révolution." *Revue historique de Toulouse*, 21 (1934), 165–85.

Le mouvement religieux dans la Haute-Garonne sous le consulat d'après la correspondance prefectorale. Toulouse, 1907.

Pages d'histoire toulousaine. Toulouse, 1935.

Coppolani, Jean. *Toulouse, étude de geographie urbaine*. Toulouse, 1954.

Correch, A. *La cour d'appel de Pau, ses originés, son histoire, son personnel*. Tarbes, 1920.

Couret de Villeneuve, L.P. *Essai d'un manuel d'agriculture . . . domaine d'Hauterive, commune de Castres*. Toulouse, 1819.

Crouzet, F. "Les origines du sous-développement économique du sud-ouest." *Annales du Midi*, LXXII (1960), 75–81.

Daudet, Ernest. *La terreur blanche, episodes et souvenirs de la réaction dans le Midi en 1815 d'après les souvenirs contemporains et des documents inédits*. Paris, 1878.

Dedieux, J. "Le romantisme à Toulouse." *Les annales romantiques*, X (1913), 1–26.

Délandine de Saint-Esprit, Jérôme. *Le panache d'Henri IV, ou les phalanges royales, en 1815*. 2 vols. Paris, 1817.

Delpa, Claude. "Etude du niveau intellectuel des émigrés toulousains (1791–1797) d'après les inventaires de bibliotheques. . . ." Toulouse, typescript, n.d. *BUT*.

Desazars de Montgaillard. *Histoire de l'académie des sciences de Toulouse, le musée, le lycée, l'athenée, 1784–1807*. Toulouse, 1908.

Droulers, Paul. *Action pastorale et problèmes sociaux sous la monarchie de juillet chez Mgr. d'Astros archévêque de Toulouse censeur de la Mennais*. Paris, 1954.

Druy de Constant-Scribe. *La vie du général baron Ramel, 1768–1815*. Paris, 1912.

Dubédat, J.-B. *Histoire du parlement de Toulouse.* 2 vols. Toulouse, 1885.

Duboul, Axel. *L'armée révolutionnaire de Toulouse: épisode d'une rivalité de clochers.* Toulouse, 1891.

———. *Les deux siècles de l'Académie des Jeux Floraux.* Toulouse, 1901.

———. *La fin du parlement de Toulouse . . . avec une introduction par M. Dubédat.* Toulouse, 1890.

———. "Un toulousain oublié, le général Verdier." *Revue des Pyrénées,* IV (1892), 633–79.

———. *Le tribunal révolutionnaire de Toulouse: 25 nivôse – 3 floréal an II.* Toulouse, 1894.

Dubourg, A. *Monseigneur du Bourg, évêque de Limoges 1751–1822.* Paris, 1907.

Dumège, Alexandre-Louis-Charles. *Histoire des institutions religieuses, politiques, judiciaires et littéraires de la ville de Toulouse.* Toulouse, 1844–46.

Duphil, J.-C. "Les notables patentés de Toulouse sous le premier Empire," Mémoire pour le diplôme d'études supérieurs, Toulouse University. Typescript, 1959. *BUT.*

Dutil, Leon. *L'état économique de Languedoc à la fin de l'Ancien Regime, 1750–1789.* Toulouse, 1911.

———. *La Haute-Garonne et sa region; géographie historique.* Toulouse, 1828–29.

———. "Un homme de 1789. Pierre Roussillon." *Mémoires de l'académie des sciences, inscriptions et belles lettres de Toulouse.* 13 ser., II (1940), 274.

———. "La réforme du capitoulat toulousain du XVIIIe siècle." *Annales du Midi,* XIX (1907), 305–63.

———. "Les 'communes' en 1792: le comité central de sections de Toulouse (septembre–decembre)," *La Révolution française,* LXV (1913), 385–412.

Escudier, Adrien. *Monographie de Labastide St.-Sernin, canton de Fronton, Haute-Garonne.* Toulouse, 1936.

Faucher, D., et al. *Les villes de la région de Toulouse.* Toulouse, 1942.

———. "Réflexions sur le destin de Toulouse." *Revue de géographie des Pyrénées et du sud-ouest,* XXX (1959), 101–15.

Forster, Robert. "The Noble as Landlord in the Region of Toulouse at the End of the Old Regime." *Journal of Economic History,* XVII (1957), 224–44.

————. *The Nobility of Toulouse in the Eighteenth Century: a Social and Economic Study.* Johns Hopkins Studies in Historical and Political Science, ser. LXXVIII (1960), no. 1. Baltimore, 1960.

Fourcassié, Jean. *Une ville à l'épôque romantique: Toulouse, Trente ans de vie française.* Paris, 1953.

Frêche, Georges. "Compoix, propriété foncière, fiscalité et démographie historique en pays de taille réelle (XVIe–XVIIIe siècles)." *Revue d'histoire moderne et contemporaine,* XVIII (1971), 321–53.

————. *Le prix des grains, des vins et des légumes à Toulouse (1486–1868).* Paris, 1967.

Gélis, M. F. de. "Les philosophes et les jeux floraux." *Mémoires de l'académie des sciences de Toulouse,* ser. 11, VIII (1920), 15–56.

Génévray, Pierre: *L'administration et la vie ecclésiastiques dans le grand diocèse de Toulouse, (Ariège, Haute-Garonne, arrondissement de Castelserrasin) pendant les dernières années de l'Empire et sous la Restauration.* Bibliothèque méridionale, ser. 2, vol. XXX. Toulouse, 1941.

Gérard, P. "L'armée révolutionnaire de la Haute-Garonne." *Annales historiques de la Révolution française,* 8 (1959).

Godechot, Jacques Léon, ed. *La Révolution de 1848 à Toulouse et dans la Haute-Garonne: études publiées sous la direction de Jacques Godechot.* Toulouse, 1948.

————. "L'histoire sociale et économique de Toulouse au XVIIIe siècle." *Annales du Midi,* 78 (1966), 363–74.

———— and G. Moncassin. "Structures et relations sociales à Toulouse, 1749, 1785." *Annales historiques de la Révolution française,* 180 (1965), 129–69.

Gros, Jean. "Le duc et la duchesse d'Angoulême dans le Midi." *Mémoires de l'Academie des sciences de Toulouse,* ser. 12, II (1923), 47–66.

————. "L'esprit public à Toulouse après la Terreur." *Mémoires de l'académie des sciences, inscriptions et belles lettres de Toulouse,* ser. 12, VIII (1929), 65–83.

————. "Les juifs de Toulouse pendant la Révolution et l'Empire." *Revue des Pyrénées,* XVIII (1906), 250–60.

————. "Un maire de Toulouse sous la Restauration: de Villèle." *Mémoires de l'académie des sciences de Toulouse,* 12 ser., I (1922), 93–110.

Jorre, G. "Le commerce des grains et la minoterie à Toulouse."

Revue géographique des Pyrénées et du Sud-Ouest. IV (1933), 30–72.

Julien, Abbé. *L'église de Toulouse pendant la période révolutionnaire ... dicourse prononcé devant S.E. le cardinal Desprez.* Toulouse, 1887.

Lacouture, Joseph. *Le mouvement royaliste dans le sud-ouest, (1797–1800).* Hosségor, 1932.

Lacroix, F. de. "Un révelateur méconnu des Cent-Jours." *Revue des Pyrénées* (1911), 527–80.

Lamouzèle, Edmond. *Essai sur l'administration de la ville de Toulouse à la fin de l'ancien régime, 1783–1790.* Paris, 1910.

————. *Précis de l'histoire de Languedoc sous l'ancien régime de 1610 à 1790 avec un résumé de l'histoire de cette province des origines au dix-septième siècle.* Toulouse, 1914.

————. "Le premier procès de presse à Toulouse sous la Révolution." *Revue des Hautes-Pyrénées,* XVII (1922), 41–53.

————. "La procédure en usage devant le tribunal révolutionnaire de Toulouse." *Recueil de l'académie de législation de Toulouse,* ser. 4, IX (1930–31), 152–56.

Lapeyrouse, Philippe Picot de. *The Agriculture of a District in the South of France.* London, 1819.

Lapierre, Eugène. *Les anciennes bibliothèques de Toulouse.* Toulouse, 1890.

————. *Le parlement de Toulouse. Extrait, La revue de législation française et étrangere.* Paris, 1875.

Lavigne, Bertrand. *Histoire de l'insurrection royaliste en l'an VII, D'après les documents officiels.* Paris, 1887.

Limouzin-Lamothe, R. "Le cardinal de Clermont-Tonnerre, archévêque de Toulouse, et le mémoire des évêques du 1er août, 1828." *Annales du Midi,* LXIX (1957), 259–65.

Loubet, Jean. "Le gouvernement toulousain du duc d'Angoulême après les Cent-Jours." *La Révolution française,* LXIV (1913), 149–65, 337–66.

Mandoul, J. *Les municipalités de Toulouse pendant la Révolution. Extrait, Recueil de Législation,* ser. 2, II (1906). Toulouse, 1906.

Marinière, G. "Les marchands d'étoffes de Toulouse à la fin du XVIIIe siècle." *Annales du Midi,* LXX (1958), 251–308.

Martin, Gaston. *Le lycée de Toulouse de 1763 à 1881.* Toulouse, 1930.

Martin, Henri. "Les biens du clergé et des émigrés deportés et condamnés, confisqués et vendus sous la Révolution d'après les archives de la Haute-Garonne." *Revue des Pyrénées,* XXVI (1914), 193–98.

Massio, Roger. "La vie économique dans le département de la Haute-Garonne de 1799 à 1830." Toulouse, 1950. Typescript, *BUT.*

Mater, André. "Le groupement régional des partis politiques à la fin de la Restauration, 1824–1830." *La Révolution française,* XLII (1902), 406–643.

Mazars, [Capitaine]. "Huit mois à Toulouse il y a un siècle, novembre 1813–juin 1814." *Revue des Pyrénées,* XXVI (1914), 401–24.

Montaugé, Théron Louis de. *L'agriculture et les classes rurales dans le pays toulousain depuis le milieu du xviii siècle.* Paris, 1869.

Morère, C. B. *Histoire de St. Félix-Caraman.* Toulouse, 1899.

Morère, Philippe. "L'établissement du consulat à Toulouse en l'an VIII." *La Révolution française,* XXXII (1897), 5–46.

Nouvelles tentatives des aristocrates de Toulouse. Bordeaux, 1791.

Ousset, P. E. *Clérmont sur Ariege, archéologie et histoire.* Toulouse, 1934.

Pariset, F. *Economie rurale, moeurs et usages du Lauragais (Aude et Haute-Garonne). Extrait, Mémoires de la société imperiale et centrale d'agriculture de France, année 1866.* Paris, 1867.

Passérieu, Jean-Bernard. "Députés de Toulouse à l'assemblée constituante du 5 mai 1789 au 30 septembre 1791." *Révolution française,* VIII (1885), 704–12.

Plégat, M. T. "L'évolution démographique d'une ville française au XIXe siècle: l'exemple de Toulouse." *Annales du Midi,* n.s., LXIV (1952), 227–48.

Poitevin-Peitavi, B. *Mémoire pour servir à l'histoire des jeux floraux, par M. Poitevin-Peitavi.* Toulouse, 1815.

Praviel, Armand. *Histoire ancedotique des jeux floraux.* Toulouse, 1923.

Précis historique de la bataille livrée le 10 avril 1814 sous les murs de Toulouse entre l'armée française et les armées combinées anglaise, espagnole et portugaise. Toulouse, [1815?].

Puntous, Th. *Un diocèse civil de Languedoc: les états particuliers du diocèse de Toulouse au XVIII siècle.* Paris, 1909.

Ramet, Henri. *Le capitole et le parlement de Toulouse.* Toulouse, 1926.

―――. "Les cours prévôtales dans le ressort de la cour d'appel de Toulouse (1816–1818)." *Recueil de l'académie de législation de Toulouse,* ser. 4, VIII (1928–29), 1–41.

―――. *Histoire de Toulouse,* préface d'Edmond Hauracourt. Toulouse, 1935.

Renaud de Vilback. *Voyages dans les départemens formés de l'ancienne province de Languedoc . . . Description de l'Hérault.* Paris, 1825.

Rességuier, Fernand. *Comte Fernand de Rességuier—pages royalistes.* Toulouse, 1903.

Richert, G. "Biens communaux et droits d'usage en Haute-Garonne pendant la réaction thermidorienne et sous le Directoire." *Annales Historiques de la Révolution Française,* XXIII (1951), 274–88.

―――. *La vie économique de la Haute-Garonne sous le Directoire.* Toulouse, 1947. Typescript, *BUT.*

Roschach, E. *Géographie de la Haute-Garonne.* Toulouse, 1866.

Roy, Joseph-Antoine. *Villèle avant 1815.* Paris, [1952?]. Typescript, Bibliothèque de la Sorbonne.

Salvan, Adrien. *Histoire générale de l'Eglise de Toulouse.* 4 vols. Toulouse, 1856–61.

Ségu, Frederic. *L'académie des jeux floraux et le romantisme de 1818 à 1824 d'après des documents inédits.* 2 vols. Paris, 1935–36.

Sentou, Jean. "Faillites et commerce à Toulouse en 1789." *Annales historiques de la Révolution française,* XXV (1953), 217–56.

―――. *Fortunes et groupes sociaux à Toulouse sous la Révolution.* Toulouse, 1969.

―――. "Impôts et citoyens actifs à Toulouse au début de la Révolution." *Annales du Midi,* n.s., LXI (1948), 159–79.

Sevrin, Ernest. *Les missions religieuses en France sous la Restauration (1815–1830).* Paris, 1948–59.

Sicard, Roger. "La guerre des nerfs à Toulouse en 1814–1815." *Auta,* n.s., 229 (March, 1953), 45–48.

Tajan, Bernard-Antoine. *Esprit et conférences des lois d'intérêt général qui ont été rendues depuis la Restauration ou qui seront rendues à l'avenir.* Toulouse, 1826–27.

Théron de Montaugé, Louis. *L'agriculture et les classes rurales dans le pays toulousain depuis le milieu du XVIII siècle.* Paris, 1869.

Thiers, Adolphe. *The Pyrénées and the South of France, during the Months of November and December 1822.* London, 1823.

Thomas-Latour, A. *Les dernières années du parlement de Toulouse, de 1788 à 1794.* Toulouse, 1851.

Thore, Pierre-Henri. "Essai de classification des catégories sociales à l'intérieur du tiers état de Toulouse." *Toulouse. Congrès national des sociétés savantes. Actes du soixante-dix-huitième congrès*, pp. 149–65. Paris, 1954.

———. "Le tiers-état de Toulouse à la veille des élections de 1789, querelles intestines et requêtes partisanes, (mai–decembre 1788)." *Annales du Midi*, LXV (1955), 181–91.

Thoumas-Schapira, Micheline. "La bourgeoisie toulousaine à la fin du XVIIe siècle." *Annales du Midi*, LXVII (1955), 313–29.

Toulouse, Université de. *L'Université de Toulouse, 1229–1929.* Toulouse, 1929.

Tournier, Clément. "Le cardinal de Clermont-Tonnerre et le drame de la petite-Eglise (1820–1830)." *Revue historique de Toulouse*, XX–XXII (1933–35).

———. "Le centenaire du retour des Bourbons." *Revue historique de Toulouse*, I (1914), 351.

———. *Le conseiller Mathias du Bourg: une famille toulousaine au moment de la Révolution. Conférence donnée a l'institut catholique de Toulouse, le 28 mai 1907.* Toulouse, 1907.

———. *Un saint Vincent de Paul toulousain, le chanoine Maurice Garrigou.* Toulouse, 1945.

Tudesq, A. J. "L'opposition légitimiste en Languedoc en 1840." *Annales du Midi*, LXVIII (1956), 391–407.

Vic, Claude de. *Histoire générale de Languedoc, avec des notes et les pièces justicatives: Composée sur les auteurs et les titres originaux, et enrichie de divers monumens, par Dom Claude de Vic et Dom Vaissete, religieux bénédictins de la congrégation de Saint-Maur: Commentée et continuée jusqu'en 1830, et augmentée d'un grand nombre de chartes et de documens inédits, par le chevalier Al. Du Mège.* Toulouse, 1840–46.

———. *Histoire générale . . . continuée jusqu'en 1790 par E. Roshach.* Toulouse, 1872–1904.

Weymss, A. "L'Angleterre et la terreur blanche de 1815 dans le Midi." *Annales du Midi*, LXXIII (1961), 287–310.

Wolff, Philippe. *Histoire de Toulouse*, 2nd ed. Toulouse, 1961.

C. Comparative Local Studies

Boussonnet, Jean-Baptiste. *Le Bourbonnais sous la seconde Restauration: l'esprit public.* Moulins, 1924.

Fizaine, Simone. *La vie politique dans la Côte-d'Or sous Louis XVIII, les élections et la presse.* Publications de l'université de Dijon, fasc. iv. Paris, 1931.

Hufton, Olwen. *Bayeux in the Late Eighteenth Century.* Oxford, 1967.

Leuilliot, Paul: *L'Alsace au début du XIXe siècle.* Paris, 1959–61.

———. *La première Restauration et les Cent-Jours en Alsace.* Bibliothèque générale de l'école pratique des hautes études, VIe section. Paris, 1958.

Ribe, Georges. *L'opinion publique et la vie politique à Lyon lors des premières années de la seconde Restauration.* Annales de L'Université de Lyon, ser. 3, fasc. xvi. Paris, 1957.

Rocal, G. *La seconde Restauration en Périgord.* Angoulême, 1956.

Vidalenc, J. *Le département de l'Eure sous la monarchie constitutionnelle.* Paris, 1952.

INDEX

Aa, confraternity of the, 97
Academy of Sciences, 158, 162
Actes des Apôtres, 28
Action Française, 1
Adresse des Catholiques de Nîmes
(1790), 28, 37
Agricultural Society of Toulouse, 168–
69
Aguilar de Bon de Margarit, Melchior-
Louis, 167
Aguin, Auguste d', 56, 172
Aiguesvives. *See* Martin d'Aiguesvives
Albi, environs of, 6, 85
Albis de Belbèze, Jean-François-Denis
de, 12
Aldéguier, Jean-Baptiste-Auguste, 38
Aldéguier, T.-Joseph-Hippolyte, 92,
96, 97, 125, 126, 131
Ami du Roi, 93, 139, 143, 157
Amilhau, Jean-Pierre-Catherine, 85
Amis de la Constitution, 30, 34, 35
Anglaret. *See* Carivent, Pierre-Louis
(*dit* Anglaret)
Anglophobia, 149–50
Angoulême, Louis de Bourbon, Duc
de, 4, 56, 57, 58, 66, 76, 91, 108,
111, 127, 128, 129, 132, 172
Angoulême, Marie-Thérèse de Bour-
bon, Duchesse de, 163
Anti-Terroriste, 41
Antraigues, Emmanuel-Louis-Henri d',
57
Arbou-Castillon, 56

Ardèche, department of, 4, 110
Ariège, department of, 47, 124, 173,
175
Armées révolutionnaires, 7
Army, 133–35
Army of the Pyrenees, 77
Arnal, Jean, 37
Arnaud Bernard, district of, 19, 75
Artois, Comte de. *See* Charles X
Aspe, President d', 34
Assignats, 7
Association Légitimiste, 173, 175
Astros, Paul-Thérèse-David, 173
Ateliers de charité, 62
Aube, department of, 111
Aubuisson de Voisins, François, 86,
141–43
Auch (Gers), 60
Aude, department of, 91
Aussaguel de Lasbordes, V.-J.-M., 125,
126, 127
Aussonne, canton of, 84
Auterrive (Haute-Garonne), 45
Authier, Jean, 81
Auvergne, 2
Avignon (Vaucluse), 74
Azais (merchant), 78

Bahuhaut, Pierre, 172
Barbasan, J.-F.-P.-J. de, 81
Barère, Bertrand de, 18, 31, 165
Baron de Montbel. *See* Montbel, Guil-
laume-Isidore, Baron de

215

Robespierre, Maximilien de, 39, 42, 133, 150
Romiguières, Dominique-Joseph-Jean-Louis, 67, 84, 93, 111, 138, 160
Romiguières, Jean-Antoine, 27, 67, 114
Roquebrune, Mr. de, 57
Roquette-Buisson, Anne-Antoine de, 96, 113
Roquette-Buisson family, 93
Roquette-Buisson, Maxime de, 132, 166
Rouergue, inhabitants of, 12
Rougé, Baron de, 44, 136
Rousseau, Jean-Jacques, 156, 158
Roussillou (committeeman), 19
Rouzet, Jacques-Marie, 27
Ruche d'Acquitaine, 154
Ruffat, Barthelémy, 163
Ruffat, Jean-Dominique-François, 163, 166
Rural industry, 6
Russian wheat, 118–19

Sabatié, Paul-Alexis, 121
Sabran family, 93
La Sagesse (masonic lodge), 175
Saint-André, J.-A.-D., 72–73
Saint Antoine du Salin, 175
Saint-Chamans, Louis-Marie-Joseph, 63, 68, 108, 133
Saint Cyprien, district of, 19, 21, 61
Saint Etienne: cathedral of, 14, 41; district of, 72, 75
Saint Exupère, church of, 175
Saint-Félix de Maurémont, Armand-Joseph, 90, 91, 92, 96, 172
Saint-Félix de Maurémont, Armand-Philippe-Germain, 44
Saint-Gaudens (Haute-Garonne), 6, 79, 113, 118, 174, 176
Saint Géry, Jean-Jacques-Augustin de Rey, 92, 97
Saint Léon, Mlle de, 93
Saint Louis, 57, 156
Saint Louis, confraternity of, 175
Saint-Lys (Haute-Garonne), 45, 77
Saint-Michel, district of, 19, 46
Saint-Raymond, François-Marie, 81, 97, 108, 178
Saint-Sardos (Haute-Garonne), 47
Saint Sernin, basilica of, 14

Saint-Simonism, proponents of, 177
Saint Sulpice-sur-Lèze (Haute-Garonne), 46
Saintegême, Ovide-Jean-François-Henri, 113
Salvan, *Abbé,* 156
Sambucy, Alexandre, 40, 90, 91
Saragossa (Spain), 46
Sarrus, François, 78
Saurimont, Jacques-Louis-Pierre, 166
Savés, Philippe-Louis, 55
Savy-Gardeilh, Hippolyte, 91
Savy-Gardeilh, Jean-François de, 57, 90, 91–92
Secrets. See Verdets
Seigneurial rights, 25
Seilh, canton of, 84
Sermet, Hyacinthe, 31
Serre brothers, 45
Serres de Colombars, J.-A.-L.-A., 166
Servat (merchant), 174
Seysses near Muret, 46
Société d'agriculture de la Haute-Garonne. See Agricultural Society of Toulouse
Société de défense mutuelle, 175
Société des bonnes études, 97, 164–66, 167
Société populaire, 30, 39
Solomiac, Noel, 129
Sorèze school, 86, 161
Sorto, Gabriel, 57
Soulé (secretary), 175
Soumet, Alexandre, 160, 167
Spain, 57, 66, 77, 85, 134, 149–50, 154, 167
Stendhal (Henri Beyle), 86

Tabac. See Tobacco factory
Taille réelle, 16
Tajan, Bernard-Antoine, 68
Tarn, department of, 85, 91, 108, 124, 173, 175
Tarn-et-Garonne, department of, 110, 124, 135, 173, 175
Tauriac, Amedée-Victor-Xavier-Silvestre-Charles, 160
Théon, Vicomte de, 92
Thésan family, 32
Thoron, Paul, 83, 113
Tobacco factory, 17, 137

THE JOHNS HOPKINS UNIVERSITY PRESS

This book was composed in Caledonia text and Bulmer
and Caledonia display by Monotype Composition Company.
It was printed on 60-lb Danforth paper and bound in
Joanna Kennett cloth by The Maple Press Company, Inc.

Library of Congress Cataloging in Publication Data

Higgs, David, 1939–
    Ultraroyalism in Toulouse.

    (The Johns Hopkins University studies in historical
and political science, 90th ser., 2)
    Bibliography: p.
    1. Toulouse—History. I. Title. II. Series:
Johns Hopkins University. Studies in historical and
political science, 90th ser., 2.
DC801.T726H5   944'.86   72-4021
ISBN 0-8018-1432-4